THE WITNESS AND SPIRIT OF TRUTH

I dedicate this book to my parents, Basil Sheets and Barbara Sheets McCullough, who instructed me in the faith, and William Graff, who took me the final step to the LORD.

I also want to honor Donald Brosseau, who taught me amateur radio, providing the foundation for my career in Electrical Engineering

"A system of morality which is based on relative emotional values is a mere illusion, a thoroughly vulgar conception which has nothing sound in it and nothing true." – **Socrates**

"Employ your time in improving yourself by other men's writings so that you shall come easily by what others have labored hard for." – **Socrates**

THE WITNESS AND SPIRIT OF TRUTH

Experiential versus Hubristic Theology

LARRY SHEETS

The Witness and Spirit of Truth by Larry Sheets
Copyright © 2021 by Larry Sheets, All Rights Reserved.
ISBN: 978-1-59755-655-2

Published by: ADVANTAGE BOOKS™ Longwood, FL - www.advbookstore.com

This book and parts thereof may not be reproduced in any form, stored in a retrieval system, or transmitted in any form by any means (electronic, mechanical, photocopy, recording or otherwise) without prior written permission of the author, except as provided by United States of America copyright law.

All material contained herein that is not original is reprinted with authorized permission or license from the authors, artists, and/or publishers with appropriate attributions, or are in the public domain, or within the publishers' gratis use guidelines.

Scriptures marked NIV are taken from the NEW INTERNATIONAL VERSION® (NIV). Copyright© 1973, 1978, 1984, 2011 by Biblica, Inc.TM. Used by permission of Zondervan

Scripture quotations marked (NASB) are taken from the NEW AMERICAN STANDARD BIBLE®, Copyright© 1960, 1962, 1963, 1968, 1971, 1972, 1973, 1975, 1977, 1995 by The Lockman Foundation. Used by permission.

Scripture quotations marked "BSB" are taken from The Holy Bible, Berean Study Bible, BSB. Copyright ©2016, 2018 by Bible Hub. Used by Permission. All Rights Reserved Worldwide. www.berean.bible

Scriptures marked ESV are taken from the The Holy Bible, ENGLISH STANDARD VERSION (ESV): Copyright© 2001 by Crossway, a publishing ministry of Good News Publishers. Used by permission.

Scripture quotations marked (NKJV) are taken from the NEW KING JAMES VERSION®. Copyright© 1982 by Thomas Nelson, Inc. Used by permission. All rights reserved.

Scriptures marked KJV are taken from the KING JAMES VERSION (KJV) Public Domain).

Scripture quotations marked "ASV" are taken from the American Standard Version Bible (Public Domain).

Edited by Leslie Reder Kleckner

Library of Congress Catalog Number: 2022932336

Sheets, Larry, Author
The Witness and Spirit of Truth / Larry Sheets
Longwood: Advantage Books, 2021
ISBN (print): 9781597556552, (mobi, epub): 9781597556699
RELIGION: Christian Bible Criticism & Interpretation
RELIGION: Christian Bible Study Books
RELIGION: Christian Theology

First Printing: March 2022
22 23 24 25 26 27 10 9 8 7 6 5 4 3 2 1

Letter to the Reader

My intention back in 2006 was to pen a brief response to the then recently published book *Mapping Postmodernism: A Survey of Christian Options* (InterVarsity Press, 2003). My friend, Robert Greer, PhD, wrote that book. Greer addressed the presence of postmodernism within Christian theology today. But as I read Greer's book, I became aware of the centuries old disregard theologians had for the Word of God. The issues I had with theology I found predated the arrival of postmodernism, having their roots in modernism and existentialism.

Possibly, the name should not be postmodernism, but hypermodernism or latemodernism instead. For now, I'm stuck with the convention that names the thought *postmodernism* that emerged somewhere between 1960 and 1980. What precedes postmodernism is existentialism, and their participants are proto-postmodernists. Greer called the current developing philosophy post-postmodernism. These naming conventions become tedious because the naming is nondescript. There should be a name for this irreverent theology. It is critical of God's Word, disputes the existence of absolute truth, and spawns and fosters so many evils in our world.

So, this response became a belated essay about a conceited theology, a system of thought that has its architects, builders, and dwellers—an evil parading as a messenger of light, embodied in an "ism," looking for its next seduction. I have the practical spirit of an electrical engineer, trained in causality and committed to field-tested truth. You should care what I think of modernism, Higher Criticism, and postmodernism. You see, the baggage I carry is not from any particular school of thought, but is a practical toolbox for a practicing faith. I hope you will appreciate the viewpoint of a natural applied study of THE BEING and His Way drawn from an engineer's heart. A Study of Abraham's God, *I am THE BEING*, as expressed in the Septuagint.

As I wrote notes on this subject, new issues came to mind, issues, which I also added and then developed. Eventually, my notes became an essay which slowly grew into this book. The process ushered us into enduring arenas of submerged thought now at last finding expression. I became singularly alarmed at the penetration of the postmodern worldview developing in the Christian Church. I see this substantial body of thought and expression as an ill-conceived system grounded in serious error: contemptuous of God by declaring Him irrelevant, and therefore a self-defining blasphemy.

Through studying this system, and its two predecessors, I came to a closer understanding of how an amoral Bavarian corporal came to be the political leader of a major Christian nation, profoundly affect its culture, and dispense so much evil into the world. I wondered if the scholars responsible for this pernicious system were such people as mentioned in Scott Peck's book, *The People of the Lie*. [1] Did their religion or their philosophy control these scholars? Were their moral and religious natures dulled by their philosophical presuppositions? Is their authority human or divine? When they claim the scientific method, do they adhere to the following order?

- Recognize and formulate a problem
- Collect data through observation and experiment

- And then formulate and test a hypothesis?

Or do they rather follow the method of self-deception that alters the order and taints the evidence?

- Formulate a hypothesis consistent with their world view
- Collect data through selective observation and contrived experiment
- And then test the hypothesis against the filtered data?

Such things are done by dishonest natural philosophers, could it be that theologians are also capable of such behavior? These radical theologians who are ashamed of the *Theo* in their discipline are a timid gaggle. They cling to the ways and methods of this world by cravenly avoiding the effective laboratory for Christian theologians -- the Scriptures and Life. Therefore, their errors are dangerously undetectable and effectively masquerade as truth. They have a deleterious effect on our culture and have begun to corrupt Christ's Church.

But who should listen to someone like me, someone who is so far removed from professional theology? After all, a large number of papers and books have already been published on it in the last decade. What value could one more opinion have in such an over – written area? Luther and Andersen advocate the contrary, however. Luther wrote,

> In the world government of course the rule holds, that the older is wiser than the younger, a learned man than a layman; but in spiritual things a child or a servant, a common woman or man can have the grace of God as well as an old person or a lord, a priest or a Pope. To sum up, let no learned person take from you the right to judge, for you have this right as well as he. [2]

The situation is somewhat like Hans Christian Andersen's immortal tale *The Emperor's New Suit* (1837): a small child observed what everyone refused to say:

> But he has nothing on at all!

We're told that the kingdom of God belongs to such a child. In his story, Andersen wrote that appealing to the fears of the rich and powerful sold the goods

> … but the clothes made of their material possessed the wonderful quality of being invisible to any man who was *unfit for his office or unpardonably stupid.*

But the child had no such fears to cow him into silence. At times, the scholarly world needs the perspective of a child like this, a child that stands outside the general intellectual, moral, and cultural climate of the profession. God calls all to learn and study about Him. Therefore, all are called to be theologians and Luther's earlier comments are applicable to all. And like a small child, I may possess perspectives that those inside the field of theology have avoided for fear of looking unpardonably stupid or unfit for their office.

Consequently, my jump to theology may not be as long a jump as first imagined. Dorothy L. Sayers, author of *The Mind of the Maker*, believes this jump is imperative,

> Our minds are not infinite; and as the volume of the world's knowledge increases, we tend more and more to confine ourselves, each to his special sphere of interest and to the specialized metaphor belonging to it. The analytic bias of the last three centuries has immensely encouraged this tendency, and it is now very difficult for the artist to speak the language of the theologian or the scientist the language of either. But the attempt must be made; and there are signs everywhere that the human mind is once more beginning to move toward a synthesis of experience.[3]

My question, then, was this: what contribution could my scientific and engineering background offer to the questions raised by Greer's book? What were some of these issues that served as triggers to my mind? Every issue revolved around irreverence of philosophical theology toward God and His Word. Disregard or disbelief in Truth, and the notion that humanity was incapable of knowing absolute Truth because of language, were pivotal positions in the conflict. There were lesser irritations; such as a disregard for Biblical promises to believers, and there was an almost universal reaction erupting from my chest as I read on,

> Don't they read their Bibles?

Focusing upon the issue of the nature of truth and the role of language as a conveyer of truth, I draw upon many different scholars to buttress my perspectives. These scholars articulate their views with much greater erudition and authority than I. Consequently, as this project developed, I saw myself as a conductor of a great symphony, with each musician skilled in the use of a magnificent instrument - and me with nothing more than a simple harmonica. To a large extent this book is dependent upon the writings of these other gentlemen, ladies, scholars, and statesmen upon whose shoulders I stand. This work has been consuming. A growing concern emerged about the survival of much of what I cherish. Following lines of least resistance, avoiding the immediate stress and ignoring the challenge were not acceptable. This problem needed addressing, so reading, taking notes, and prayer was the rule. I address the effects of philosophical theology on the moral fabric of Christ's Bride. Christianity without Truth is no light of the world-no city upon a hill, not even a candle under a basket, but only the charred remains of a bonfire long since extinguished. This foul cloud threatens to hide the light. I needed a plan.

[1] M. Scott Peck, M.D., *People Of The Lie*, Simon & Schuster, New York, 1983

[2] Martin Luther, *Complete Sermons of Martin Luther*, Vol. 2.2, *Eighth Sunday After Trinity*, Baker Books, Grand Rapids, MI, 2000, p. 241

[3] Dorothy L. Sayers, *The Mind of the Maker*, HarperCollins Publishers, New York, 1987, p.p. 30,31

Larry Sheets

Table of Contents

LETTER TO THE READER 5

PART ONE – THE FOUNDATION LANGUAGE, TRUTH, AND THE WORDS OF LIFE 13

  1) INTRODUCTION 13
  1.1) THE PLAN OF THE ESSAY 13
  1.2) THE SUBSTITUTION OF KNOWLEDGE FOR WISDOM 15
  1.3) THE KING OF TRUTH BEARS WITNESS TO THE TRUTH 21

2: FIRST PRINCIPLES THE FIRST PRINCIPLE IS ONE PRINCIPAL. FIRST GOD... 23

  2.1) GOD 23
    2.1.1) THE CHARACTER AND PERSONALITY OF GOD 23
    2.1.1.1) INTRODUCTION 23
    2.1.1.1) GOD BY GOD FROM HIS PERSPECTIVE 24
    2.1.2) GOD THE CREATOR 28
    2.1.3) THE UNITY VS. THE TRINITY OF GOD 28
    2.1.4) GOD'S NAME 32
  2.2) THE BIBLE AND THE CREEDS 32

3) WE LOOK TO THE PAST 51

  3.1) SCHOLASTICISM 51
  3.2) DESCARTES' RADICAL DOUBT 54
  3.3) THE COGITO 57
  3.4) YOU WILL BE LIKE GOD 59
  3.5) THE DRIFT TOWARD PANTHEISM 61
  3.6) PREJUDICIAL HIGHER CRITICISM 64
  3.7) THE BEAUTIFUL BIG BANG THEORY 67

PART TWO - IF (A) LINGUISTIC UNIVERSALS EXISTS AND A UNIVERSAL LANGUAGE IS POSSIBLE 71

4) LANGUAGE AND TRUTH 71

  4.1) THE CRUX OF THE MATTER 71
  4.2) AN EMOTIONAL ASIDE 71
  4.3) LINGUISTIC UNIVERSALS 72
  4.4) LANGUAGE OF THE BRAIN 74

5) ON THE NATURE OF AN IDEAL LANGUAGE 83

  5.1) THE POETIC MATHEMATICIAN 84
  5.2) WHAT'S IN A NAME? 89
  5.5) LOVE POSSESSES WHAT REASON CANNOT COMPREHEND 94

PART THREE- IF (B) TRUTH IS AVAILABLE TO MEN 99

6) TRUTH 99

6.1) Absolute Truth 99

THE PRESENT CRISIS [14] 103

6.2) Partitioned Truth 104
6.3) Quotation Orchestration 105
6.4) The Abiding Truth and an Analogy of Synchronization 107

PART FOUR - THEN (C) THE POSTMODERN UNDERSTANDING OF LANGUAGE THEORY 111

7) THE POLLUTED STREAMS WE SWIM IN 111

7.1) Heidegger's Dossier 111
7.2) Heidegger's Spawn 112
7.3) Heidegger's Grand-fathered Legacy 113
7.4) The Devil's Triangle 115
7.5) Club Theology 117
7.6) Concluding Comments on Postmodernism 121

PART FIVE – ON REPRESENTATIONS, NAMES AND REALITY 129

8) ON THAT WHICH IS AND WHAT IT'S CALLED 129

8.1) On Representations, and Names 129
8.2) On Representations and Reality –The Trouble With Models 129
8.3) God's Representation, Name, and Reality 132

PART SIX – A LOOK AT SPURIOUS BELIEFS 136

9) THE ECUMENICAL IMPERATIVE 136

9.1) Logical Statements of Love 136
9.2) Evidence of the Ecumenical Nurturing and Protective Imperative 138
9.3) The True "Ecumenical Imperative" 147
9.4) On the Sacraments 149
9.5) It All Depends On What *Is* Is 152

10) FOUR-DIMENSIONAL THINKING 155

10.1) The Issue 155
10.2) Definitions 155
10.3) Time, Light, and Creation 156

11) THE BELIEVER'S TRANSFIGURATION 157

11.1) Finite Or Infinite 157
11.2) Nothing Will Be Impossible For You 158

PART SEVEN – A WAY OF EQUIVALENCE RELATION THINKING 161

12) EQUIVALENCE RELATION THINKING 161

12.1) Equivalence Relation and Sanctification 162
12.2) Examples 162

PART EIGHT – ANALOGIC AND ALGEBRAIC THINKING 169

13: ANALOGY, PARABLE AND METAPHOR 169

13.1: Analogies 169
13.2) THE PARABLES OF JESUS 170
13.2) Parable Conclusions 172

14 -THE DIVINE SYSTEM – AN ANALOGY TO PONDER 176

14.1) Graphical System Representations 176
14.3) A Star of David 180

15: CONCLUSIONS 181

APPENDIX A: THE NECESSARY CONDITIONS FOR AN ENTITY TO BE CONCEIVED AS A SYSTEM 185

APPENDIX B THE RELEVANT PORTIONS OF THREE CHRISTIAN CREEDS 187

APPENDIX C DESCARTES' LAWS OF LEARNING 189

APPENDIX D ANTIMONY OF THE LIAR 191

APPENDIX E – MOUNTAIN MOVING CALCULATIONS 193

APPENDIX F THE FUNDAMENTAL LIFE – ANOTHER OSCILLATOR ANALOGY 195

APPENDIX G THE INVERSE FUNCTION FOR SIN 199

G.2) The Synthesis of an Inverse 201
G.3) God's Plan of Sin Inversion Using A Sinless Substitute 202

APPENDIX H PARABLES OF JESUS 205

Parable Kingdom Secrets Revealed 205

L.L. SHEETS PATENTS 211

Part One – The Foundation

LANGUAGE, TRUTH, AND THE WORDS OF LIFE

1) Introduction

1.1) The Plan of the Essay

Our plan is to orchestrate the comments of exemplary minds to bring the best thoughts to the front, to refute the fundamentals of postmodernism with empirical evidence, and employ well-established and proven principles from natural philosophy and applied mathematics into the field of theology. Although I rely on the words of masters, the arrangement is significant, as Blaise Pascal said,

> Let no one say that I have said nothing new; the arrangement of the subject is new.... I had as soon it said that I used words employed before. And in the same way if the same thoughts in a different arrangement do not form a different discourse, no more do the same words in their different arrangement form different thoughts! Words differently arranged have a different meaning, and meanings differently arranged have different effects.[1]

So, it should also follow that quotations differently arranged have a different meaning, and those meanings differently arranged have different effects. This effort has been somewhat like using quotations for words rather than the usual symbols. Although I am conducting the orchestra, the audience really can only accept the symphony due to extraordinary fame and talent of the masters on their separate instruments. In any event, this quotation orchestration honors the thinker and conveys the desired thought. I am trying to follow my Master's advice, found in John 7:18. He who speaks on his own does so to gain honor for himself, but he who works for the honor of the one who sent him is a man of truth; there is nothing false about him.

Our primary concern is the question of language and truth. I hope to disprove the argument dominant in the philosophical and theological world that all language is relative to culture by demonstrating the existence of language universals in the brain leading to the feasibility of a universal language. With this achieved, I believe we can (a) conclude why and how the postmodern study of the methodological principles of interpretation of God is fatally flawed, and (b) introduce what would be a more correct Biblical hermeneutical replacement.

This is not a book written to atheists, but to theists. It is written more to a Theophilus than to a theologian, that is, more to the lover of God than the thinker of God. I will carefully explain our *first principles*, those ideas that define our spiritual nature and beliefs.

This is provided for the reader so he may understand a later statement or question. It is not an attempt to convince anyone of the correctness of my nature, but rather for insight into my thinking, which has changed during this journey. One might say I'm a child of the enlightenment and can only see through those lenses, while another might believe me a first century believer trying to get to the essence of the faith. A Calvinist or a Lutheran or Evangelical or a bigot or whatever I might be called for better or for worse, I hope these *first principles* simply express my Christianity and awe of my Maker.

Next, we seriously address the notion that men cannot think without language and how that belief helped create postmodernism. I then employ the works of Avram Noam Chomsky, Stephen Crain, Bishop George Berkeley, and Patrick Suppes to test that notion, and then approach the subject of an ideal language. The mathematical, musical and graphical nature of language and thought is described. Super languages, Intuitional Rational languages, and a hierarchy of "essentially rich" languages are considered. Greer's and Tarski's thoughts on language are summarized, chewed on and partially digested. The importance of Gödel's Incompleteness Theorem is discussed. Interesting conclusions are made at this juncture on the feasibility of an ideal language.

I consider the availability of Truth to men, and whether absolute Truth is a global concept or confined to the West. Prophets who publicly support or oppose the work of the Spirit of Truth are discussed. There is then an orchestration of quotations from around the world, from various times and persons. I will show by analogy how God's abiding Truth stabilizes a society and makes it lock to the Truth.

After taking Blaise Pascal's lead on poking fun at philosophy, we do the same to theology by referring to them as *Club Theology*. The spiritual distance between the faithful and the theologian is attributed to the theologian's rejection of Scripture. Having written, and hopefully shown, what I wanted to expose about postmodernism, I provide our concluding remarks and sum up the argument against it. We then move on to other subjects that relate to this study.

An Aid For the Reader
Because of the complexity of this endeavor, years ago Dr. Greer suggested that if this were to be read by others, I should help the reader by breaking this paper down into subparts. The first three chapters comprise the first part, *The Foundation*. The next three of these sections, composed of four chapters, will take on the form of an Aristotelian syllogism:
if (a) and if (b) then (c). Specifically, the three points of our syllogism are the following:

• *If (a)* Linguistic Universals exists and *a* universal language is possible, and *if (b)* Truth is available to men, *then* (c) the postmodern understanding of language theory fails in the real world, giving rise to many spurious belief-systems that are not only anti-biblical but also anti-humanitarian.

On this final point, I will draw upon the works of Friedrich Nietzsche and Martin Heidegger (two prominent proto-postmodernists), demonstrating that a consistent application of their understandings of language and truth have given needed philosophical energy to the system of Nazism in the mid-twentieth century that was a scourge to the world.

Beyond Part Four, the syllogism is over and, in the remaining parts, other paths are taken to study the way, truth and life of our glorious Redeemer. I hope you will continue with me on our journey.

1.2) The Substitution of Knowledge for Wisdom

There is persuasive evidence that a concerted effort was made in the last 200 years to blur the divine and secular wisdom of the past ages. One might argue that subterranean forces swept through history causing certain thoughts and events to happen. History teaches us the contrary, though, in that change is caused by strength of personalities and characters appearing on the scene to alter the courses. These changes may be for the better or for the worse, depending on the character of the leader. In this case, the spiritual intent appears malicious; the 20th century consequences were too horrific to be accidental. Or, perhaps instead, those responsible were *unfit for their office or unpardonably stupid.* Albert Einstein (1879-1955) noted this long-term trend in the first half of the twentieth century.

> During the last century, and part of the one before, it was widely held that there was an unreconcilable conflict between knowledge and belief. The opinion prevailed among advanced minds that it was time that belief should be replaced increasingly by knowledge; belief that did not itself rest on knowledge was superstition, and as such had to be opposed. According to this conception, the sole function of education was to open the way to thinking and knowing, and the school, as the outstanding organ for the people's education, must serve that end exclusively.[2]

On other occasions, he added, The intuitive mind is a sacred gift and the rational mind is a faithful servant. We have created a society that honors the servant and has forgotten the gift.[3]

> The intellect has little to do on the road to discovery. There comes a leap in consciousness, call it Intuition or what you will, the solution comes to you and you don't know how or why.[4]

His point is that rationality is a faithful servant, but the gift of intuition is too valuable to forget; any society that diminishes intuition will soon itself diminish. By Einstein's estimate, the year 1800 AD is roughly the commencement in Western societies of this detriment to intuition. It is of interest to note that the origin of the word *superstition* comes from the idea of *standing over as a witness or standing over and staring.* That is, *intuition* relates to *looking down to apprehend.* In contrast, the word *understanding* obviously relates to *looking up to comprehend.*

The world of thought underwent an odd convolution of perspectives between the Reformation and the Enlightenment. First, for approximately a millennium, the European mind had been subject to the uninspired unbiblical Roman Church bureaucracy that worked against the Holy Spirit's flame in the human heart. Further, it practiced the methods of Greek Logic but used axioms and premises that ran counter to the Gospel and the human heart. The same Roman Church fought against the scientific method of extracting the truth from nature by experiment. Thus, the papal forces thwarted both inspiration and reason.

Secondly, the antagonism the Roman Church had with science spread itself across all the churches in the minds of philosophers and scholars by a method akin to *guilt by association*. The natural philosophers, or scientists, did not hold this antagonism, however. The great discovers in science in times past were nearly always devout Christian men; Galileo, Kepler, Bacon, Newton, Faraday, Brewster, Kelvin, and a host of others were in this class. These Christian scientists maintained a reverential attitude toward the Scriptures and the Person of Jesus Christ. They were inspired reasonable men, capable of accepting the gifts of insight when the Holy Spirit of Truth offered them. Their students, however, didn't get to read of the inspiration; only of the flawless logic and mathematics they brought to the world.

Thirdly, the scientists that followed the start of the 19th century were attempting, or professing, to think reasonably without the gift of inspiration. The gift was inappropriately rejected because of its guilt by association. It is most unfortunate that many scholars that benefited directly from the Divine enlightenment of the Reformation were unable to embrace the gift to further the secular Enlightenment.

The time frame referred to by Einstein is coincident with the works and derivative works of Immanuel Kant. Kant's religious teachings were based on rationalism rather than revelation and were so unorthodox as to bring him into religious conflict with Frederick William II, King of Prussia. Nevertheless, Kant had a greater influence than any other philosopher of modern times. The German philosopher Georg Wilhelm Friedrich Hegel developed Kantian philosophy to the point where it was the basis on which the structure of Marxism was built. His dialectical method was used by both Hegel and Karl Marx and was an outgrowth of the method of reasoning by antimonies that Kant used. Johann Gottlieb Fichte was a student of Kant and developed a philosophy that greatly influenced 19th century socialists.

These were the scholars that Einstein spoke against. He was humble enough to explain the gift as unrelated to intellect but was associated with personhood or being. The neglect of intuition truncates, stagnates, and eventually inhibits the human spirit and renders it sterile, while a repudiation of reason results in superstition. Consequently, as we pursue knowledge, we must be mindful to nurture both.

Another instance of a change in thinking from wisdom to knowledge occurred in the 19th and 20th centuries. This was the "rise to power," noted by philologists, of the two words, "problem" and "solution" as dominating terms of public debate. Their "rise to power" is synchronized with a parallel disregard for wisdom and a "rise to power" of the word "happiness." L.P. Jacks in the Stevenson Lectures of 1926-7 first expressed this awareness,

> Like "happiness," our two terms "problem" and "solution" are not to be found in the Bible—a point which gives to that wonderful literature a singular charm and cogency.... On the whole, the influence of these words is malign, and becomes increasingly so. They have deluded poor men with Messianic expectations ... which are fatal to steadfast persistence in good workmanship and to well-doing in general ... Let the valiant citizen never be ashamed to confess that he has no "solution of the social problem" to offer to his fellowmen. Let him offer them rather the service of his skill, his vigilance, his fortitude and his probity. For the matter in question is not, primarily, a "problem," nor the answer to it a "solution." [5]

This lecture occurred in the 1920s, and was recorded in *The Mind of the Maker,* by Dorothy L. Sayers in 1941, the year of our entry into the Second World War. It was there and then that our fathers and grandfathers fought so valiantly against the Nazi protopostmodernists' "Final Solution" that was to establish happiness in Germany. The National Socialism (Nazi) and postmodernism connection will be discussed later.

C.S. Lewis (1898 – 1963) in his book, *The Abolition of Man*, wrote of the Chinese Tao, the reality beyond all predicates, and relates education absent of virtue to social problems. He then argues that if we fail to teach the youth specific standards of right and wrong, of what is valuable or worthless, commendable, or shameful, then we must share the responsibility for the resulting failings of character.

> Hence, the educational problem is wholly different according as you stand within or without the *Tao*. For those within, the task is to train in the pupil those responses which are in themselves appropriate, whether anyone is making them or not, and in making which the very nature of man consists. Those without, if they are logical, must regard all sentiments as equally nonrational, as mere mists between us and the real objects. As a result, they must either decide to remove all sentiments, as far as possible, from the pupil's mind: or else to encourage some sentiments for reasons that have nothing to do with their intrinsic 'justness' or 'ordinacy.' The latter course involves them in the questionable process of creating in others by 'suggestion' or incantation a mirage which their own reason has successfully dissipated...

> And all the time — such is the tragicomedy of our situation – we continue to clamor for the very qualities we are rendering impossible. You can hardly open a periodical without coming across the statement that what our civilization needs is more 'drive,' or dynamism, or self-sacrifice, or 'creativity.' *In a sort of ghastly simplicity, we remove the organ and demand the function. We make men without chests and expect of them virtue and enterprise. We laugh at honor and are shocked to find traitors in our midst. We castrate and bid the geldings be fruitful.*[6] (emphasis added)

Societies not grounded or synchronized to the Truth by both comprehension and apprehension, by reason and intuition, by justice and mercy, are capable of the most obscene and brutal behavior. Certain minimum requirements have proven essential through the millennia, as Confucius rightly said in the concluding words of *Analects,* Chapter 20.

> Without recognizing the ordinances of Heaven,
> > it is impossible to be a superior man.
>
> Without an acquaintance with the rules of Propriety,
> > it is impossible for the character to be established.
>
> Without knowing the force of words,
> > it is impossible to know men.

In his book *Nietzsche*[7], Martin Heidegger argued that absolute truth is a Western invention, beginning in early Hellenistic thought and moving onward until the latter nineteenth century, ending with Friedrich Nietzsche. Although Confucius was neither Christian nor Western, his words were true. In order to know and love God, know and love yourself, and know and love man, you must:

- recognize the ordinances of Heaven
- be acquainted with the rules of Propriety
- know the force of words

We know *the ordinances of Heaven* from the Scriptures – that is, from Genesis to Revelation and a few others from the *Septuagint*. They are available to anyone who wishes to read them. It is impossible to be a righteous man without the Word of God. All Scripture judges the thoughts and attitudes of the heart because it is the Breath of God. The Apostle Paul and the writer to the Hebrews made this point abundantly clear:

> *All Scripture is God-breathed* and is useful for teaching, rebuking, correcting and training in righteousness, so that the man of God may be thoroughly equipped for every good work. - 2 Tim 3:16,17 (NIV)

> For the Word of God is alive and active. Sharper than any double-edged sword, it penetrates even to dividing soul and spirit, joints and marrow; *it judges the thoughts and attitudes of the heart.* ... - Heb 4:12 (NIV)

With respect to *the rules of Propriety*, Emily Post shows how the character is involved with those deciding whether to follow certain norms. She says that the decision to follow a rule is based on the following questions:

- What is the purpose of this rule?
- Does it help to make life pleasanter?
- Does it make the social machinery run more smoothly?
- Is it essential to the code of good taste or to ethics? [8]

She goes on to say,

> Etiquette, if it is to be of more than trifling use, must go far beyond the mere mechanical rules of procedure or the equally automatic precepts of conventional behavior. Actual etiquette is most deeply concerned with every phase of ethical impulse or judgment and with every choice or expression of taste, since what one is, is of far greater importance than what one appears to be. A knowledge of etiquette is of course essential to one's decent behavior, ... [9]

This, then, becomes our field of empirical analysis: *theology must yield a "decent behavior" if it is to be trusted*. Moving on to Confucius' third point, we next address the *force of words*.

With respect to *the force of words*, we must become acquainted with the rules of language. A lack of regard for language and meaning of words undermines the most important concepts like *The Living Word* and *The Word of God*. Noah Webster was a devoted Christian dedicated to the American language.

> Noah Webster recognized that each age is subject to the demoralization of its language by the '*literary*' or '*modish*' segment of society. Thus he put, as a check and balance upon each other, *universal undisputed practice* and the *common law of language*, or established principles of analogy. Change for the sake of change, vulgarity, cant, slang for its own sake, was to Webster like the principle of motion in physics – if not controlled it became the principle of destruction.[10]

Death and life are in the power of the tongue (Proverbs 18:21.) (NIV)

Are languages the constructs of individual cultures with vocabulary, grammar, and syntax unique to themselves, or are there common threads that tie them all together? Must we think with language, or can we think in a fashion independent of language? What is the relationship of a *word* (human language) with the *Word* (God's statements)? What is the relationship of both to a *pure* language? And what is the relationship of a *pure* language to the internal language of the *brain*? Confucius said that without knowledge of the force of words, it is impossible to know men. If he is correct, then questions such as this need answering, because it is impossible to love a man without knowing him. And no Christian theology is worthy of the name if it doesn't support love.

If theology is to have its value to Christians, it must be relative to the world our neighbor is in. And there must be axioms employed in our languages if we are to arrive at the truth – a fact explained later in the section *On The Nature of an Ideal Language*. There is zero difference between axioms and faith. Faith somehow relates to the intuition of what could be, powered by the love of the Creator. Therefore, if we are to discover truth and our relationship to it, we must accept axioms from a credible source. One such credible source is the Bible– a fact explained later in the section *First Principles*. The second, but less credible, source is applied natural philosophy employing its precise mathematical languages to describe God's creation. Philosophy without faith could not be Christian theology. Vain philosophy is not the object of our concern. It is only Christian theology that I seek to synchronize to the Words of Life.

In short, the pursuit of knowledge of God requires more than the construction of philosophical substructure whereupon we construct our theological system. We must construct an axiom-based substructure and system in the real world where our resultant behavior is examined. Do they cause us to trust God in faith and then to love our neighbors as ourselves? Do they remain focused and draw strength from the death, burial, and resurrection of Jesus Christ? According to the Apostle Paul, the cross of Christ is foolishness to the Gentiles. His words written to the church in Corinth long ago are words for us as well:

Where is the wise man? Where is the scholar? Where is the philosopher of this age? Has not God made foolish the wisdom of this world? .... Jews demand signs and Greeks look for wisdom, but we preach Christ crucified: a stumbling block to Jews and foolishness to Gentiles, but to those whom God has called, both Jews and Greeks, Christ the power of God and the wisdom of God. For the foolishness of God is wiser than man's wisdom, and the weakness of God is stronger than man's strength. - 1 Cor. 1:20-25 (NIV)

Such an empirical analysis of our study of the Way of the God of Abraham will make us politically incorrect, as Christianity is politically incorrect. As Martin Luther once said," The devil and the world, for the sake of the Word and of confession of Christ, will sting, torture, and plague you."[11] Nevertheless, we must be careful not to fall into the trap of espousing politically correct falsehood.

Undoubtedly, the same situation will result with theology as resulted in Andersen's tale. In that tale, after the child declared the king was naked, and the people along the route of the king's procession were encouraged and loudly declared that the king was naked, the royal company and courtiers continued on with the gag pretending that they could still see the clothes in order to save face: "And the chamberlains walked with still greater dignity, as if they carried the train which did not exist."

The philosophizing theologians say, "God is dead." Their words mean: "That there once was a God to whom adoration, praise and trust were appropriate, possible, and even necessary, but that now there is no such God."[12] I declare, simple child that I am, "God is not dead, nor does He sleep." Arguments to the contrary are proud but vain. They have proven empirically baseless. They depend on false premises and logic that is incapable of proving or disproving the essential statements relating to the Living God.

The real issues of knowledge do not revolve around man's ability to approach God. They revolve around the accessibility of man when God approaches. I agree with Blaise Pascal when he said, "The knowledge of God is very far from the love of Him." [13] Our worship and loving of God is the only way He finds appropriate to reveal Himself to us. But we love God because He first loved us. Thus, the entire knowledge of God is revelation instigated by God. When the Word says, "God is Love," God effectively says, "I AM the Existence of Love" God who names Himself *I AM* is the God of the living (Matt. 22:32) and is the Living God. (1Sam.17:26 &36, 2Kings 19:4 & 16, Ps.42:2, etc.) We then live and know God because He loves us. There is no living without love.

I AM denotes Existence, Awareness and Expression; it connotes God's Self-given Name. Existence, awareness, expression, and words are all connected in a conjugate manner. Taken in overlapping pairs, we are linked together from words to the great I AM. Existence is the Father of all. Awareness of all that exists is the Essence of Truth. Expression of Truth is thus born of Existence through Awareness. Alternatively, the Witness of Truth is born of the Father of Truth through the power of the Awareness of Truth.

The order of Creation, however, is a slightly different order than the Procreation of the Word. If we think of creation as the authoring of a book [14], the Great I AM is the-Book-as-Thought, the actual structure of the universe is the-Book-as-Written, and we are the-Book-as-Read. That is, the Idea, the Activity, and the Awareness; these three correspond with Existence, Expression, and Awareness. With God as Creator, and we as His image, we are motivated also to be a creator. I am encouraged to express my thoughts since I know that I am because our God spoke. I write for our loving and Almighty Yahweh Who says to us "*I AM*, therefore, you think." so that we might individually say with Descartes "I think, therefore I am."

1.3) The King of Truth Bears Witness to the Truth

You say correctly that I am a king, for this I was born, and for this I have come into the world, to testify to the Truth. Everyone who is of the Truth hears My voice- John 18:37. (AMP)

I am the way and the truth and the life: no man comes to the Father except through Me. – John 14:6 (KJV)

These words, of course, come from Jesus. He spoke them while standing before Pontius Pilate, hours before His own crucifixion. Several hours earlier He said to His disciples

Jesus comments are revealing. What Jesus was saying was this: (a) He bears witness to the truth, and (b) anyone who is of the truth will hear His voice, and (c) He is the truth. What is more, Jesus is not just *a* truth—He is *the* truth, truth in its most pure and absolute form. This implies that absolute truth exists and we are capable of being grounded in such truth if we are *of* the truth.

This suggests that Truth and the Word (both the written and living Word) are bound together. Taken a step further, Absolute Truth and Language are divinely conjoined. Turn around, look back, and you will see that Jesus said He is the *King of Truth*. If there were no Truth, He would either reign Supreme over a desolate Kingdom, or be remembered as that lunatic who thought himself a king - for those are the choices left to us once truth is abandoned.

In this essay, we will look at truth with this idea in mind; how God, Absolute truth and Language are related. I will insist here that Absolute Truth exists in the Person of Jesus and that an Absolute Language also exists. By Absolute I mean perfect in quality and nature; complete and not derived from temporal events; pure. Thus, if something exists Absolutely, it exists independently of time or circumstance. If an Absolute pure gift is from the Hand of God, then it was, and is and ever shall be. This will, of course, move us in a direction diametrically opposed to postmodern thought and closer to the spiritual war that engulfs our Christian society. But then, faith, a child, a sling and five smooth stones have won such wars.

[1] Blaise Pascal, *PENSfES*, 1660, translated by W. F. Trotter, #22-23

[2] "On Education," Address to the State University of New York at Albany, in Ideas and Opinions

[3] "What Life Means to Einstein: An Interview by George Sylvester Viereck," for the October 26, 1929 issue of The Saturday Evening Post.

[4] Albert Einstein Quotes, http://www.sfheart.com/einstein.html

[5] L. P. Jacks as quoted by Dorothy L. Sayers, *The Mind of the Maker*, HarperCollins Publishers, NY, 1987, p.179

[6] C.S. Lewis, *The Abolition of Man*, Edited by William J. Bennett, The Book of Virtues, Simon & Schuster, N.Y., 1993, p.p. 264,265

[7] Martin Heidegger, Nietzsche, transl., David Farrell Krell (SanFrancisco: HarpeSanFrancisco, 1991)

[8] Emily Post, *Etiquette*, Funk & Wagnalls. New York, 1945, p.1

[9] Ibid., p. 2

[10] Noah Webster, American Dictionary of the English Language, Foundation for American Christian Education, 1967 & 1995 by Rosalie J. Slater, In Preface, p.10

[11] Martin Luther, Complete Sermons of Martin Luther, Vol. 2.1, *Pentecost Sunday*, Baker Books, Grand Rapids, MI, 2000, p333

[12] Thomas J. J. Altizer and William Hamilton, *Radical Theology and the Death of God* (Indianapolis: Bobbs-Merrill, 1966), p.x.

[13] Blaise Pascal, *PENSfES*, 1660, translated by W. F. Trotter, #280

[14] Dorothy L. Sayers, *The Mind of the Maker*, HarperCollins Publishers, NY, 1987, p.p.122,123

2: First Principles The first Principle is One Principal. First God…

2.1) God

2.1.1) The Character and Personality of God

2.1.1.1) Introduction

1.1 Prophesy has the common meaning of revealing or foretelling something, or a future event by, or as if by divine inspiration. It has, however another meaning in the Church of giving instruction in religious subjects.

This second meaning is what the Holy Spirit was promised to do in John 14:26. I quote Jesus,

> "But the Helper, the Holy Spirit, whom the Father will send in My name, He will teach you all things, and bring to your remembrance all that I said to you."

I have not revealed or foretold the future in God's Name, never cast out demons, and never did any mighty works in God's Name. But in Matthew 7:21-23, God has told others who have done these things

> 'I never knew you; depart from me, you workers of lawlessness.'

This verse worried me, so I searched the Scriptures for an answer to the question: How do I become known by God?

I finally found the two-step answer in two verses, Psalm 9:10 and Nahum 1:7 (NKJV)

> *"And they who know Your name will lean on and confidently put their trust in You, for You, Lord, have not forsaken those who seek You ."* Psalm 9:10 *(NKJV)*

> *"The Lord is good, A stronghold in the day of trouble; And He KNOWS those who TRUST in Him."* Nahum 1:7 *(NKJV)*

Thus, we become known by God by seeking His Name. The process creates Trust and eventually friendship. The LORD said in John 15:15: (NKJV)

> *"15 No longer do I call you servants, for the servant does not know what his master is doing; but I have called you friends, for all that I have heard from my Father I have made known to you."*

As a Spirit Filled Christian, I believe that God has chosen to dwell within me. Further, as a Christian I believe that Jesus, the Holy Spirit, and the Father are all one God, and God is everywhere but not anywhere divisible. This belief makes me accept what God now asks of me. I believe our God wants us to write for Him. At this time, I make myself available to do just that.

2.1.1.1) God By God From His Perspective

So, this servant Larry, who wrote this, will represent Me by quoting My written Word. He understands full well he is not Me.

Scholars often speak of My Attributes or Characteristics, but I want you to know ME as a Father and as a friend.

You learn to trust a friend, but you can't be My friend if you don't know me. I want you to know my person. (Personalized Scripture)

First, I want to speak about the difference of two words: Jealousy and Envy. They relate to Me and My Adversary,

- *Jealousy is an emotion regarding the potential loss of a cherished person or thing to another.*

- *Envy is an emotion regarding the desire to have what another possesses.* (*Covet*)

This is obvious when a husband becomes jealous when another man is envious of his wife.

You should know my Name if you are serious. *My Name is Jealous! Yes, Jealous! And I AM your God.*

- In Exodus 34:14 (NIV) I had written, *"for you shall not worship any other god, for the LORD, whose name is Jealous, is a jealous God—"*

Besides that, My Son calls me Truth in John 18:37 :

- *"You are a king, then!" said Pilate. "You say that I am a king, Jesus answered. ""You say that I am a king. In fact, the reason I was born and came into the world is to testify to the truth. Everyone on the side of truth listens to me."* (NIV)

Did you know My adversary is Envy! – I had it written in <u>Isaiah -14</u> about Lucifer's envy.
¹³ *'For you have said in your heart: I will ascend into heaven, I will exalt my throne above the stars of God; I will also sit on the mount of the congregation On the farthest sides of the north;*(That is, in the most prestigious place) ¹⁴ *I will ascend above the heights of the clouds, I will be like the Most High.' (NKJV)*

And he is a liar and the father of lies.

- In John 8:44 I had it written *"You are of your father the devil, and the desires of your father you want to do. He was a murderer from the beginning, and does not stand in the truth, because there is no truth in him. When he speaks a lie, he speaks from his own resources, for he is a liar and the father of it." (NIV)*

So if I AM the Father of Truth, and Jesus the Witness of Truth, then the Antichrist should be called "The Witness to the Lie."

- First, because his fraudulent claim to be the real Christ will be the greatest falsehood palmed off upon humanity.
- Second, because he is the direct antithesis of My Son, who is "The Witness to the Truth." (John 18:37) (NIV)
- Third, because he is the son of Satan who is the arch liar.

But let's no longer speak of him. Know Me:
Did you know that I AM Reciprocal?

- If you seek Me, I will be found by you;
- But if you forsake Me, I will forsake you. – 2 Chronicles 15:2
- Judge not, and you will not be judged.
- Condemn not, and you will not be condemned.
- Forgive, and you will be forgiven. Luke 6:36-42
- Jesus says, give, and it will be given to you. …For with the measure you use it will be measured back to you.
- I will give you the keys of the kingdom of heaven; whatever you bind on earth will be bound in heaven, and whatever you loose on earth will be loosed in heaven." Matthew 16:19
- "We love, because He first loved us." 1 John 4:19
- If you endure, you will also reign with Me;
- If you deny Me, I also will deny you; 2 Timothy 2:12

This is the law of reciprocity: I will judge you according to how you have judged others (see Matthew 7:2)

- Man offered his son to Me and I offered My Son to Man

- Genesis 22:1-19 ESV - The Sacrifice of Isaac

- Luke 23:26-43 - The Crucifixion of Jesus

- "I AM with you while you are with Me. (2 Chronicles 15:2) However, in contrast:
- If you are faithless, I remain faithful, for I cannot deny Myself-(2Timothy 2:13)

I, the Creator of the universe and your DNA. Yes, I AM also Humble. As men you say "An acorn doesn't fall far from the tree." My Son presented Me to you in Matthew 11:28,30,

> "Come to Me, all you who are weary and burdened, and I will give you rest. 29Take My yoke upon you and learn from Me; for I am gentle and humble in heart, and you will find rest for your souls. 30For My yoke is easy and My burden is light...."

When I came as Jesus, I was as I had the Psalmist write:

> Psalm 22:6 But I am a worm and not a man, scorned by everyone, despised by the people.
> Psalm 22:7 All who see Me mock me; they hurl insults, shaking their heads.

By these words I was showing you how I am. And in Isaiah 53:2, I stated how I chose to appear to you as My Son:

- For Jesus grew up before Me like a tender shoot, And like a root out of parched ground;
- He has no stately form or majesty That you should look upon Him,
- Nor appearance that you should be attracted to Him.
- He was despised and forsaken of men,
- A man of sorrows and acquainted with grief;
- And like one from whom men hide their face
- He was despised, and you did not esteem Him.
- Surely your griefs He Himself bore, and your sorrows He carried;
- Yet you esteemed Him stricken, Smitten by Me, and afflicted....

And what kind of man do I choose to lead MY people? I had it written in Numbers 12:3, "Now the man Moses was very humble, more than any man who was on the face of the earth." Why do you think I had that included?

I walked and talked with Adam and talked with Moses and Abraham.

So, what should you have read in the Bible about MY character so that you could have decided if I would make a good friend? Here is a partial list:

- First, I AM trustworthy. (Hebrews 13:8) "Jesus Christ is the same yesterday and today and forever".
- Second, I AM love (1 John 4:8). Jesus made that very clear. He loved the people that society spit out. He embraced children. He invited tax collectors to follow him. Sharing God's love with prostitutes was more important to him than his reputation.
- Third, I AM righteous. (Deuteronomy 32:4) "A God of faithfulness and without iniquity, just and upright AM I". I love truth and justice, and I hate lies and injustice.
- Fourth, I AM holy. Isaiah 6:3 says "Holy, holy, holy am I Lord of hosts; the whole earth is full of MY glory!" I AM glorious, and MY glory sets ME apart from sin; that is, I AM holy. Because this same holiness is in Jesus, He is called 'the Holy One of God' (John 6:69).

But this glory is not the glory of a king. Instead, it is the glory of one removed from the distortion of the lie. One who has a brilliant laser beam of Truth cutting through the work of the Adversary!

- Fifth, I AM merciful. I appeared to Moses on the mountain, and the next thing you read in Exodus 34:6-7 is: "The LORD passed before him and proclaimed, "The LORD, the LORD,
  - a God merciful and gracious,
  - slow to anger, and
  - abounding in steadfast love and faithfulness,
  - keeping steadfast love for thousands,
  - forgiving iniquity and transgression and sin,
  - *And in* Exodus 20:5 regarding false gods I said :

"You shall not worship them or serve them; for I, the LORD your God, am a jealous God, visiting the iniquity of the fathers on the children, on the third and the fourth generations of those who hate Me, 6 but showing lovingkindness to thousands of generations, to those who love Me and keep My commandments.

In Summary,

I am just through my reciprocity

I am merciful through my love

I am humble before you my children

And now, so that My acorns don't fall far from this Oak, Do justly, love mercy, and walk humbly with Me.

Micah 6:8

o And if you must boast, boast in this,
- That you understand and know Me,
- That I am the Lord, exercising lovingkindness, judgment, and righteousness in the earth.

For in these I delight,"- Jeremiah 9:24

2.1.2) God The Creator

In Genesis 1:1 God is immediately identified as the Creator of the heavens and the earth. He is the Father of creation. In Genesis 1:27 He creates man and woman in His own image-that would make man and woman also creators in the image of God. In Genesis 2:7, God was reported to have made man from the dust of the earth, but woman was some manner of gender-altered derivative taken from man's side. There could be no concern about recessive genes with Adam's perfect genetics. Then, in Genesis 3:15 He tells the serpent about a seed of woman that is coming. In Matthew 1:18 we first hear of Jesus Christ being the Child of God through His Holy Spirit, the very same Holy Spirit mentioned in Genesis 1:2 as the Prime Mover.

Thus, God creates human life in three ways: first He makes man from dust, then He makes woman from man, and lastly, He makes man from woman. He therefore likes to be varied in His method of creation, not just varied in His creations. He further wants us to be creators in His image. Lastly, His image has been revealed to us as having three projections. These projections we refer to by Name as the Father and the Son and the Holy Spirit. These projections are on three different axes, but the three superimpose into one unified hologram.

2.1.3) The Unity vs. the Trinity of God

I am sensitive to the fact that men of other religions believe that we worship three gods. The core fault lies in the use of the word "person" to describe each of the three modes of being in the Trinitarian Godhead as understood by Christians. The fundamental definition of "person" is *Human Being* or *Individual*. Thus we have used human characteristics to describe God. That is a natural consequence of God appearing as a Man in Christ Jesus. However, the use of human terms to describe the other manifestations of God is inappropriate except by analogy.

The difficulty with using more appropriate terms can lead to language that carries with it a lack of warmth or human connection. The word "Entity" perfectly states the existence of God but does not describe His attributes. This word "Entity" is cold, and could easily describe an uncaring system of power. As we will see in the Appendix *Necessary Conditions for an Entity, S, to be a System*, God is more than an entity, and can be viewed as a System. Such a view has no reverence until the purpose of that System is described.

Such views, even with the details added, do not provide the soul with the image of its Creator. Describing God is like describing Love. It is only possible to describe by experience. Men who can only describe the chemical reactions that happen in the brain when a man falls in love don't have a clue what they are missing. Terms of endearment that we relate to are necessary to describe this Entity.

So we are told that the Trinity is a mystery, an enigma, an inscrutable puzzle. I don't think, however, that God intends to hide by revealing. He reveals His existence and His essence in His Word. And He insisted that His chosen people repeat the phrase, "The LORD our God is One Lord" God is One God, not three Gods. He is not three Lords, but One Lord. But like a jewel, He has multiple facets. He has appeared for us, and to us, in three manifestations.

- *There is one God and Father of all, who is over all and through all and in all. – Eph.4:6 (NIV)*
- *There is but one God, the Father, from whom all things came and for whom we live; and there is but one Lord, Jesus Christ, through whom all things came and through whom we live. – 1Cor.8:6*
- *For there is one God and one mediator between God and men, the man, Jesus Christ – 1 Tim.2:5 (NIV)*
- *A mediator, however, implies more than one party; but God is one. – Gal.3:20 (NIV)*
- *Hear O Israel: The Lord our God is one Lord. – Deut. 6:4, Mark 12:29*
- *And the Spirit of God was hovering over the waters. – Gen.1:2 (NIV)*
- *The Spirit of God has made me; the breath of the Almighty gives me life.- Job 33.4 (NIV)*
- *You believe that God is one; you do well: the demons also believe, and shudder." James 2:19 (NIV)*
- *Therefore go and make followers of all nations, baptizing them in the **name** of the Father and of the Son and of the Holy Spirit. - Matt.28:19 (NIV)*

The New Testament does not promote the doctrine of the Trinity as three individual Persons. Jesus answered Philip and said:

> *Don't you know me, Philip, even after I have been among you such a long time? Anyone who has seen me has seen the Father. How can you say, `Show us the Father'? - John 14:9 (NIV)*

For the Scriptures declare that the Father, Son and Holy Ghost are only manifestations of the One God; and God is One Entity. God was manifested as: Aravat, the Father of creation (Invisible Spirit - John 1:18, 4:24) and later revealed as Yahweh, the Great I AM; Yah –Yeshua , I AM Salvation, or Yeshua the Son in salvation (Spirit in body - Col. 1: 1315, 2:9); and Ruach HaKodesh, the Holy Spirit (Spirit in believers - Acts 2:4, 17, Rom. 8:9, Eph 4:6) in emanation.

On the Unity of God consider the following:

- The Lord God is Almighty. Gen. 17:1.
- The Lord Jesus is Almighty. Rev. 1:8.
- The Lord God is the Creator. Is. 42:5.
- The Lord Jesus is the Creator. John 1:3, 10.
- The Lord God is the First and the Last. Is. 44:6.
- The Lord Jesus is the First and the Last. Rev. 1:8.
- The Lord God said, "I am *He*." Is. 43:10.
- The Lord Jesus said, "I am *He*." John 8:24.
- The Lord God is the King of Israel. Is. 43:15.
- The Lord Jesus is the King of Israel. Matt. 27:37.
- The Lord God is the only Savior. Is. 43:11.
- The Lord Jesus is the Savior Titus 1:4.

"There are three that bear record in heaven, the Father, the Word, and the Holy Ghost: and these three are ONE." I John 5:7. So, our God is one with a singular ***name*** "Father and Son and Holy Spirit. The word "Trinity" never appears in our Bibles, but Matt. 28:19 certainly ascribes a singular ***name*** that describes the triple manifestation. He partitioned, or sanctified, His appearance for our sake.

This single entity below that is viewed as three is called the **Triquetra**.

A Single Entity
Viewed as Three

Contained in God is all that *Is,* all that *has being.* God is *Immense,* and all that is God is *Good; Kindhearted and Well-intentioned.* He is *Just* and *Merciful, Graceful* and *Holy*; *Perfect* in His Attributes. God penetrates everything even though He contains all things. God dwells in His universe and yet the universe dwells in God. How can such a thing be? A. W. Tozer gives us an analogous answer.

> "The bucket that is sunk into the depths of the ocean is full of the ocean. The ocean is in the bucket, but also the bucket is in the ocean—surrounded by it." [1]

Further, God is infinite and indivisible. How can this be? Blaise Pascal addressed this beautifully in ***PENSfES***,

> 231.　Do you believe it to be impossible that God is infinite, without parts? Yes. I wish therefore to show you an infinite and indivisible thing. It is a point moving everywhere with an infinite velocity; for it is one in all places and is all totality in every place. Let this effect of nature, which previously seemed to you impossible, make you know that there may be others of which you are still ignorant. Do not draw this conclusion from your experiment, that there remains nothing for you to know; but rather that there remains an infinity for you to know.

> 232.　Infinite movement, the point which fills everything, the moment of rest; infinite without quantity, indivisible and infinite.[2]

2.1.4) God's NAME

There are 22 Characters in the Hebrew alphabet. Each has a meaning, and also a core meaning. For example, the first letter, Aleph, has a meaning of king or ruler, but its core or literal meaning is Bull or Ox. This signifies, I guess, raw power. One can find these tables of Hebrew alphabet meaning on the internet easily. Hebrew is written from right to left like Aramaic. This fascinated me, and I wondered about God's NAME, written as the TETRAGRAMATION:

יהוה

Reading from right to left, we have Yod, Hey, Vav, Hey - With literal meanings respectively: Closed Fist, Behold, Nails or Pegs, Behold.

I take the meaning to be: Behold, I AM the ONE with the Nails in MY Hands!

Further, when we read, it's from left to right, but we can easily read words from top to bottom. For example, when driving and looking for a diner, we easily recognize EAT written vertically. When one writes God's NAME, it becomes the stick figure of a man!

When King David decided, and Solomon built a Temple for God's NAME it was understood that the whole world was God's footstool. This Temple was for God's people!

We are walking billboards for God's NAME!
We are like Him and in kind, as it says in Genesis, an also in a visual sense.

2.2) The Bible and The Creeds

I cannot accept a theology that rejects verbal inspiration of the Scriptures and stresses a nonliteral revelation, nor one that favors a subjective view of atonement and a tendency to belief in universal salvation when the Scriptures say otherwise. I doubt the value of any such religious belief, except as an opiate for the masses. I think religion so established would generally be increasingly ignored. This essay conveys meaning and truth if and only if the Bible, the Word of

God, is True. The Bible is True if and only if it is completely true. It must have no real contradictions. Let's focus on the Bible and the Creeds.

The Bible and the Creeds are a privileged text and a privileged mode of explanation. The Holy Scriptures and creeds were given to the church through the helpful counsel of the Holy Spirit. They were not a reasoned product of Gnosticism, Scholasticism, or modernity. There were roughly fifteen hundred years elapsed between the writing of the Bible's first and last pages. There were scores of authors involved in its writing, including shepherds, fishermen, statesmen and kings.

2.2.1) The Inspired, Inerrant, Infallible, and Indestructible Bible

What is it if not inspired? Just what is meant for a document to be called "inspired?" [3]. Inspiration is not revelation, illumination, or human genius, but the terminating work of the Holy Spirit on the original record and not a copy or translation. In 1893 the General Assembly of the Presbyterian Church of America in Washington, D.C., proclaimed the following statement on Biblical Inerrancy in the face of the then current Higher Criticism to the contrary. "The Bible as we now have it, in its various translations and revisions, when freed from all error and mistakes of translators, copyists and printers, (is) the very Word of God, and consequently wholly without error."[4]

But There are Mistakes

But there *are* mistakes of translators and copyists and worse. It does not serve the body of Christ to ignore the errors. The LORD intended for us to read His Word, not alternatives. Christ said, Seek and you will find! So, we seek in older texts the undistorted Word. I have come to envy the Eastern Churches because of their ancient Greek ***Septuagint*** translation of the Old Testament and Aramaic ***Peshitta***. First a Septuagint background provided by Sir Lancelot C. L. Brenton:

The ***Septuagint*** text proved successful converting Jews to Christianity after Jesus fulfilled its message. The non-messianic Jewish reaction resulted in three new Greek translations by them to their liking.

> "The first of the Greek versions of the Old Testament executed in the second century was that of AQUILA. He is described as a Jew or Jewish proselyte of Pontus, and the date commonly attributed to his version is about the year A.D. 126. His version is said to have been executed for the express purpose of opposing the authority of the Septuagint: his version was in consequence upheld by the Jews. His labour was evidently directed in opposing the passages which Christians were accustomed to cite from the Septuagint as applicable to the Lord Jesus."[6]

Larry Sheets

Talmudic Influences on Scripture

You shall not add to the word which I command you,

Do not add to what I command you and do not subtract from it, but keep the commands of the Lord.
Deut. 4:2a

The *Masorites* were Jewish scholars who scribed and published Hebrew scriptures. *Masorah* refers to Jewish tradition. In the Masoretic text, though, it has the specific meaning of the notes written in the margins of the Scriptures. They didn't alter the text known as the "Emendations of the Scribes", they only passed down the product of the earlier *Sopherim* Scribes. Rabbi Simon ben Pazzi (third century) calls these readings "Emendations of the Scribes " or "Emendations of the Sopherim" (*tikkune Soferim*; Midrash Genesis Rabbah xlix. 7). These assumed changes are of four general types:

- Redacting of unseemly expressions referencing to God;
- Removing YHWH and substituting Elohim
- Removal of any false god names to YHWH
- Protecting Jerusalem as the place for worship

The first Talmud was written during the Babylonian exile, and later brought to Israel. The language of the Masoretic text is composed of both Hebrew and partly Palestinian Aramaic writings. The Hebrew word *masorah* ("tradition".) evolved with use. The term *masorah* originally meant "fetter. The notes in the margins were to be a fetter upon its exposition. *Masorah* was later given the meaning of "tradition," because of its use. These writings and thoughts of men, called traditions, were objected to by our Lord Jesus.

> You have let go of the commands of God and are holding on to the traditions of men. - Mark 7:8

> And he said to them: "You have a fine way of setting aside the commands of God in order to observe your own traditions. - Mark 7:9 (NIV)

The Scribes (*Sopherim*) modified the name of God, the Tetragrammaton *YHVH*, to read *Adonai*, or Lord, in the Hebrew Scriptures. They believed His name should not be used in certain contexts. These scribes kept records of these changes so that others later would know where changes had been made to the text. These records were kept as notes in the margins of the handwritten Scripture texts. This collection of marginal notes is called the *Masorah*. The writing in the upper and lower margins is called the Great *Masorah*, while that found in the side margins and between the columns is called the Small *Masorah*. I quote the works of E. W. Bullinger, in his Appendix #30, p. 31, of *The Companion Bible*, {Zondervan Bible Publishers, Grand Rapids, 1974. The Holy Bible, (King Games Version), Oxford University Press, London.} where he discusses the relationship between the *Sopherim* and the *Masorites*:

> "The Text itself had been fixed before the *Massorites* were put in charge of it. This had been the work of the *Sopherim* (from *saphar*, to *count*, or *number*). Their work, under Ezra and

Nehemiah, was to set the Text in order after the return from Babylon; and we read of it in Neh. 8.8 (cp. Ezra 7.6,11). The men of 'the Great Synagogue' completed the work. This work lasted about 110 years, from Nehemiah to Simon the first, 410-300 B.C.

The *Sopherim* were the authorized revisers of the Sacred Text; and, their work being completed, the Massorites were the authorized custodians of it. Their work was to preserve it. The *Masorah* is called 'A Fence to the Scriptures,' because it locked all words and letters in their places. ... "

As technology improved with the printing press, the altered Scripture was produced without the margin notes to explain what changes had been made. Thus, when the Hebrew text was translated into other languages, the Masorah was missing for use by the translators. E. W. Bullinger continues:

"When translators came to the printed Hebrew Text, they were necessarily destitute of the information contained in the *Massorah*; so that the Revisers as well as the Translators of the Authorized Version carried out their work without any idea of the treasures contained in the *Massorah*; and therefore, without giving a hint of it to their readers. "

Masoretic Text
(from **Hebrew** *masoreth,* "tradition")

The **Masoretic Text (MT)** is the Hebrew text of the Tanakh approved for general use in Judaism. *It is the oldest complete manuscripts of the Masoretic Text known to still exist date from approximately the ninth century* It was written by the Talmudic Jews known as the Masoretic Sect of the Talmudic Jews between the first and tenth centuries AD. There are many small and large differences between it and the Septuagint.

It was first printed in 1425 AD. William Tyndale 1494-1536 translated it into the English language. Tyndale was found guilty of treason and heresy against the Church. He was strangled in the courtyard of the prison and then burned at the stake. Tyndale's Bible was the basis of the

Bishop's Bible, the Geneva Bible and the subsequent King James Bible. Wycliff had earlier translated the Latin Vulgate into English, so the English had knowledge of the Anglicized Septuagint variant which included the Apocrypha. The Apocrypha was included with the Masoretic Text in the original 1611 King James Bible..

The Septuagint is representative of a 3rd century BC Hebrew text anticipating the coming Messiah; the Masoretic is representative of a 7th-9th century AD revision of the original Scriptures. The Masoretic Text was, therefore, a "Johnny come a millennium lately" text received from the Talmudic Jewish scholars of the Masorah who had no fondness for the messianic prophecies in the LXX that were cherished by the Christians of the first Christian millennium.

So, this anti Messianic ***Masoretic Text*** is the basis for most of the Old Testament in the 1611 King James Version, with the Apocrypha from Wycliff's earlier work. The ***Masoretic Text*** permeates many subsequent Bibles since the 1600's, including the NIV. The KJV uses the 16th century ***Textus Receptus*** as its basis for the New Testament. A few examples are included here to demonstrate the point.

Example 1:

In the King James Version, we hear of a man who is two years older than his father! II Chronicles 21:20-22:1-2 reads:

> "Thirty and two years old was he [Jehoram] when he began to reign, and he reigned in Jerusalem eight years, and departed without being desired. Howbeit they buried him in the city of David, but not in the sepulchres of the kings. And the inhabitants of Jerusalem made Ahaziah his youngest son king in his stead: for the band of men that came with the Arabians to the camp had slain all the eldest. So Ahaziah the son of Jehoram king of Judah reigned. Forty and two years old was Ahaziah when he began to reign ... "

In the Greek ***Septuagint*** (II Chr. 22:2 LXX) the last verse reads Ahaziah's (Ahaziah = Ochozias) age:

> ... began to reign when he was twenty years old...

Example 2:

In the King James Version, II Kings 24:8 reads: Jehoiachin was eighteen years old when he began to reign...

But in the King James Version, II Chronicles 36:9 reads: Jehoiachin was eight years old when he began to reign...

The Greek ***Septuagint*** (Alexandrine Text) reads 'eighteen years' in both instance

Consider the evidence supporting the Septuagint that exists between the New Testament and the Old Testament quotations:

Romans 3:11-18. These verses are quoted from **Psalms 14:1-3 (Psalm 13 in LXX).** These quotations of over 60 Greek words differ only by three letters. In the Masoretic Text, however, verses 11 and 12 are only partially present. Further, Verses 13-18 are entirely absent. The Apostle Paul made it clear that he was quoting the Scriptures. Thus, Paul's scriptural source had to be the Septuagint. Paul was a scholar of repute, a Pharisee, a Jew's Jew, and he quoted from the Septuagint. ***The Septuagint was the Bible of the first century Christians.***

In *The Bible in Greek Christian Antiquity,* Edited by Paul M. Blowers, (1997 from Notre Dame University), Paul Lamarche writes:

> "In what version was the Old Testament used and commented on by early Christians? ... it is the Septuagint, the Greek translation which, directly or indirectly, was fundamentally for all writings of the early Christian centuries, and even after Jerome it is the text which the Greek Fathers, including the Antiochenes, customarily used."

Lamarche states that the consensus opinion after the discovery of the Dead Sea Scrolls is that problem verses lie not with the Septuagint but with the corrupted Masoretic Text. Scholars have taken this position for centuries, primarily because of the quotations from the New Testament which parallel exactly with the Greek Septuagint (LXX) but differ greatly from the Masoretic Text.

Rom. 3:11-18 NIV	Psalms 14:2-7 NIV	Psalm 14 LXX
3:11 there is no one who understands; there is no one who seeks God.	14:1 The fool[a] says in his heart, There is no God." They are corrupt, their deeds are vile; there is no one who does good.	14:1 The fool has said in his heart, There is no God. They have corrupted [themselves], and become abominable in their devices; there is none that does goodness, there is not even so much as one.
	14:2 The LORD looks down from heaven on all mankind to see if there are any who understand, any who seek God.	14:2 The Lord looked down from heaven upon the sons of men, to see if there were any that understood, or sought-after God.
3:12 All have turned away, they have together become worthless; there is no one who does good, not even one."[a]	14:3 All have turned away, all have become corrupt; there is no one who does good, not even one.	14:3 They are all gone out of the way, they are together become good for nothing, there is none that does good, no not one. Their throat is an open sepulchre; with their tongues they have used deceit;
3:13 "Their throats are open graves; their tongues practice deceit."[b] "The poison of vipers is on their lips."[c]		
3:14 "Their mouths are full of cursing and bitterness."[d] 3:15 "Their feet are swift to shed blood; 3:16 ruin and misery mark their ways, 3:17 and the way of peace they do not know."[e] 3:18 "There is no fear of God before their eyes."[f]		the poison of asps is under their lips: whose mouth is full of cursing and bitterness; their feet are swift to shed blood destruction and misery are in their ways; and the way of peace they have not known: there is no fear of God before their eyes.
	14:4 Do all these evildoers know nothing? They devour my people as though eating bread; they never call on the LORD.	14:4 Will not all the workers of iniquity know, who eat up my people as they would eat bread? they have not called upon the Lord.
	14:5 But there they are, overwhelmed with dread, for God is present in the company of the righteous.	14:5 There were they alarmed with fear, where there was no fear; for God is in the righteous generation.
	14:6 You evildoers frustrate the plans of the poor, but the LORD is their refuge.	14:6 Ye have shamed the counsel of the poor, because the Lord is his hope.

	14:7 Oh, that salvation for Israel would come out of Zion! When the LORD restores his people, let Jacob rejoice and Israel be glad.	14:7 Who will bring the salvation of Israel out of Zion{gr.Sion}? when the Lord brings back the captivity of his people, let Jacob exult, and Israel be glad.

The three most revered manuscripts of the LXX known are the 1) Vatican, "Codex Vaticanus" (fourth century); 2) the Alexandrian, "Codex Alexandrinus" (fifth century), now in the British Museum, London; and 3) that of Sinai, "Codex Sinaiticus" (fourth century). The "Codex Vaticanus" is the purest of the three; it generally gives the more ancient text, while the "Codex Alexandrinus" borrows much from the hexaplar text and is changed according to the Masoretic text.

How do the Masoretic and Septuagint compare with the Dead Sea Scrolls? All Hebrew manuscripts found at Qumran are more aligned with the Greek Septuagint than with the Masoretic Text.

For the skeptical, convincing internal evidence supporting the Septuagint exists between the New Testament and the Old Testament quotations. A table is provided by physicist R. Grant Jones and made available *Notes on The Septuagint,* ©2000 on the Internet at: http://home.earthlink.net/~rgjones3/Septuagint/spindex.htm, and http://home.earthlink.net/~rgjones3/Septuagint/spexecsum.htm

New Testament Peshitta

However, even the acceptance of the ***Septuagint*** would not rid our Bible of all the discrepancies.

Example 3:

> Matthew 27:9 has been a mystery verse to me. The quote is not found in Jeremiah in either the Hebrew Masoretic Text or the Greek Septuagint, but is found in Zechariah 11:12,13 instead!

> Then that which was spoken through Jeremiah the prophet was fulfilled:
> "AND THEY TOOK THE THIRTY PIECES OF SILVER, THE PRICE OF THE ONE WHOSE PRICE HAD BEEN SET by the sons of Israel;"

If this is a transcribing error it must have happened early in the process, as seems to be the case, because the same verse in the Aramaic ***Peshitta*** uses only the word "prophet" instead of the name "Jeremiah." Since Aramaic was the language spoken in Israel at the time of Christ, except in the synagogues, it is thought to be the original form of the text.

The saying about the "eye of a needle" never seemed to ring true. The Lord's other sayings were all universally understandable without the need of extra knowledge such as the speck of sawdust in one eye and a log in another. As it is presently explained, it requires knowledge of the structure of the gates into Jerusalem to understand. However, in the Peshitta, the parable says,

> ***And again, I say to you that it is easier for a rope to enter into the eye of a needle than for someone who is rich to enter into the kingdom of God. – Matthew 19:24***

Now you have to admit, that sounds more like His voice! My guess is that the "camel" of the Greek and Latin texts was a literal translation for a slang name for a camel hair rope. Our culture has had its horsehair ropes. We know John the Baptist wore camel hair clothes. It seems possible that camel hair ropes were simple called "the camel." Don't we say, "Pass the china." When we mean porcelain dishes that were made in china? Don't we say a "Monkey wrench" when no animal is involved? Or maybe, "Needle nose" when we want pointed pliers? And we won't even delve into all the "male or female" connectors and fittings that never reproduce! Regardless of my weak guesses, the word "Rope" was in the oldest document and in the original language.

Thus, as we seek earlier manuscripts, we find that the errors were introduced as time passed without benefit of printing press or Xerox machines. We may never find the first document but is sufficient to observe that the errors diminish as we observe older documents. If the contrary were true, the results would surely have been fudged! But there is more to this Word than the scientist can measure. It may rather require a good physician to explain it.

It Is Alive!

We are but feebly aware of the wonderful fact that the Word of God is not just a document. It is a LIVING Word. It is extraordinary that the property of Life, or vitality, is attributed to the Word of God. It is in fact more alive than the creatures we call "living," which may just as appropriately be regarded as "dying." The so-called "land of the living" may be better described as the "land of the dying." There is between the Bible and all other books the same difference as between Jesus and all other men. In Jesus there was Life capable of the resurrection, and the Bible has the Word of Life capable of the new birth. Jesus' appearance did not reveal His Deity, nor demonstrate that "in Him was life" (John 1:4) (NIV). Similarly, there is nothing in the outward appearance of the Bible to reveal its characteristic and divine life.

The Bible is never exhausted, trite, or unresponsive to the redeemed soul who comes to it. In this it is comparable only to a loved one to whom we go for companionship and comfort. Thus, the Word of God may be compared to a living person while the books of men are comparable only to statues of living persons. And like a living person with resolve, it has its enemies.

There is no other book in the world that is so truly reviled. This hatred is unrelenting, acrid, and murderous, and has been kept alive from one generation to the next for thousands of years.

Surely this continuous display of hostility towards the Bible has a supernatural explanation, since that Book has a supernatural enemy who has felt its power (Matt. 4:110).

It is no wonder that the Bible is hated; it presents the truth about man and his world. It does not say that man is a dignified being, ever reaching for the stars and aspiring towards the attainment of lofty principles. It does not say that mans' tenure has demonstrated "progress," as the successful courageous struggle against the evils of his world; to the contrary, it describes it as a disobedient departure from God, choosing darkness over light "because their deeds are evil." We continue with the thoughts of Philip Mauro:

> "There may be books which men dislike, and such they simply let alone But the Bible is, and always has been, hated to the death. It is the *one book* that has been pursued from century to century, as men pursue a mortal foe. At first its destruction has been sought by violence. All human powers, political and ecclesiastical, have combined to put it out of existence. Death has been the penalty for possessing or reading a copy; and such copies as were found have been turned over to the public executioner to be treated as was the Incarnate Word. ...
>
> One explanation alone will account for the astounding fact that such a Book should be the only one now or ever in existence to provoke active and persistent animosity among men who refuse to acknowledge it as from God; namely, that it declares that man is a fallen creature. ... It is the only thing *in* the whole world that is hostile *to* the whole world-system. ... Like a living person, the Bible has made its way into all lands, has adapted itself to all environments, entered into relations of the most intimate kind with all peoples, and has exerted upon them all its own unique influence. ... it not only speaks to all peoples in their mother tongue, but it addresses itself to all classes of society".[7]

When we write or speak about the Word of God, we are discussing both Christ and the Bible. The Incarnate Word and the Written Word are so referenced in Scripture that it is not always clear which is referred to. Furthermore, both are repeatedly referred to as food for the children of God.

> "Christ and the Bible are inseparable. If we follow Christ, He will teach us of the Bible; and if we study our Bible, it will point us to Christ. Each is called the Word of God. ... A word is an oral or visible expression of an invisible thought. The thought needs the word for its expression, and the word is intended to represent the thought accurately, even if not completely. .... He came, among other things, to bear witness to the truth (John 18:37), and it is a necessary outcome of this purpose that He should bear infallible witness. He came to reveal God and God's will, and this implies and requires special knowledge. It demands that every assertion of His be true. The Divine knowledge did not, because it could not, undergo any change by the Incarnation. He continued to subsist in the form of God even while He existed in the form of man".[8]

Life begets life, and life nourishes life. We eat what lived before us, and we eventually become food for some life. We don't really understand the details of digestion and integration of nourishment into our bodies, and we understand even less the digestion of spiritual food. Jesus was quite insistent that He was the food of life, "*I am the living bread that came down from heaven. Whoever eats this bread will live forever. This bread is my flesh, which I will give for the life of the world.*" –John 6:51 (NIV)

> "Looking more particularly at what is said in this connection concerning the written or spoken Word of God we find that the Word of God is "living" in the sense that, like other living substance, it has the property of furnishing nutrition, and thereby sustaining life. It is a life-sustaining Word. ... The passages which present the Word of God as the food for His children are very familiar; and in bringing them to mind again we would impress it upon our readers that these statements are not to be taken as if they were poetical or figurative, but as very literal, practical and immensely important. [9]
> ...
>
> This is the wonderful provision of God for the deliverance of dying men. In order that they might not die, and because God wills not that any should perish (2 Peter 3:9), He has sent this dying world a Word of Life. For God is not the God of the dead, but of the living (Matt. 22:32). ...What men need is not morality, but life; not to make death respectable, but to receive the gift of eternal life; not decent interment, but a pathway out of the realm of death."[10]

How shall we view this living pathway, this bridge between the land of the living and the land of the dying, this banquet prepared for us in the presence of our enemies?

> "Look at its structure; look at its completeness; look at it in the clearness and fullness and holiness of its teachings; look at it in its sufficiency to guide every soul that truly seeks light unto the saving knowledge of God. Take the Book as a whole, in its whole, in its whole purpose, its whole spirit, its whole aim and tendency, and the whole setting of it, and ask, Is there not manifest the power which you can only trace back, as it traces back itself, to God's Holy Spirit really in the men who wrote it?"[11]

The Bible[12]

> *We search the world for truth. We cull the good, the true, the beautiful,*
> *From graven stone and written scroll, and all old flower-fields of the soul;*
> *And weary seekers of the best, we come back laden from our quest,*
> *To find that all the sages said is in the Book our mothers read.*
> -John Greenleaf Whittier

2.2.2) Creeds

> *"We must give in a definition the briefest possible statement*
> *of such qualities as are sufficient to distinguish the class from other classes."*
> – W.S. Jevons: *Lessons in Logic*

"A definition must be carefully thought out and should have the following properties:

- *The terms used must be simpler than the term defined.*
- *The term defined must be placed in its nearest class.*
- *The difference between the term defined and other similar terms must be pointed out.*
- *The definition must be reversible."* [13]

As is discussed later, plane geometry is a study of unchangeable shapes, while algebra relates to time and things flowing in time. God does not change, but what He does causes change for us. Thus, if we study God, or His Word, certain rules might apply that relate to those used in geometry. Those rules are:[14]

i. The only instruments that can be used in making constructions are compasses and an unmarked straightedge.
ii. A reason must be given for every statement made.
iii. The only reasons that can be given are: the facts that are given, definitions, postulates and axioms, and previously proved theorems The first rule on this list begs an analogy for theology:

I will make justice the measuring line and righteousness the level; then hail will sweep away the refuge of lies and the waters will overflow the secret place- Isaiah 28:17.

We won't consider that further at this time. The other rules address the reasoning process separate and distinct from intuition.

Postulates and axioms constitute the firm underpinnings, or foundational ideas that are not provable, unless they are not independent, and may be able to "prove" each other in a cyclical way. Furthermore, as in any field, there are undefined terms. In geometry, such are the terms point, line, straight line, surface, and angle since the ideas they represent are so fundamental that they cannot be defined in simpler terms.

The postulates and axioms in Christianity are the statements of faith, derived by revelation, called Creeds. The theorems are the doctrines created from the Creeds by reason, and the undefined terms such as *life* are employed many places in the Bible and the Creeds. The most ancient and succinct summary of the Biblical revelations of God is found in the *Apostles' Creed*.

"I believe in God the Father Almighty, Maker of heaven and earth.

And in Jesus Christ his only Son our Lord; who was conceived by the Holy Ghost, born of the Virgin Mary, suffered under Pontius Pilate, was crucified, dead, and buried; he descended into hell; the third day he rose again from the dead; he ascended into heaven, and sitteth on the right hand of God the Father Almighty; from thence he shall come to judge the quick and the dead.

I believe in the Holy Ghost; the holy catholic Church; the communion of saints; the forgiveness of sins; the resurrection of the body; and the life everlasting. AMEN."

Creeds are not necessarily **complete**. The enumerated statements of a creed may all be **necessary**, but not **sufficient** for a complete statement of faith. I have to include the statement, "The LORD our God is One Lord." Before I can accept this amended Apostles' Creed as complete. There may also be other such supplementary statements that should be added to properly reflect the revelations in the Scriptures. A perfect creed would include the truth, the whole truth, and nothing but the truth, so help us God.

Appendix B includes other Christian Creeds for reference. The chapter on *The Divine System* considers this difficulty in a different manner. Our faith, however, refers only to the Word and the Creeds inspired by the Holy Spirit. We do not, however, stand firmly behind every interpretation found outside of the Word.

2.2.3) No Dogmatic Theory of Geology

For example, some beloved true believers interpret the Bible as recording the Creation to be less than six thousand years. I believe this is true for the arrival of Adam and his derived wife, Eve. I don't believe the Bible ever stated this is true for the heavens and the earth. The Sun and Moon were not even created until the 4th "day." Without a natural sunrise and sunset, I find it unreasonable and presumptive to assume God's "day" means 24 hours, at least before the 4th day. One might well ask, as Augustine did long before geology was a known discipline, what kind of "days" these were that cycled through time before the sun was appointed the task? These "days" are certainly indefinitely long periods of time, and it would do no violence to the narrative to mentally substitute "aeonic" days. I believe as that English Baptist Charles Spurgeon believed that this earth is very old

> In the 2d verse of the first chapter of Genesis, we read, 'And the earth was without form, and void; and darkness was upon the face of the deep. And the Spirit of God moved upon the face of the waters.' We know not how remote the period of the creation of this globe may be—certainly many millions of years before the time of Adam. Our planet has passed through various stages of existence, and different kinds of creatures have lived on its surface, all of which have been fashioned by God. But before that era came, wherein man should be its principal tenant and monarch, the Creator gave up the world to confusion. He allowed the inward fires to burst up from beneath, and melt all the

solid matter, so that all kinds of substances were commingled in one vast mass of disorder.[15]

Later in his mid-19th century ministry, he would reiterate his biblical understanding. I will not venture upon any dogmatic theory of geology, but there seems to be every probability that this world has been fitted up and destroyed, refitted and then destroyed again, many times before the last arranging of it for the habitation of men.[16]

Careful readers, like Charles Spurgeon, who considered our blood on their hands if they misspoke, never rewrite the Bible to their own liking. Such men, though, have been led by the Holy Spirit to believe every Word that is *God-breathed*.

The six-day Creation interpretation is just one of the methods that unbelievers have held the Holy Writ up for ridicule for something not even written in it. Please understand me, I am a creationist by first principles. Evolutionists have a publicly failed religion with the general acceptance of the Big Bang theory. It has been generally understood that trillions of years would be required for the improbable random or accidental emergence of life to happen. The Big Bang is thought to be 13 billion, give or take 3 billion years. The most current estimate I am aware of is a 13-billion-year-old universe and a 4-billion-year-old earth. That is clearly orders of magnitude too brief for evolution. Nevertheless, the priests of evolution continue to espouse a known lie to keep from acknowledging the real Creator.

> And the chamberlains walked with still greater dignity, as if they carried the train which did not exist. – Andersen

2.2.4) The Harmony of the Gospels

Another example is where there appears to some to be a conflict in the harmony of the Gospels. In Matthew, Mark, and in Luke the account is that rich disciple Joseph of Arimathea went to Pilate and asked for the body of Jesus after crucifixion. He then took it and wrapped it in clean linen and laid it in his own tomb. In John it is recorded that Joseph of Arimathea was a secret disciple who asked Pilate for Jesus' body. It also says that Nicodemus came with Joseph to take the body. It says that this Nicodemus was the one who first came to Jesus by night. To the tomb, that day, Nicodemus reportedly brought a mixture of myrrh and aloes weighing about 100 pounds, and he and Joseph wrapped Jesus in the linen and these spices. So why wasn't Nicodemus mentioned in the first three Gospels?

The answer to this question and others like it is that these Gospels are testimonies. A God-Man had just been crucified and raised from the dead and had thereby changed our relationship with the Creator forever. In light of what these men were testifying about, how significant is the mention or lack of mention of Nicodemus? Let us consider a different story that demonstrates the nature of the doubt in the Harmony of the Gospels

2.2.4.1) Harmony of the Equivalence of Mass and Energy

The year is 1942. The Nazi SS has infiltrated the U.S. intelligence agency with a number of U.S. born poorly trained sympathizers. Up to this point, the war has gone well for the Fatherland. Japan has bogged the U.S. down in the Far East, and Russia has retreated to the North East. Rumor has it that the U.S. has begun a nuclear weapons program that could affect the long-term plans of the Fuhrer. Everyone in the German high command knows that the degenerate democratic society to the West couldn't do anything as complicated as that in the time frame necessary to make a difference. However, the great leader wants assurances, so the German intelligence group jumps to.

The sympathizers advise the German command through coded short-wave transmissions that a meeting of Allied intelligence and their political leaders is to be held on April 1, 1942, and three of the sympathizers will be in attendance. They are advised to take copious independent notes and report back as soon as possible.

Gretta Schmidt submits her report via the German- American Bund connection. Her report read as follows:

> *Agent Alpha attended a meeting on April 1, 1942. In attendance were Winston Churchill, Franklin D. Roosevelt, a degenerate Jew called Albert Einstein, a young English Intelligence officer named Margaret Thatcher, a pilot named Billy Mitchell, and a group of unnamed assistants that included, among others, the other sympathizers. Ms. Thatcher wore a stunning blue suit that created interest among the degenerates. Winston Churchill looked like he was half drunk while he polluted the air with his disgusting cigar. The crippled degenerate U.S. leader was propped-up to appear significant. The disheveled Einstein (you wouldn't believe what his hair looked like!) muttered and droned on about the letter E being equal to some mass times some squared sea. Imagine that, a sea that was somehow made square! They all were acting excited as if they understood what this degenerate was saying. The pilot, a scraggly looking specimen compared with our glorious Luftwaffen pilots, kept insisting, "He could do it! " It was all punctuated with the cripple declaring, "He'll get the chance." Tell the führer we have nothing to fear from these clowns.*

Bruno Wilhelm submitted his report via coded telephone message to Canada where it was subsequent carried to South America where a U-boat radioed it to Berlin.

> *Agent Beta was present at the April 1, 1942 meeting in Fort Meade, where the subject of a bomb design that could alter the course of the war was discussed. An intelligent European man named Einstein explained his long known theory of special relativity where mass and energy are shown to be equivalent through the equation $E = mc^2$. The delivery system is planned to be a rather large bomb, but an experienced pilot named William Mitchell declared the task doable. There was a young lady named Margaret Thatcher, who was a*

regular wallflower with her drab uniform, who had no apparent reason for being there. Old Grumpy Winston Churchill was present listening intently to every word spoken. He has an excellent taste in cigars, though! President Roosevelt told Mitchell that he hoped he'd get the chance to drop it. Don't underestimate this guy Roosevelt.

Johann Schwarz delivered his report in person after crossing the border to Mexico and flying to Argentina illegally. His destination was Berlin after a roundabout trip through Africa and the Middle East.

Agent Gamma attended the April 1, 1942 meeting in Maryland, USA about the possible development of a super bomb. Agents Alpha and Beta were also present. Albert Einstein and Billy Mitchell were the featured speakers. Einstein boasted that with his Jewish brains, this bomb was possible, while the simple Yankee Pilot Billy Mitchell said, "He could drop any bomb you brains could make!" Einstein said that an equation of just three variables could destroy the Reich! These Jewish dogs! There was some lady in red there that Churchill admired. He said she was an Iron Lady. I don't know what that old drunk meant. President Roosevelt maintained a cautious reserve, except in reply to that boasting pilot, when he said, "You might just get a chance to drop it!." That shut him up, I suspect the man is a coward. I think these guys are puffing smoke when they say $E = mc^2$ could threaten the Third Reich.

These three agents each reported that $E = mc^2$ was a defining equation that would help build a bomb. They each reported the names of the attendees, but they didn't agree perfectly. Is Billy Mitchell William Mitchell? They reported Einstein being present, but their take on him was each different. Each reported Mitchell present, but their view to his competence was quite varied. Each reported Thatcher's apparel differently, and each reported her relation to the persons and the process differently. One reported that this should concern the Führer, while two agents blew off the meeting as a meeting of degenerate buffoons. There were so many disharmonies in the reports, that they were dismissed as fanciful, reported to the Führer as such, and ignored.

Although this story is fiction, it expresses how people who report on an actual event do so using their own personalities. The common elements should have been believed, and the differences considered part of the game of using untrained witnesses to report the facts. The final report should have revealed the use of the known equation, the belief that a bomb so designed could be made small and light enough to be delivered by air, the United States' President thought that the bomb could be built and deployed soon, and that there was no disputing between governments on the matter. They ignored the imbedded truth because of the discrepancies, to their peril. The same picayune differences retard the delivery of the Gospel Message that has nothing to do with spices or angels or secondary characters.

2.2.4.2) The Testaments Bear Witness

There are other such "discrepancies" like where the angel was when the women went to the tomb, etc. Can you imagine your own emotional state if you met with your dearest friend three days after you had buried him? Can you say with certainty that your testimony of those moments would be dispassionately and accurately recorded?

If these stories had been completely identical, right down to where the angel sat, and whether the women knew about the 100 pounds of spice that the secret disciples brought, who could have believed then that these were independent testimonies. If they were all perfect down to the minutia, we would expect fraud and conspiracy.

This Holy Writ that we call the Bible is a collection of written records of people testifying about the action, nature and Words of God. So, when I say that I take the Word of God as Truth, understand that we apply the same "reasonable man" view of what we read as what we would if we were in the Jury of a legal trial. We are not trained in the Law, but neither is a member of a jury. A jury of lay decision-makers, not experts, determines the truth or falsehood of a witness. In these courts of Law, lives often depend upon the decisions of untrained Jurors. But a trial by jury is not a curse, but a right highly defended by all.

So as a member of the jury debating the veracity of the Gospels, how do we frame our questions? By determining the truthfulness of eyewitnesses. How do we gather our intelligence? By reading written testimony. And how do we come to conclusions? The decision of whether the Gospel writer presents a true account does not depend upon his recollection of ordinary events, but instead upon the extraordinary events he records that the other Gospel authors corroborate. Let me suggest that the decision of whether or not a Gospel writer was accurate does not depend upon the picayune points, but whether his testimony agrees with the salient points outlined in our Creeds and confessions of faith. They are in fact the sum and substance of the gospel record. And lastly, did they stand by their testimony? The answer, a resounding Yes! Their testimony remained solid to the point of torture and death.

I highlighted Christ's Identity in the introduction as the King of Truth, but He is also the Bridegroom. We will soon look to the history of His Bride, the Church. Much could be said about its first 1000 years, but I find it more instructive to dive into the history at its midpoint and discuss the history most relevant to the current times. That is where our introductory background story begins. It is here where brother fights brother over the meaning of the past and the correct view of the future. So as a great President said during another war between brothers,

With malice toward none, with charity for all, with firmness in the right as God gives us to see the right, let us strive on to finish the work we are in. [17]

Early in Section 2.2.1 we quote the works of E. W. Bullinger, in his Appendix #30, p. 31, of *The Companion Bible*, {Zondervan Bible Publishers, Grand Rapids, 1974. The Holy Bible, (King Games Version), Oxford University Press, London.} where he discusses the relationship between the *Sopherim* and the *Masorites*.

[1]   A.W. Tozer, *The Attributes of God*, Christian Publications, Inc., Camp Hill, PA,1997,p.138

[2]   Blaise Pascal, *PENSfES*, 1660, translated by W. F. Trotter, #231,232

[3]   R. A. Torrey, A. C. Dixon and Others, The Fundamentals, Vol. II, Ch. I *"The Inspiration of the Bible-Definition, Extent and Proof", Rev. James M. Gray, D. D.,* 1917, Baker Books reprint, 2003, p.p. 10,12

[4]   R. A. Torrey, A. C. Dixon and Others, The Fundamentals, Vol. II, Ch. I *"The Inspiration of the Bible-Definition, Extent and Proof", Rev. James M. Gray, D. D.,* 1917, Baker Books reprint, 2003, p.p.42,43

[5]   Sir Lancelot C. L. Brenton, The Septuagint With Apocrypha: Greek And English, *Introduction*, Samuel Bagster & Sons, Ltd., London, 1851, Hendrickson Publishers reprint 2003, p.p. ii, iv

[6]   Sir Lancelot C. L. Brenton, The Septuagint With Apocrypha: Greek And English, *Introduction*, Samuel Bagster & Sons, Ltd., London, 1851, Hendrickson Publishers reprint 2003, p. v

[7]   R. A. Torrey, A. C. Dixon and Others, The Fundamentals, Vol. II, Ch. VII *"Life In The Word, Philip Mauro, Attorney at Law* 1917, Baker Books reprint, 2003, p.p. 158,173

[8]   R. A. Torrey, A. C. Dixon and Others, The Fundamentals, Vol. I, Ch.VII *"Old Testament Criticism and New Testament Christianity,* W.H. Griffith Thomas, D.D., 1917, Baker Books reprint, 2003, p144

[9]   R. A. Torrey, A. C. Dixon and Others, The Fundamentals, Vol. II, Ch. VII *"Life In The Word, Philip Mauro, Attorney at Law* 1917, Baker Books reprint, 2003, p.p. 198,199

[10] Ibid p.207

[11] R. A. Torrey, A. C. Dixon and Others, The Fundamentals, Vol.1, Ch. V *"Holy Scripture and Modern Negations",* James Orr, D. D., 1917, Baker Books reprint, 2003, p. 110

[12] Marjorie Barrows, One Thousand Beautiful Things, Spencer Press, New York, 1947, p169

[13] Virgil S. Mallory, *New Plane Geometry*, Revised Edition, p.p. 4,5, Benj H. Sanborn & Co.,1943,Chicago

[14] Virgil S. Mallory, *New Plane Geometry*, Revised Edition, p.p. 38,39, Benj H. Sanborn & Co.,1943,Chicago

[15] C.H Spurgeon, Spurgeon's Sermons, Vol 1, Sermon *"Power of the Holy Spirit"*, p. 115, BakerBooks 1999,Grand Rapids, Michigan.

[16] C.H Spurgeon, Spurgeon's Sermons, Vol 9, Sermon *"The Holy Spirit"*, p.369, BakerBooks 1999,Grand Rapids, Michigan

[17] Abraham Lincoln, *Second Inaugural Address*, Edited by William J. Bennett, The Book of Virtues, Simon & Schuster, N.Y., 1993, p.797

3) We Look to the Past

"The best way to suppose what may come, is to remember what is past."
-- George Savile

"Those who cannot remember the past are condemned to repeat it.
-- George Santayana

As we look to the past we need to consider the modus operandi of the spirit of error that would lead even the elect away from the Word of God, if that were possible. What is the nature of the spirit?

His is a philosophical rather than a religious spirit. Such was Gnosticism in the early centuries. "It construed Christ and Christianity through the categories of the Graeco-Oriental philosophy and thus was compelled to reject some of the essentials of Christianity. Such was the Scholasticism of the Middle Ages, which construed Christianity through the categories of the Aristotelian Logic and the Neo-platonic Philosophy. Such is Higher Criticism which construes everything through the hypothesis of evolution. The spirit of the movement is thus essentially scholastic and rationalistic….the movement was entirely intellectual, an attempt in reality to intellectualize all religious phenomena. … it was a partial and one-sided intellectualism, with a strong bias against the fundamental tenets of Biblical Christianity." [1]

3.1) Scholasticism

Look back a full millennium. The comforting Spirit of Truth had already been making His home in the hearts of the Son's believers for a full millennium. At the start of that first Christian millennium Saint Paul had warned,

> *"See to it that no one takes you captive through hollow and deceptive philosophy, which depends on human tradition and the elemental spiritual forces [a] of this world rather than on Christ." – Col. 2:8 (NIV)*

But by the year 1000, the Greeks had practiced the branching, growing, and forking methods of Aristotelian syllogisms to yield its fruit of the knowledge of the true and the false for 1300 years. That decision tree of knowledge continually beckoned, and after a millennium of temptation, the Church saw that logic provided sustenance, and was a joy to see accomplished, and would make the practitioner wise, so She took from its fruit, ingested it, and called it Scholasticism.

Scholasticism attempted to integrate human reasoning and science with divine revelation to understand the supernatural content of Christian revelation. It ran its course in the medieval Christian schools and Universities of Europe from the 11th century to the mid 15th century. Its purpose was not in looking for new facts, but just to understand old ones. The philosophy and science of the Greek philosopher Aristotle was the basis for its natural reasoning. The revelation that formed the basis for its arguments were the Bible and a collection of the theological opinions of the early Church Fathers: the *Four Books of Sentences* (*Sententiarum Libri Quatuor*) by the Italian theologian and Prelate Peter the Lombard (1100? -1160).

One major flaw with this integration was the Scholastics' misguided faith in Aristotle's scientific views. This severe limitation in Scholasticism was one of the primary reasons for its contemptuous denunciation by scientists during the Renaissance and later. The other major defect was the assumed inerrancy of the Church Fathers. In 1522, Martin Luther stated that the spiritual blindness that plagued the Church had been in place "for nearly four hundred years,"[2] which agrees well with the arrival of *the Four Books of Sentences*.

In later sermons Luther reiterated the timeframe of the Churches' error toward works righteousness based on the philosophy of men.

> Here Madam Huldah with her scornful nose – human nature – steps in and dares to contradict her God and to charge him with falsehood. She hangs upon herself her old frippery, her straw armor – natural light, reason, free-will and human powers. She introduces the heathenish books and doctrines of men, and proceeds to harp upon these, saying; 'Good works do precede justification. And they are not, as God says, the work of Cain. They are good to the extent of justifying. For Aristotle taught that he who does much good will thereby become good,' ... This satanic doctrine universally reigns at present in all the high schools and other institutions, and in the cloisters. .... Indeed, faith is condemned and banished as the worst heresy, and all who teach and endorse it are condemned with it. The Pope, the bishops, charitable institutions, cloisters, high schools, unanimously opposed it for nearly four hundred years, and simply drove the world violently into hell.[3]

The early Scholastics critical commentaries adhered closely to the biblical text with which they were dealing. Scholastics believed that revelation was the direct instruction of the Almighty. They were more certain of God's word than the product of natural human reasoning. In conflicts between religious faith and philosophical reasoning, faith won; the theologian's decision overruled the philosopher's. Throughout the Scholastic period philosophy was referred to as the handmaid of theology. This was because the conclusions of philosophy were subordinated to those of theology, and because the theologian used philosophy to understand and explain revelation—as if an axiom could be explained.

Enter the 13th century theologian, Saint Thomas Aquinas (1225 – 1274) who merged Scholastic theology with philosophy in his *Summa Theologica*. In the same period, the 13th century supplementary commentaries provided by critical readers began to include the personal opinions of the expositors. These opinions became the largest and most central part of the commentaries, resulting in the literal part of the Biblical text being reduced to a small part of each commentary.

Martin Luther, writing as if he were one of that period discussing Biblical commands, said

> He did not command it, but merely suggested it to such as wished to be perfect. Again, the perfect are not under obligation to be so, it suffices, if they strive after perfection. Many large books, called *Formas conscientiarum*, treaties to comfort and acquit the consciences, have been written on this subject. Thomas Aquinas was about the leading heretic in this line. Later the same doctrine was confirmed by the Pope, and diffused throughout the world; this explains the later origin of the Orders, which aimed at perfection. Well, God be praised that we have understood the error, so it can be avoided.[4]

Luther went on to say that

> The clergy also quote St. Thomas of Aquin, who teaches that perfection is not necessary; that it is sufficient to be in a state of perfection and looking forward to that end. ... A 'state of perfection' now means monk, cap and pate. ...If St. Thomas Aquinas was holy which I doubt he surely attained his holiness in an extraordinary way, judging from his pernicious and poisonous doctrines.[5]

After the time of Aquinas, Scholasticism emphasized increased independence of philosophy within its own domain. With the rise of philosophy and the theological opinions of the early Church Fathers, and the diminished influence of the Bible, the Church no longer regarded Saint Paul's warning of Colossians 2:8. Without the truth, without the axioms, any argument goes uncontested; Paul says in 2 Tim 4:3,4 (NIV)

> *"For the time will come when people will not put up with sound doctrine. Instead, to suit their own desires, they will gather around them a great number of teachers to say what their itching ears want to hear. They will turn their ears away from the truth and turn aside to myths.*

It is at this time, after *Summa Theologica* and Aquinas' influence had been felt throughout the Holy Roman Empire, that bad things started happening to good people.

In his 1302 Bull UNAM SANCTAM Pope Boniface VIII (1294-1303) declared it
...absolutely necessary for the salvation of every human creature to be subject to the Roman Pontiff.

Roughly a century later, John Wycliffe and John Huss were both declared heretics. As mentioned in the section on the Ecumenical Imperative, Wycliffe was blessed by dying naturally before the Papists could kill him, but John Huss was not so lucky. Biblical Scholasticism and Biblical Christianity almost died together from the Aquinas touch - the elevation of philosophy and tradition at the expense of Biblical revelation.

Nominalism dominated the 14th century as Scholasticism began to fade. The chief nominalist was the English philosopher William of Ockham, famous for his Razor, that one should pursue the simplest hypothesis. This is referred to as the principle of economy (parsimony) in formal logic. He was a rigorous logician who applied logic to show that many of the truths held by Christian philosophers could not be proved by natural reason, but only by divine revelation. He was denounced by Pope John XXII for dangerous teachings and held in house detention for four years (1324-28). He fled to Munich in 1328 for the protection of Louis IV. The Pope subsequently excommunicated him, and he died in 1347.

A brief revival of Scholasticism occurred in Spain in the 16th century. Francisco de Vitoria (1483? – 1546) and Francisco Suarez (1548 – 1617) exemplify the Spanish theologians involved. René Descartes (1596-1650) lived during this revival. He must have known the failings of the science of Aristotle and the assumptions that finally diminished Scholasticism. After Aquinas the

> Scholastics applied the requirements for scientific demonstration, as first specified in Aristotle's *Organon*, much more rigorously than previous philosophers had done. … It was this trend that led finally to the loss of confidence in natural human reason and philosophy that is characteristic of the early Renaissance and of the first Protestant religious reformers, such as the German theologian Martin Luther.[6]

Thus, Descartes' philosophy of doubt had its origins in the demise of Scholasticism, the beginnings of religious protests and reformation, and the awakening Renaissance. Descartes lived in an age that was one of the greatest intellectual periods in the history of man. Gilbert, who founded the science of electromagnetism, died when Descartes was seven. Descartes was twelve when Milton was born. Shakespeare died when Descartes was twenty. Pascal and Fermat were his mathematical contemporaries. Newton was born on Christmas day, the year Galileo died, and Descartes died eight years later. Harvey, the discoverer of the circulation of the blood, died seven years after Descartes. [7]

3.2) Descartes' Radical Doubt

Descartes was schooled at the Jesuit College at La Fleche, where he became a proficient classicist.

> The authoritative dogmas of philosophy, ethics, and morals offered for his blind acceptance began to take on the aspect of baseless superstitions. … From this he rapidly passed to the fundamental doubt which was to inspire his life-work: how do we know anything? And further, perhaps more importantly, if we cannot say definitely that we know anything, how are we ever to find out those things which we may be capable of knowing?[8]

He left school at the age of 17 in the year 1612. In 1619 Descartes gave himself the task of doubting everything in order to build a foundation of certainty upon which to construct an entire philosophy. E.T. Bell continues,

> As a first fruit of his meditations he apprehended the heretical truth that logic of itself – the great method of the school-men of the Middle Ages which still hung on tenaciously in humanistic education – is as barren as a mule for any creative human purpose. His second conclusion was closely allied to his first: compared to the demonstrations of mathematics – to which he took like a bird to the air as soon as he found his wings – those of philosophy, ethics, and morals are tawdry shams and frauds. How then, he asked, shall we ever find out anything? By the scientific method, although Descartes did not call it that: by *controlled experiment* and the application of ridged mathematical reasoning to the results of such experiment.[9]

Of Descartes' desire to be sure of every premise, he wrote,

> … : but as for the opinions which up to that time I had embraced, I thought that I could not do better than resolve at once to sweep them wholly away, that I might afterwards be in a position to admit either others more correct, or even perhaps the same when they had undergone the scrutiny of reason. I firmly believed that in this way I should much better succeed in the conduct of my life, than if I built only upon old foundations, and leaned upon principles which, in my youth, I had taken upon trust.[10]

So this is the method that some call *radical doubt*. Descartes never in his *Methods* expressed any doubt in God. In fact, he expressed a statement of faith, "It is thus quite certain that the constitution of the true religion, the ordinances of which are derived from God, must be incomparably superior to that of every other."[11] The problem with Descartes' faith was in his belief that God was only active in the creation, and afterwards just a detached spectator. Blaise Pascal would have disdain for Descartes' belief in an absentee God.

3.2.1) Descartes' Character

Descartes seemed hostile to most philosophers and theologians, and they reciprocated. He wrote,

> Of philosophy I will say nothing, except that when I saw that it had been cultivated for many ages by the most distinguished men, and that yet there is not a single matter within its sphere which is not still in dispute, and nothing, therefore, which is above doubt, I did not presume to anticipate that my success would be greater in it than that of others; and further, when I considered the number of conflicting opinions touching a single matter that may be upheld by learned men, while there can be but one true, I reckoned as well-nigh false all that was only probable. [12]

He had some flaws in character that irritated many scientists and philosophers. Descartes repeatedly, and obviously falsely, claimed that nothing in his work was influenced by the work of others. This flaw would cause substantial repercussions as time goes on, as we shall discuss later. He was a genius, though, and one of the shoulders Newton stood on.

3.2.3) Descartes' Interaction with Blaise Pascal

Starting in 1646, Pascal conducted experiments on atmospheric pressure. By 1647, he had proved to his own satisfaction that a vacuum could exist. Descartes visited Pascal on September 23rd of that year. His visit only lasted two days. The two argued because Descartes did not believe in a vacuum. Descartes wrote a rather cruel letter to a noted scientist, Huygens, after this visit in which he commented that Pascal...*has too much vacuum in his head.*

Descartes wrote to Carcavi in June 1647 claiming credit for Pascal's experiments saying: *It was I who two years ago advised him to do it, for although I have not performed it myself, I did not doubt of its success ...* By October of the same year, Pascal wrote *New Experiments Concerning Vacuums*. In August of 1648 Pascal observed that the pressure of the atmosphere decreases with height and deduced that a vacuum existed above the atmosphere.

Pascal was brilliant, and Descartes' ridiculing of his capabilities does not say much for Descartes' character. He responded negatively and cryptically to Descartes in PENS*f*ES:[13]

76. To write against those who made too profound a study of science: Descartes.

77. I cannot forgive Descartes. In all his philosophy he would have been quite willing to dispense with God. But he had to make Him give a fillip to set the world in motion; beyond this, he has no further need of God.

78. Descartes useless and uncertain.

79. Descartes.—We must say summarily: "This is made by figure and motion," for it is true. But to say what these are, and to compose the machine, is ridiculous. For it is useless, uncertain, and painful. And were it true, we do not think all Philosophy is worth one hour of pain.

80. How comes it that a cripple does not offend us, but that a fool does? Because a cripple recognizes that we walk straight, whereas a fool declares that it is we who are silly; if it were not so, we should feel pity and not anger.

As a side note, Blaise Pascal was also known for his famous wager:[14]

God does or He does not exist, and we must bet for or against Him.

- If I bet *for* and God *is*: infinite gain;
- If I bet *for* and God *is not*: no loss.
- If I bet *against* and God *is*: infinite loss;
- If I bet *against* and God *is not*: no loss, no gain.

If I bet against God, I am exposed to the loss of everything. Thus, I should make the bet that ensures my winning all or, at worst losing nothing.

I have said enough about Blaise Pascal for now. Suffice it to say that his heart and style were both beautiful, and it is my observation that his manner and approach was reminiscent of Confucius. I believe Descartes' treatment of this saint, and his belief in the complete originality of his own work, is what earned him the disrespect shown him today. Greater men than Descartes acknowledged the work of their predecessors.

3.3) The Cogito

This insight came about as Descartes speculated upon his existence and the possibility that all was false and unreal,

> But immediately upon this I observed that, whilst I thus wished to think that all was false, it was absolutely necessary that I, who thus thought, should be somewhat; and as I observed that this truth, I think, therefore I am (COGITO ERGO SUM), was so certain and of such evidence that no ground of doubt, however extravagant, could be alleged by the skeptics capable of shaking it, I concluded that I might, without scruple, accept it as the first principle of the philosophy of which I was in search.[15]

Considering the many years of religious training that Descartes enjoyed, and his reputed character flaw for falsely claiming that nothing in his work was influenced by the work of others, it seems likely that Descartes transformed God's statement of existence ("I AM") into his own ("I am"). This seems plausible although he may have actually believed it original.

Eberhard Jüngel in his book, *God as the Mystery of the World,* placed the responsibility for the genesis of modern metaphysics at René Descartes' feet. "Descartes' approach, which determines the metaphysics of the modern period, is, judged objectively, the beginning of the disintegration of the presupposed understanding of God and thus of the certainty of God which had developed until now." [16] Why is this? According to Jungles,

> It is very significant that Descartes, in calling this insight the Archimedean point of certainty, establishes the existence and the essence of the human person as being, in fact, one and the same. 'I think, therefore I am' means then 'I am a thinking essence."
> ...Descartes does realize his knowledge of the existence of man and his knowledge of man's essence *one after the other* in both the Discourse and the Meditations. That accords with his requirement that every problem should be divided "into as many parts as possible." ... I am (exist) because I am what I am. A part of my essence as a 'thinking thing' (*res cogitans*) is thus the knowledge that I am because I am this essence. [17]

This is where things start to go wrong. We just read that the Cogito "establishes the existence and the essence of the human person as being, in fact, one and the same." The idea that I am a "thinking thing" is a complete statement of my essence, is false and misleading. My essence also depends on what I think. Are my thoughts loving and lovely, or selfish and merciless? Are my thoughts pure, or vile? As a man, my existence does not specify or prove my essence, however, any part of my essence will demonstrate my existence.

The fundamental flaw with Descartes' Cogito is that it is incomplete in origins. That is, Descartes had a noted character flaw that he refused to acknowledge the previous work his work stood upon. In this case, the previous work was God's. "I think, therefore I am," should have been preceded by "God spoke, therefore I think." The fundamental trace of consciousness is God Speaking, ***"I Am, therefore I Spoke; I Spoke therefore you are; you are, therefore you think."*** God is forever the fountainhead, the I Am of the I ams, the beginning and the end. Such was not said; the Cogito thus orphaned becomes convoled with origins, and theology loses its real source.

Cause and effect, proof and reality, God and man; these have become confused in the metaphysically challenged theology since Descartes. Existence can be proven by partial essence, but essence cannot be proven by existence—unless it is the existence of the essence itself. Existence, like geometry, is fixed and independent of time; and if you so believe as God reveals, even death doesn't alter existence. Essence, like algebra, is involved with relations that vary with time, except if you so believe as God reveals, God's Essence never varies.

Descartes' conduct toward Blaise Pascal was reprehensible; his belief that he didn't base his results upon anyone else's work was arrogant, but he was educated to believe in God and His revelations and was a Christian theologian and mathematician. I wanted to believe the best of Descartes, but his worship of thought blinded his faith. The term *Cogito* is often used disparagingly because of the *radical doubt* that was part of Descartes' philosophy [18]. Leaning on

Eberhard Jüngel's insight, let us try to unwind 350 years of philosophy, beginning with Descartes and ending with Freidrich Nietzsche.

3.4) You Will Be Like God

Descartes' Cogito was a statement about his own existence. Also, his rules for doubt were very logical and reasonable and can be read in Appendix C. It is the doubt directed at the Almighty and the confusion of cause and effect, proof and reality, God and man that creates the radical conclusions of postmodernism. The postmodern Cogito is really, "I think, therefore, I AM." The difference is the postmodernist believes his thoughts create the great "I AM." Let me demonstrate this in what follows in the indentation.

> According to Jüngel, a theologian named Johann Fichte (1762-1814), a student of Immanuel Kant, thought himself more consistently Cartesian than Descartes himself. Fichte decided to also doubt God, but concluded that He exists based upon *activity*. God reveals Himself as the One who acts. Believing the metaphysical principle that the finite can't comprehend the infinite[19], he believes man is compensated for the unthinkability of God by the immediacy of God. In this process, he defines God as an object of reason, and then declares that such reason is unavailable to us because we are finite. The knowability of God is then reduced to His effect on the world, his activity[20]. He bought into the notion that nothing can be known in part, in that he believes that we cannot know God because He is infinite. *He has unwittingly defined God as a being without personality; an infinity without personhood.*
>
> Georg Wilhelm Friedrich Hegel developed Immanuel Kant's philosophy. Hegel's work formed the basis upon which Marxism and socialism would later be built. Lugwig Feuerbach (1804-1872), student of Hegel and son of Paul Johann Anselm, used Anselm of Canterbury's description of God as a being than which nothing greater can be conceived.[21]

In this manner, God became the ultimate object of the thinking process-purified thought. To Feuerbach, God is a thought: thinking is a creator and God is its finest creation.[22] Thus, the intellectual descendent of this philosophy believes his thoughts create the great "I AM." QED.

Albert Einstein's response to this kind of thinking was

> We should take care not to make the intellect our god; it has, of course, powerful muscles, but no personality.[23]
>
> God, Who is indivisible, has also been artificially divided into His Existence and His

Essence. This is utter folly to try to separate God from Himself, since He names Himself Existence or "I AM". This is anthropomorphic nonsense to ascribe finite and divisible human characteristics to the infinite Divine. God doesn't just have attributes; He *is* each of the attributes, for example, God *is* Love. Further, there is a submerged idea of *that which proves is that which causes*, and *that* isn't true. The proof of existence becomes the source of existence for Descartes and his followers. Discovering a dinosaur does not create the beast. Fichte at least demanded that for the sake of divinity, God not be considered a thought, but yet definable by an abstract system of principles. Feuerbach also wished to preserve the metaphysically defined divine, not for God's divinity but so the divinity of man could be secured.

> The existence of God had to fall so that the divine essence as the essence of humanity could be claimed. ... Like Fichte, Feuerbach had to declare that God's essence and God's existence were mutually irreconcilable, so that the concept of God as the highest and infinite being which combines all perfections and lacks all imperfections could be preserved. Only in this way could Feuerbach realize his rigorous intention of elevating the mortality of human existence to the heights of the divine essence.[24]

Friedrich Nietzsche (1844-1900), following Feuerbach and Fichte, defined God as unknowable, and therefore irrelevant.[25] Man is therefore left to rule himself, but as a superman. The intellect, however, is not necessary for salvation; therefore, it cannot be sufficient. It might be the intellect that separates man from the animals, but it is the heart that separates us from the damned. The love of God is much more important than knowledge of Him.

Love is the weakness God chooses for Himself so that His Existence is perfect and He is altogether lovely. In that singular chosen weakness, we have made Him Jealous, grieved, beaten, despised and "pushed out of the world on to the cross"[26] to be crucified. But He overcame all that to maintain His loving relationship with us. We, on the other hand, philosophically divided God in our minds into His existence and His essence, for the sole purpose of usurping His essence and destroying His existence, much like Christ's parable of the workers of the vineyard.

> *"But those husbandmen said among themselves, This is the heir; come, let us kill him, and the inheritance shall be ours." Mark 12: 7 (NIV)*

This is a rook's philosophy. In the bowels of philosophy, as in the tomb of Joseph of Arimathea, He arose, and was resurrected by the Holy Spirit of Truth. God is alive, but Immanuel Kant, Johann Fichte, Georg Wilhelm Friedrich Hegel, Lugwig Feuerbach, and Friedrich Nietzsche are all dead.

We now have a problem with theologians who equate the quagmire they're in with the act of reasoning. To a practical natural philosopher, or engineer, it is unreasonable of Kant to regard the objects of the material world as fundamentally unknowable. It is a vain imagination that, from the vantage point of reason, to regard the objects of the material world as serving merely as the raw material from which sensations are formed. It is like Fantasy Island to believe, like Kant, that object of themselves have no existence, and space and time exist only as part of the mind, as "intuitions" by which perceptions are measured and judged. This makes no sense to a soldier dodging bullets or an architect designing a building. It is a denial of the most measurable and repeatable properties that science deals with, such as *inertia, mass, energy, and momentum*. This is the basis of an ostrich philosophy.

Furthermore, it was unreasonable for Johann Fichte to treat God as an object for radical doubt. A navigator may doubt which direction a ship is headed, but not doubt the North Star. Petty minds require consistency, but great ones require veracity. *It was totally unreasonable for Fichte to believe that something is totally unknowable because its totality is unknowable. This notion is oblivious to probability and statistics and the whole concept of human interaction.* He is more like the man who was *unpardonably stupid* rather than *unfit for his office* because he wanted to honor God, but could not. This is the dodo's philosophy.

Fichte is like the mathematician just married to a beautiful woman. He is told by his master that he can only half the remaining distance between himself and his bride with each step he takes toward her. The poor man is beside himself because he knows from a pure theory that he can never reach her. Fortunately, his best man was an engineer who advised him that he could reach her for all practical purposes! We know people, oceans, mathematics, physics, biology, and all things in fact in part. That is not to say we know nothing of them.

It was short sighted for Anselm of Canterbury to believe that the infinite God was limited, or defined, by our capacity to conceive. I am told that Crows count one, two, infinity. They cannot distinguish between three and four or more. And if, for example, 100 were the largest number we could conceive, would it be reasonable to use it as a measure of an infinite God? I think this definition is patently flawed. Feuerbach's choice of Anselm of Canterbury's definition for a premise is blatantly transparent and willfully precludes successful reasoning of the infinite. This then is a crow's philosophy.

It is unreasonable for Lugwig Feuerbach to believe that God is just a perfect thought. To believe so is to believe we have created God. That would then make us super Gods who create God. Lugwig Feuerbach would like that! This manner of thinking plays well with our pride, but does not illuminate the soul or even rid us of a headache. Friedrich Nietzsche demonstrates this thinking with arrogance and pride, but he is really only restating Feuerbach and Fichte. Feuerbach and Nietzsche were each like the man *unfit for his office,* because that office requires humility and a sense of awe. So from Nietzsche we learn of the peacock's philosophy. From Kant to Nietzsche we grow from an ostrich to a peacock philosophy. These philosophies are for the birds; let's walk a different path than Descartes, but first let's see *the rest of the story*.

3.5) The Drift Toward Pantheism

Centuries later Dietrich Bonhoeffer, while in his Nazi prison cell, relates the history of thought with the growing assertion of the autonomy of man.

"On the historical side I should say there is *one* great development which leads to the idea of the autonomy of the world. In theology it is first discernable in Lord Herbert of Cherbury, with his assertion that reason is the sufficient instrument of religious knowledge. In ethics it first appears in Montaigne and Bodin with their substitution of moral principles for the Ten Commandments. In politics, Machiavelli, who emancipates politics from the tutelage of morality, and founds the doctrine of 'reasons of state'. Later, and very differently, though like Machiavelli tending towards the autonomy of human society, comes Grotius, with his international law as the law of nature, a law which would still be valid, *etsi deus non daretur*. The process is completed in philosophy. On the one hand we have the deism of Descartes, who holds that the world is a mechanism which runs on its own without any intervention of God. On the other hand there is a pantheism of Spinoza, with its identification of God with nature. In the last resort Kant is a deist, Fichte and Hegel pantheists. All along the line there is a growing tendency to assert the autonomy of man and the world.

In the natural sciences the process seems to start with Nicolas of Cusa and Giordano Bruno with their 'heretical' doctrine of the infinity of space. An infinite universe, however it be conceived, is self-subsisting *etsi deus non daretur*. It is true that modern physics is not so sure as it was about the infinity of the universe, but it has not returned to the earlier conceptions of its finitude."[27]

The result of this type of theology was to undermine the faith and divert the youth toward other more *intellectual* and *philosophical* religions. By 1909, in the "Hibbert Lectures" the talk "The Present Situation in Philosophy," was delivered by Professor William James, of Harvard University, at Manchester College, Oxford. These lectures have been published in a volume entitled "A Pluralistic Universe" (Longmans, Green & Co.). In that lecture, he made the following comment:

Dualistic theism is professed as firmly as ever at all Catholic seats of learning, whereas it has of late years tended to disappear at our British and American Universities, and be replaced by a monistic pantheism more or less open or disguised[28]

Let us first thank these Catholic Colleges for carrying the truth forward at that time as the Protestants had done in the reformation. Next let me explain that last sentence more fully. The schools of philosophy that have flourished through the ages have been partitioned into two main classes, namely, *theistic* and *atheistic*. Theistic class assumes a god of some sort to make and sustain the universe. The atheistic are irrelevant to this discussion. Of the theistic philosophies, there are *Dualistic* and *Pantheistic*.[29]

Dualism maintains that God (or the "First Cause") willfully created the universe distinct from Himself. This is called *dualistic* because God is counted as one entity and the universe as another. When a learned professor of philosophy speaks of "dualism" he really has Christianity in mind.[30]

Pantheism maintains that God and the universe are one being. It is divided today into *monism* and *pluralism*. Both forms identify human substance with divine substance. The most favored form is Monism. It assumes as the basis of reality an "absolute" or "allknower" that comprehends in its vast being all things and all their relations and activities. Monism asserts that there is but one entity - that God has no existence apart from the universe, and never did: the universe is therefore eternal and there has been no creation. Pluralism essentially in cleverly disguised words proposes a distribution of gods with or without a known unifying absolute collected god. For computer scientists, Monism has a central processor, while Pluralism involves a distributed processor with unspecified linkages. I have not read, but I surmise that today's Pantheists would describe their god in terms akin to a quantum computer. In any case, the processor is dreaming us at this moment.[31]

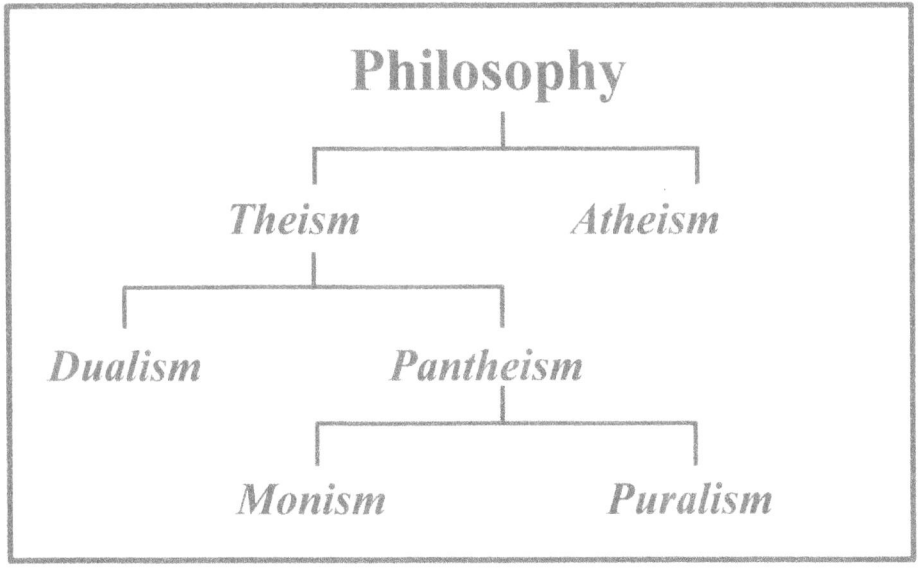

The positions of atheists and pantheists are such as to restrict their vision of the power of God to perform miracles. The atheist cannot accept a miracle, for to him there is no God to work miracles. The pantheist cannot admit a miracle, since he sees God and nature as one.

A problem with Pantheism is that it follows Satan's Pledge that "You will be like God," when it asserts the human substance is the divine substance. What Satan gets out of this system is to get God's image to believe that "God will be like you." In this system, all is essentially being dreamt by God, all monstrous crimes, cruelties, wickedness and abominations come directly from Him. That makes Him the major participant in all sin. This too is the devil's lie to blaspheme the holy God.

Professor William James continues,

> I shall leave cynical materialism entirely out of our discussion as not calling for treatment before this present audience, and I shall ignore *old-fashioned dualistic theism for the same reason*.[32]

From a 1919 commentary we learn the reason for treating Christianity and atheism alike,

> It is also important for our purposes to note the *suddenness* of the great change which has taken place at our universities, whereby Christian doctrine has been relegated to a position of obscurity so profound that it calls for no consideration in a discussion of this sort. The lecturer, after remarking that he has been told by Hindus that 'the great obstacle to the spread of Christianity in their country was the puerility of our dogma of creation,' added: 'Assuredly, most members of this audience are ready to side with Hinduism in this matter.'[33]

3.6) Prejudicial Higher Criticism

So by the roaring twenties, the learned professors agreed with eastern religionists that the story of Genesis was a childish tale. Philosophy in theology and Higher Criticism were two instruments of doubt discouraging the Church at the start of the Twentieth Century. Bonhoeffer's list didn't mention Eichhorn (1752-1827), who first coined the name "the higher criticism." Zenos, in *The Elements of the Higher Criticism*, provides the name with a benign definition.

> The discovery and verification of the facts regarding the origin, form and value of literary productions upon the basis of their internal characters.[34]

But what were these higher critics saying at the start of the 20th century?

> These critics say that God, not being a man, cannot speak; consequently, there is no word of God! Also, God cannot manifest Himself in visible form; therefore, all the accounts of such epiphanies are mystical tales! Inspiration, they tell us, is unthinkable; hence all representations of such acts are diseased imagination! Of prophecy there is

none; what purports to be such was written after the events! Miracles are impossible; therefore, all the reports of them, as given in the Bible, are mere fiction! Men always seek; thus it is explained, their own advantage and personal glory, and just so it was with those 'prophets of Israel.'

Such is what they call 'impartial science,' 'unprejudiced research,' 'objective demonstration.'[35]

Let us review the men who were the higher critics, one by one, and see if they were *unfit for their office or unpardonably stupid*.

Spinoza repudiated absolutely a supernatural revelation. And Spinoza was one of their greatest. Eichhorn discarded the miraculous, and considered the so-called supernatural element was an Oriental exaggeration; and Eichhorn has been called the father of Higher Criticism and was the first man to use the term. De Wette's views as to inspiration were entirely infidel. Vatke and Leopold George were Hegelian rationalists and regarded the first four books of the Old Testament as entirely mythical. Kuenen, says Professor Sanday, wrote in the interests of an almost avowed Naturalism. That is, he was a free thinker, an agnostic; a man who did not believe in the Revelation of the one true and living God. (Brampton Lectures, 1893, page 117.) He wrote from an avowedly naturalistic standpoint, says Driver (Dr. S.R. Driver, *Introduction to the Literature of the Old Testament,* page 205). According to Wellhausen the religion of Israel was a naturalistic evolution from heathendom, an emanation from an imperfect monotheistic kind of semi-pagan idolatry. It was simply human religion.

In one word, the formative forces of the Higher Critical movement were rationalistic forces, and the men who were its chief authors and expositors, who 'on account of purely philosophical criticism have acquired an appalling authority,' were men who had discarded belief in God and Jesus Christ Whom He had sent.[36]

The most significant scholarly counterforce in effect at the start of the 20th Century was Archaeology. That field actively found new discoveries supporting the Biblical record,

In short, from the origin of the higher criticism till this present time" (early 20th century)" the discoveries in the field of archaeology have given it a succession of serious blows. The higher critics were shocked when the passion of the ancient world for writing and the preservation of documents was discovered. They were shocked when primitive Babylonia appeared as the land of Abraham. They were shocked when early Palestine appeared as the land of Joshua and the Judges. They were shocked when Amraphel came back from the grave as a real historical character bearing his code of laws. They were shocked when the stele of the Pharaoh of the exodus was read, and it was proved that he knew a people called Israel, that they had no settled place of abode, that they were 'without grain' for food, and that in these particulars they were quite as they were represented by the Scriptures to have been when they had fled from Egypt into the wilderness [37]

These heroes of Archaeology are little known, their hardships and adventures are only felt. Their contributions to truth and integrity are but apprehended, yet the feeling is true; and they are popularly represented as enemies of the Nazi system of thought as expressed in the Indiana Jones persona. *"Well done, Junior."*

At the beginning of the last century the stage was set for man's inhumanity to man. Morality had been divorced from the intercourse of nations, the philosophers had abandoned truth, and the Bible had been trashed by the higher critics. Much of this disease was grown in Germany, with the rest of the world lagging by decades. But there was resistance to these higher critics in the land of Luther. BF. Bettex, D. D., Professor Emeritus, Stuttgart, Germany wrote a telling article on the subject, *The Bible and Modern Criticism* and published in 1917 in *The Fundamentals*. He writes on Higher Criticism,

> "In the study-room it ensnares, in lecture-halls it makes great pretenses, for mere popular lectures, it is still serviceable; but when the thunders of God's power break in upon the soul, when despair at the loss of all one has loved takes possession of the mind, when remembrance of a miserable lost life or of past misdeeds is felt and realized, when one is on a sick-bed and death approaches, and the soul, appreciating that it is now on the brink of eternity, calls for a savior—just at this time when help is most needed, this modern religion utterly fails. ...
>
> Let us then, by repudiating this modern criticism, show our contempt of it. What does it offer us? Nothing. What does it take away? Everything. Do we have any use for it? No! It neither helps us in life nor comforts us in death; it will not judge us in the world to come. ...
>
> Just as for our present life this criticism offers us no consolation, no forgiveness of sins, no deliverance from 'the fear of death, through which we are all our lifetime subject to bondage,' so also it knows nothing respecting the great beyond—nothing with regard to that new heaven and new earth wherein righteousness shall dwell, nothing with regard to a God who wipes away all tears from our eyes. It is utterly ignorant of the glory of God, and on that account it stands condemned."[38]

How unusual was the behavior of the German people toward the Jews in their midst! These Germans were presumably Christians, and Jesus was a Jew. How could they hate the race of their Savior? This was unreasonable and illogical. While most of them wouldn't qualify for the title "born again Christian," some Christians did help the Jew, and some died because of it. What was the difference between the beliefs of these two groups of "Christians?" After reviewing the effects of philosophy on theology, and the effects of the Higher Criticism on the belief in the Bible, especially the first five books written by Moses, I conclude the German of 1938 was divorced from the truth and dubious of divine inspiration. They, therefore, made no connection between Jesus the Jewish man, and Jesus our God and Savior.

The world had lost the connection between language and the truth, between the Word of God and the Spirit of Truth, between Jesus and the Prime Mover. Further, there was no appreciation for the relationship between the pair, Abraham and Isaac, and the analogous pair, God the Father and Jesus the Son. Absolute Truth was thought to be a myth of the past, but the technologists kept creating absolutely wondrous machines and absolutely deadly weapons with their sure knowledge of the physical. Here was a dilemma for the rejecters of truth; the more the philosophers denied its existence, the more the natural sciences demonstrated its ubiquity by its utility. But then, it shouldn't have taken the engineers' knowledge to threaten these arrogant Pilates. God's creation demonstrates absolute truth far better than our feeble designs.

3.7) The Beautiful Big Bang Theory

The learned professors and pantheists insisted that any fool should know the universe eternal! But a *small child observed what everyone refused to say*: in 1927, the Belgian *priest* Georges Lemaître proposed that *the universe began with the explosion of a primeval atom*. Years later, Edwin Hubble found that distant galaxies in every direction are going away from us with speeds proportional to their distance. This experimental evidence helped justify Lemaître's theory. Hubble also found the Big Bang Theory predicts the existence of cosmic background radiation (the glow left over from the explosion itself). The Big Bang Theory received its strongest confirmation when two astronomers Arno Penzias and Robert Wilson discovered this radiation in 1964. Both later won the Nobel Prize for this discovery.

This cosmological theory states that elementary particles and antiparticles were created within a minute fraction of a second after the big bang, subsequently followed by photons of radiation. Minutes later, deuterium and helium nuclei were formed, and after the temperature had dropped sufficiently, neutral hydrogen atoms emerged. At this point in the expansion process, matter became decoupled from radiation, and interacted to form stars and galaxies, causing a further cooling to the present observed temperature of the microwave background noise. This theory has been successful in explaining the observed expansion of the universe, the measured abundance of helium in the cosmos, and the microwave background noise.

The beauty and importance of the *Big Bang* theory is that it has destroyed any basis for faith in *Pantheism* by annihilating the steady-state theory of the universe and its associated god, or gods. It does this by evidentiary proofs of the spontaneous creation of the universe. It has reduced the infinite universe to an ever-expanding one. It has destroyed biological evolution as a credible theory by defining an age to the universe, not in the trillions of years needed for evolution, but in roughly 13 billion years instead. The Belgian Priest deserves a *well done,* while the Harvard philosopher was *unfit for his office or unpardonably stupid*.

[1]   R. A. Torrey, A. C. Dixon and Others, <u>The Fundamentals</u>, Vol. I, Ch. XIX, "*My Experience With Higher Criticism*", Prof. J. J. Reeve, , 1917, Baker Books reprint, 2003, p.p. 360,361

[2]   Martin Luther, <u>Complete Sermons of Martin Luther</u>, Vol. 2.2, *Twelfth Sunday after Trinity*, Baker Books, Grand Rapids, MI, 2000, p373

[3]   Martin Luther, <u>Complete Sermons of Martin Luther</u>, Vol. 3.2, *Sunday After Christmas*, Baker Books, Grand Rapids, MI, 2000, p.p. 225,230

[4]   Martin Luther, <u>Complete Sermons of Martin Luther</u>, Vol. 2.2, *Sixth Sunday after Trinity*, Baker Books, Grand Rapids, MI, 2000, p183

[5]   Martin Luther, <u>Complete Sermons of Martin Luther</u>, Vol. 3.2, *New Years Day*, Baker Books, Grand Rapids, MI, 2000, p.p. 304,305

[6]   *Funk & Wagnalls New Encyclopedia*, 21, RUSSI - SOMAL, Funk & Wagnalls, Inc., New York, Scholasticism, ., p.p.167,168

[7]   E.T. Bell, *Men of Mathematics*, Simon and Schuster, New York, 1937, p.36

[8]   Ibid, p. 37

[9]   Ibid., p.p.37,38

[10] Descartes - A Discourse on Method, Part 2

[11] Descartes - A Discourse on Method, Part 2

[12] Descartes, A Discourse on Method, Part 1

[13] Blaise Pascal, *PENSfES*, 1660, translated by W. F. Trotter, #76-80

[14] Blaise Pascal, *PENSfES*, 1660, translated by W. F. Trotter, #233

[15] Descartes - A Discourse on Method, Part 4

[16] Eberhard Jüngel, *God as the Mystery of the World*, transl.: Darell L. Guder (Grand Rapids: Eerdmans Publishing Company, 1983), p123

[17] Ibid., p115

[18] René Descartes, *Discourse on Method*, 1637

[19] Jüngel, p140

[20] Ibid.

[21] Ibid., p.146

[22] Ibid.

[23] Albert Einstein, "Religion and Science", New York Times Magazine, 9 November 1930]

[24] Eberhard Jüngel, *God as the Mystery of the World*, transl.: Darell L. Guder (Grand Rapids: Eerdmans Publishing Company, 1983), p151

[25] Ibid., p.149 Dietrich Bonhoeffer, *Prisoner for God, Letters and Papers from Prison*, Edited by Eberhard Bethge, The Macmillan Co., New York, 1954, p.164

[26] Dietrich Bonhoeffer, *Prisoner for God, Letters and Papers from Prison*, Edited by Eberhard Bethge, The Macmillan Co., New York, 1954, p.p.162,163

[27] R. A. Torrey, A. C. Dixon and Others, The Fundamentals, Vol. IV, Ch. I, "*Modern Philosophy*", Philip Mauro, Counsellor-at-Law, 1917, Baker Books reprint, 2003, p. 17

[28] Ibid., p. 15

[29] Ibid.,p. 16

[30] Ibid.

[31] Ibid., p.19

[32] Ibid.

[33] R. A. Torrey, A. C. Dixon and Others, The Fundamentals, Vol. I, Ch. III "*Fallacies of the Higher Criticism*", Franklin Johnson, D.D., LL.,D. 1917,Baker Books reprint, *2003*, p. 55

[34] R. A. Torrey, A. C. Dixon and Others, The Fundamentals, Vol. I, Ch. III" Fallacies of the Higher Criticism", Franklin Johnson, D.D., LL., D. 1917, Baker Books reprint, 2003, p. 5

[35] R. A. Torrey, A. C. Dixon and Others, The Fundamentals, Vol. I, Ch.IV "*The Bible and Modern Criticism*", F. Bettex, D.D., Trans. David Heagle, D.D. 1917, Baker Books reprint, 2003, p. 85

[36] R. A. Torrey, A. C. Dixon and Others, The Fundamentals, Vol. I, Ch.I "*The History of the Higher Criticism*", Canon Dyson Hague, M.A.,1917, Baker Books reprint, 2003, p. 20

[37] R. A. Torrey, A. C. Dixon and Others, The Fundamentals, Vol. I, Ch. III "*Fallacies of the Higher Criticism*", Franklin Johnson, D.D., LL.,D. 1917,Baker Books reprint, *2003*, p.p. 67,68

[38] R. A. Torrey, A. C. Dixon and Others, The Fundamentals, Vol. I, Ch.IV "*The Bible and Modern Criticism*", F. Bettex, D.D., Trans. David Heagle, D.D. 1917, Baker Books reprint, 2003, p.p.90,93

Larry Sheets

Part Two - *If (a)* Linguistic Universals exists and *a* universal language is possible

4) **Language and Truth**

4.1) The Crux of The Matter

The chief enemy of Absolute Truth today is the notion that men cannot think without language, and that language is solely determined by regional society. Therefore, any idea or thought to be true is true for that society and the time in which it was spoken. There could then not be any Absolute Truth, because there is no absolute language. This is Jacques Derrida's contribution to postmodernism. According to Greer,

> Postmodernism … insists that within one's mind is language (words, syntax, and grammar) and that people think within the context of such language, whether a language be spoken (e.g., German, Spanish, Chinese) or unspoken (e.g., hand signs, facial expressions). Language provides the framework from which thoughts are identified and organized, and therefore makes thinking possible. …
>
> A central premise of postmodernism, then, is that language is prior to knowledge. One cannot think apart from vocabulary, syntax or grammar. In the context of language, thoughts give shape to systems of truth. And since language is the product of culture and many different languages exist in the world, truth is relative to individual cultures.[1]

We will show here and now that this notion is false and has been known so for half a century! The behaviorist view of language that dominated American linguistics since the 1920s was that language was a set of stimulus-response mechanisms. However, in the early 1960s, the renowned American linguist, Avram Noam Chomsky, proposed the Innateness Hypothesis Theory.[2] In it, the faculty of language is an innate idea. That is, an inbuilt knowledge of a set of linguistic universals that is genetically available to a child. An innate knowledge is considered the explanation for the ease of acquisition of the first language.

4.2) An Emotional Aside

Without absolutes, or genetic universals, at work in the world, there would be no world, as we know it. Consider the birds that know their destination even though they have not been shown the route. Even more, consider the lowly Monarch butterfly that flutters south to Mexico from North America. That butterfly is necessarily preprogrammed for the flight. Cats pounce on their prey and dogs chase theirs' down (sometimes cars too!). By the grace of God, so many living creatures are surviving by the pre-programming of their small, but effective brains.

But there stands Homer, the mighty and proud Homo Sapien, so pleased with himself that he wants to believe that he creates reality, or his lens determines the world he sees. "I have no instincts like these lesser beings." He says. "Perception is reality and I perceive no absolutes." But he deceives himself, because he also perceives birds in flight, the strong will to survive, a baby's cry, his own autonomic nervous system, the urge to preserve his species and sometimes, even those lesser ones too. His statements about having no instincts can also not be grounded in awareness, because instinct is "behavior that is mediated by reactions below the conscious level." – Webster. They are, therefore, unperceivable to the owner.

I am more inclined to say that instinct is behavior mediated by reactions *above* the conscious level because the solutions provided by instinct are superior to those of reason, given the available knowledge, time, and intellectual capacity of the organism to respond. Above or below the conscious level, instincts are unperceivable to their owners

So we look again upon that proud Homer, standing securely atop the food chain. He surveys the teaming life forms God has provided. He has no difficulty understanding how instincts help the lesser animals survive. Why is it, when he sees himself the most survivable, that he attributes none of that success to instinct? He wants to claim his success is due only to his outstanding intellect and his acquired knowledge. If he is that smart, and claims his success is due totally to his ability to think, and his ability to think is due to his language, and his language is due totally to experiences in the environment, then how did he survive long enough to establish such an environment, such a society? Surely God in His good Graces also gave us our portion to allow us to prosper in the manner of our kind. We had to be given innate language universals in our brains to begin the whole process.

4.3) Linguistic Universals

Chomsky proposed the *Theory of Rationalism* in Linguistics[3]. In this theory, Chomsky drew on the theory of innate knowledge propounded by the rationalist philosophers, (e.g., René Descartes and the linguists of the Port-Royal grammar.) In this work, Chomsky opposes the Behaviorism and Empiricism of postmodern linguistics. By the 1970s, Chomsky had proposed the *Theory of Modularity*[4] that claims that language is a separate mental organ. Recent linguistic generativists view the mind as a number of distinct but interacting "modules." The principal modules are linguistic, cognitive, and perceptual. These new views of the mind are consistent with what Chomsky postulated.

Quoting Stephen Crain[5] of the University of Maryland, College Park from his paper *Language and Brain:*

> It is wrong, however, to exaggerate the similarity between language and other cognitive skills, because language stands apart in several ways. For one thing, the use of language is universal—all normally developing children learn to speak at least one language, and many learn more than one. By contrast, not everyone becomes proficient at

complex mathematical reasoning, few people learn to paint well, and many people cannot carry a tune. Because everyone is capable of learning to speak and understand language, it may seem to be simple. But just the opposite is true—language is one of the most complex of all human cognitive abilities.

Later in the same paper, Crain states

> All preschool children, for example, have mastered several complex aspects of the syntax and semantics of the language they are learning. This suggests that certain aspects of syntax and semantics are not taught to children. Further underscoring this conclusion is the finding, from experimental studies with children, that knowledge about some aspects of syntax and semantics sometimes develops in the absence of corresponding evidence from the environment.

Crain goes on to say,

> There is another way in which knowledge of language and real-world experiences are kept apart in the minds of the children; they do not always base understanding of language on what they have come to know from experience. For example, children do not combine the words of the sentence 'mice chase cats' in a way that conforms with their experience, if they did, they would understand it to mean that cats chase mice, not the reverse. In other words, children are able to tell when sentences are false, as when they are true. This means that children use their knowledge of language structure in comprehending sentences, even if it means ignoring their wishes and the beliefs they have formed about the world around them.

This is reminiscent of Socrates' philosophy that stated that there was a realm of the Forms where even uneducated slave boys knew certain things mathematical. Contrary to Socrates, in the eighteenth century, John Locke's theory of human understanding [6] included a structural pillar that every infant was born with a clean slate. All that any child would know, he would learn by experience. Based on this pillar, Locke generated his theory of abstract ideas. But Bishop Berkeley [7] criticized Locke's theory. David Hume succinctly summarized Berkeley's argument.

> A great philosopher {Berkeley} has disputed the received opinion in this particular and has asserted that all general ideas are nothing but particular ones, annexed to certain term, which gives them more extensive signification, and makes them recall upon occasion other individuals, which are similar to them.[8] If Berkeley were right, and given Chomsky's and Crain's conclusions, the mind would start off with a select set of primitive thoughts or images, and the application of experience would add complexity to those primitives by attaching annexes to the originals to provide more complex ideas or images.

4.4) Language of the Brain

In a paper[9] by the eclectic genius Patrick Suppes (Center for the Study of Language and Information, Stanford University, Stanford, CA 94305-4115); and his associates Bing Han, Julie Epelboim, and Zhong-Lin Lu, Entitled *Invariance of Brain-wave Representations of Simple Visual Images and Their Names*, some fundamental philosophical conclusions were reached. This paper was concerned with what has been done recently to infer how words and sentences are represented in the brain.

The first task of the study is like that of speech recognition. Instead of speech, however, now brain-wave recognition of words being processed in the cortex is the task. This study lasted three years using EEG recordings and extensive computational analysis. The next task was to find invariances in brain-wave representations of words and sentences. There was demonstrated a surprising invariance of brain waves for sentences from one person to the next.

> In highly structured linguistic tasks different individuals have remarkably similar brain waves for the same spoken or visually presented sentence.

He went on to say in his paper

> By averaging over different subjects as well as trials, we created prototypes from brain waves evoked by simple visual images and test samples from brain waves evoked by auditory or visual words naming the visual images...The general conclusion is that simple shapes such as circles and single-color displays generate brain-waves surprisingly similar to those generated by their verbal names. *These results, taken together with extensive psychological studies of auditory and visual memory, strongly support the solution proposed for visual shapes, by Bishop Berkeley and David Hume in the 18th century, to the long-standing problem of how the mind represents simple abstract ideas.*

With Chomsky, then, the notion of language as genetic (and thereby innate and universal) achieved scientific accepted scholastic status. His vision, and the present scientific community's position stand in stark opposition to the postmodern view. With Chomsky, Crain, and Suppes, the very foundations of postmodern understanding of language and recognition are undermined.

It is not surprising that opponents of Chomsky continue to bite at his heals. He is a mathematical type with surprising personal characteristics. He stepped all over the behaviorists' theories that were tightly linked with liberal philosophy. Allott[10], Deacon,[11] and Tomasello[12] are but three authors that have troubles with Chomsky.. Mario Vaneechoutte, and John R. Skoyles[13] are additional detractors.

The last two authors have taken a perfectly intriguing subject of the musical basis for speech and language universals and twisted it into a Darwinian debate with support for the area of memetics. Not surprisingly, their paper was presented in the Journal of Memetics. . In section 5.2.entitled, *Music and language development*, I hear the strain between the subjective and the objective,

Do we need Chomskyan theory, borrowed from mathematics and logic?[14]

It appears to this linguistic novice that turf battles, philosophy, and pride have more to do with the objections than the facts.

Consider the following quote from Vaneechoutte and Skoyles[15] that shows the filtering of ideas accepted relative to their Darwinian religion,

> Pinker [16] and Pinker & Bloom [17] have suggested that the Chomskyan innate Universal Grammar arose by natural selection. There are many problems with this proposal. Bickerton [18], for example, in spite of being committed to the idea that an innate Universal Grammar arose by natural selection, felt the problems of this happening were so great that it could only be explained by a single and extraordinary macromutation, *which is clearly unacceptable to any evolutionary biologist.*

You see how God appears in History and is subsequently ruled out because He doesn't fit well with the Darwinian Sect.

4.4.1) A Beast with Two "Solutions."

We see that the presumption that language was totally social and temporal is false, but still debated. The theory that it is genetic in nature, and thereby innate to all, is current. If a property is genetic, innate, inbred, then it is itself unalterable by society. A behavior may be learned that appears to "undo" or mask the instinct, (e.g., allowing a human trainer's head in a lion's mouth). Thus, a "working copy" of proper behavior is taught the beast that varies greatly from the original, but the instinct remains active for the first opportunity or necessity to be engaged. Some animal trainers have found this out to their dismay. The beast has two "solutions." One is the response to a forced situation, and one is the natural mode.

If the brain is provisioned with a language module equipped with innate genetic language universals, and if the brain builds upon these universals by appending new meanings, images, or names, to comply with society, then all men have language fundamental functions that are themselves unmodified by time or environment but have working copies for current use that have appendages suitable for the time and place. Again, a beast with two "solutions."

4.4.2) Thought Eigenfunctions

If the brain has language fundamental functions that are unmodified by time or environment, then these functions must span the language space necessary for thought, albeit subconscious, or intuitive thought. Such must be if the local language is to grow onto the fundamental functions and append new meanings, etc., as a child learns.

If communication by language is to be considered a transformation between thought and sound waves, and subsequently in the listener, sound waves and understanding, then such a (thought to thought) transformation is subject to "natural modes," otherwise called: characteristic functions, eigenfunctions, or eigenvectors [19]. That is, a (thought to thought) linear transformation from thought to sound and from sound to thought will experience natural modes of resonance. Eigenfunction analysis is one of the most common analysis tools to optimize system performance, or to insure stability. It basically answers the question "How does this system like to vibrate, or respond?"

When an input is applied to a system, the output is generally a complicated convolved function of past values. It is generally difficult to "see" the input appearing in a scaled form at the output. So it is natural to ask, what inputs will appear as a purely scaled version at the system output? Such inputs are the "natural" or "characteristic" types of functions for the system under consideration. Sometimes, the "system" is a simple string, or organ pipe. Sometimes, the system is as complicated as a suspension bridge oscillating in the wind.

Input = x → **SOME SYSTEM CALLED A(x)** → Output = y = A(x)

So we ask the question, when is the output y equal to some scaled version of the input of x?

$$y = \lambda x = A(x)$$

That is when is the solution of this problem generally has the form of a number of different functions x_i and differing values for their respective λ_i.

$$\begin{pmatrix} \lambda_1 & x_1 \\ \lambda_2 & x_2 \\ \lambda_3 & x_3 \\ \cdot & \cdot \\ \cdot & \cdot \\ \cdot & \cdot \\ \lambda_n & x_n \end{pmatrix}$$

Where the l_i are scaling constants and the x_i are generally functions of time.

The x_i are called eigenvalues and the x_i are called eigenfunctions. The number of them depends on the system. The relative sizes of the l_i determine their relative importance in describing the system. I will not solve any such problems here, but simply mention the meaning of such strange sounding functions that are different for different systems. It seems natural that the functions interfacing the brain to the world would be the same as those used in the brain in the slow speed serial communications channels of the brain.

**FIGURE 4.1 Thought-to-Thought System
One Way Thought to Thought Transmission Without Physical Detail**

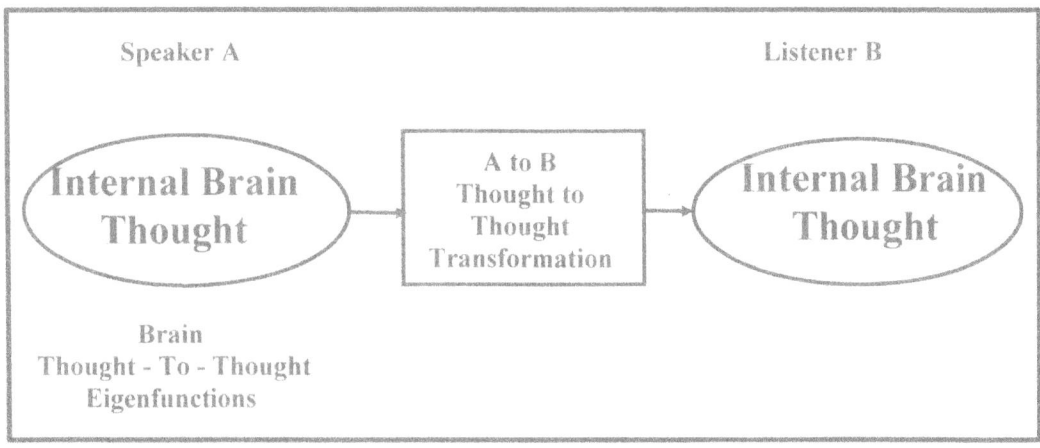

If as stated above, the brain has language fundamental functions that are unmodified by time or environment, and these functions span the language space necessary for thought, albeit subconscious, or intuitive thought, then the only way that the (thought to thought) eigenfunctions would change would be if the makeup of the communicating minds would change.

Existing external language might be able to be represented by linear combinations of the internal eigenfunctions, and maybe not. These characteristic functions may not be able to be represented in existing language if the existing language has not built upon one or more of these internal language fundamental functions. Let's be clear, the eigenfunctions I've been referring to are those internal to the brain that relate to thought-to-thought transformations. There might be different eigenfunctions working in the physical realm of sound that probably are different. An example of the physical "natural modes" is described below.

Suppose a species had 11 organic tuning forks in an acoustic chamber in its body. Each fork rings at a different frequency than the other forks. Suppose for simplicity that together the forks cover (span) the audio range of the species, and that range is less than an octave to prevent coupling between the individual animal's forks. To "talk", the species tweaks one or more of the forks in succession. The "listening" mate senses one or more of its forks sympathetically vibrating (resonating) because of the impinging sound waves.

Information is therefore carried between the two critters by sound and resonant structures. The basic functions are the sound waves at the individual fork frequencies. If for sociological reasons, one of the fork frequencies is not used (It might be a predator's listening frequency, for example), the species adapts by being wordier with the other forks. If the species has avoided the use of one fork frequency, there will be no element of that frequency in the "speech" and the function created by the unused fork could not be detected by listening to the speech. This is why I say that external eigenfunctions might be used to represent existing external speech, but not necessarily conversely.

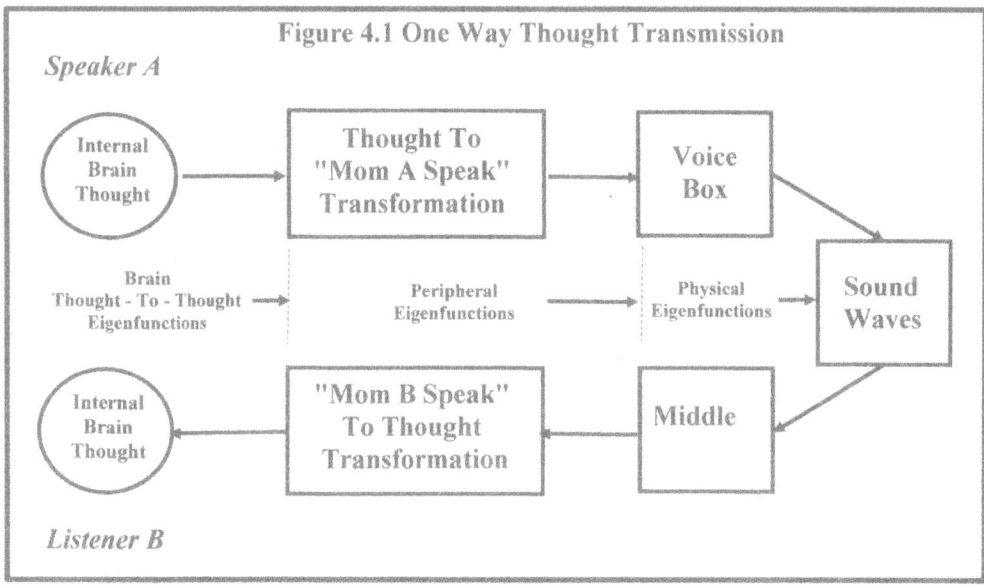

In the above example, however, I glossed over the most hidden part of the communication process. There is a sentence above worth considering again, "To 'talk', the species tweaks one or more of the forks in succession." This sentence avoids discussing the process of converting the speaking critter's thoughts into "tweaks." Similarly, there is no mention how the resonating listener converts the sympathetic vibrations into thought. The sound vibrations and the physical structure are not as important to us as the originating idea's transformation from the internal language of the brain into a sociologically agreed to utterance, or word. It is becoming ever so clear that animals and humans think in some genetic language of the brain, but only humans have the ability to effectively convert those internal thoughts into the flowing spoken languages our mothers taught us.

In communication systems, when the data source is jerky and the information arrives in fits and spurts, but there is a need to convey it smoothly, the solution is called a "buffer." The jerky data is fed into the buffer and is then subsequently read smoothly out of it. Provided the buffer is large enough, all erratic variations of input are smoothed-over in the resulting output. The requirement to do this job is that the system has adequate memory to construct the buffer of necessary length. It is possible that the flowing spoken languages our mothers taught us require considerable memory to implement-memory unavailable to animals.

4.4.3) The Imperfect Thought to Language Interface

> "The Pure, the beautiful ... the impulse to a wordless prayer, ... these things can never die."[20] – Doudney.

We have all been made aware that the words that we use to represent our thoughts do not equal our thoughts. We seek for more precise equivalence between the thought and the words used. We grope for the right words. Education helps us find those suitable symbols for our ideas. The problem is not just in the speaker, however. A precisely spoken sentence in a close equivalence with the original thought may nevertheless be imperfectly interpreted by the listener and rendered into an idea far removed from the original thought. In that case, the listener is modeling the spoken word into a framework that is different from the speaker's.

A mathematician might say that a matrix transforms (i.e., convolves) the thinker's ideas into a spoken sentence, while the speaker expects the listener to employ his inverse matrix (i.e., deconvolves) to recover the thought. Well, the speaker doesn't control the listener's inverse matrix, and mistakes are made. This idea of incorrect inverse matrices is exemplified in figure 4.2. The speaker A's thoughts are transformed by 'Thought to "Mom A Speak" Transformation." The exact inverse of that matrix would be '"Mom A Speak" to Thought Transformation,' but the listener only has the '"Mom B Speak" to Thought Transformation.' The difference between these two "decoders" is an error of some kind.

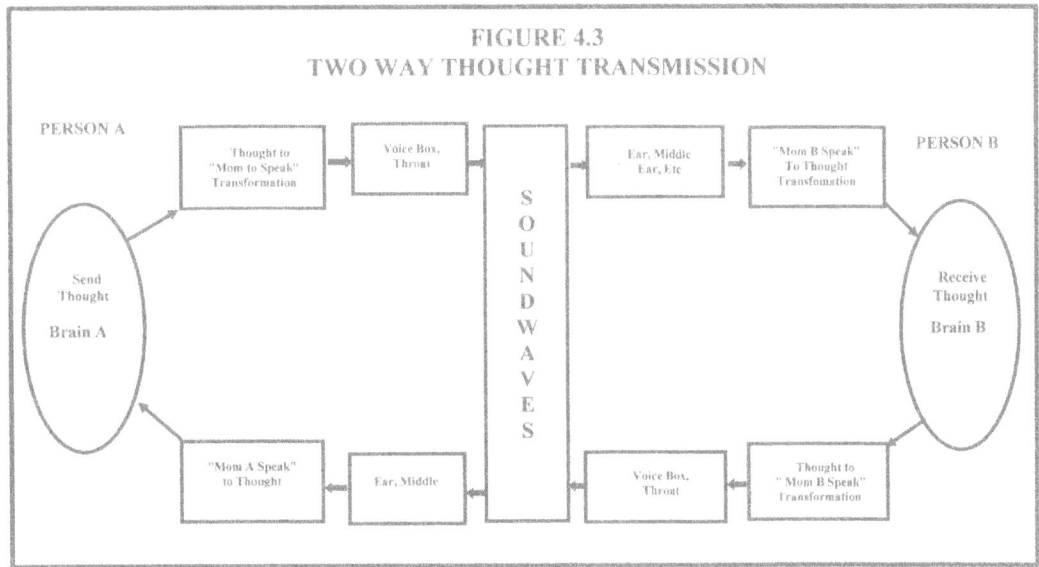

Because of the expense of faulty listening in business, the Carl Roger's rule of active listening is often employed.

> Active listening restates or paraphrases the speaker's message. It clarifies and obtains accurate facts and gives feedback to the speaker. In 'active listening,' a clarity check designed by Carl Rogers, a listener responds to a speaker with, 'What I heard you say was ...,' and then gives comments.[21]

With such an approach, both speaking matrices and both listening inverse matrices are exercised. If the speaker receives his original thought echoed back, he is satisfied the listener understood, i.e., got the right thought.

The same process happens in the sciences. The difference is that all creation speaks and we use our inverse matrices to try to understand what has been spoken. If our inverse matrices are not correct, we understand imperfectly. So we set up experiments to communicate with nature, and see if she agrees with our hypothesis. Since she cannot lie and change her nature, if the hypothesis is false, nature returns a different message in the experiment.

When the functions expressed in nature are measurable, they can be quantified and correlated with other functions. Often, our mathematics language is used to describe such relationships. Our inverse matrices influence our choice of mathematical representations. Since we have all bounced or rolled a ball, thrown a rock, hopped, skipped, and jumped, we all have similar thought/reality transformations at work, and can communicate well about such reality. When it comes to the obscure, like the "potential well problem with the wave equation" that leads to quantum theory, then we have difficulty with the other's inverse matrices. When we communicate about the speed of light, and the representations of reality that evokes, then too we doubt others' ability to think properly.

[1]   Robert C. Greer, *Mapping Postmodernism*, InterVarsity Press, Downers Grove, Illinois, 2003, *Postmodernism*, p. 225

[2]   N. Chomsky, *Cartesian Linguistics* (New York, 1966)

[3]   Ibid

[4]   J. A. Fodor, *The Modularity of Mind* (Cambridge, Mass., 1983)

[5]   Stephen Crain, *Language and Brain, The Domain of Study,* University of Maryland, College Park Cover Article for Linguistic Society of America Web page, http://www.lsadc.org/ 2003

[6]   John Locke, *An Essay Concerning Human Understanding*, Henry Regnery Company, Chicago, Illinois, 1956

[7]   . Berkeley, G. (1710) Principles of Human Knowledge. (Jeremy Pepyat, Dublin).

[8]   D. Hume, *A Treatise on Human Nature*. (John Noon, London, 1739). p.17

[9]   Patrick Suppes (Center for the Study of Language and Information, Stanford University, Stanford, CA 94305-4115); and his associates Bing Han, Julie Epelboim, and Zhong-Lin Lu, Entitled *Invariance of Brain-wave Representations of Simple Visual Images and Their Names.* Paper gratuitously emailed to me 2003 by Patrick Suppes, CSLI,

Ventura Hall, Stanford University, Stanford, CA 94305-4115, Phone: (650) 7256030, Fax: (650) 470-7606, Email: suppes@ockham.stanford.edu

[10] Allott, R. 1997. Pinker's language instinct: gradualistic natural selection is not a good enough explanation. http://www.percep.demon.co.uk/pinker.htm

[11] Deacon, T.W. 1997. The Symbolic Species: The Co-evolution of Language and *the Brain*. W.W. Norton & Cy, New York.

[12] Tomasello, M. 1995. Language is not an instinct. *Cognitive Development* 10: 131-156.

[13] Vaneechoutte, M. and Skoyles, J.R., 1998; The memetic origin of language: modern humans as musical primates. Journal of Memetics - Evolutionary Models of Information Transmission, **2**.

[14] Ibid

[15] Ibid.

[16] Pinker, S. 1994. The Language Instinct: How the Mind Creates Language. Morrow, New York.

[17] Pinker, S., and P. Bloom. 1990. Natural language and natural selection. *Behavioral and Brain Sciences* 13: 707-784.

[18] Bickerton, D. 1990. *Language and Species*. University of Chicago Press, Chicago.

[19] Peter B. Kahn, *Mathematical Methods For Scientists & Engineers*, John Wily & Sons, New York, 1990, p. 27

[20] Marjorie Barrows, One Thousand Beautiful Things, Spencer Press, New York, 1947, p68

[21] Robert W. Rasberry and Laura Fleche Lemoine, *Effective Managerial Communication*, PWS-KENT, Boston, 1986, p. 165

Larry Sheets

5) On The Nature of an Ideal Language

> ... *for you know the Kingdom of Christ is founded upon the Word, which cannot be apprehended or understood except by these two organs, the ear and the tongue, and he rules in the hearts of men alone by the Word and by faith. The ears apprehend the Word, the heart believes it; the tongue, however, speaks or confesses that which the heart believes.*[1]

What if language is not limited to the known language groups of this world? What would it mean if from His Throne, God broke in and spoke in this world? Surely God is capable of approaching us, communicating with us, and living among us. Is not this what Pentecost was about? God has further declared that He will give all peoples a pure language so that we can all worship Him coherently in unison.

> *For then will I turn to the people a pure language, that they may all call upon the name of the LORD, to serve him with one consent. (Zephaniah 3:9) (ASV).*

Different translations quote this verse otherwise, but the term "consent" translated here comes from "shoulder" conveying the idea of synchronous rowing or equally yoked oxen. The word "language" here comes from the Hebrew "lip", which is the same word used in the Biblical texts describing the Tower of Babel. The Septuagint translated it "tongue", which the Greek use to describe language.

What would a language be like? Well, we should not expect it to be radically different sounding from what we use now, because, before Babel we naturally had a common language. However, in the above scripture He didn't just say, "I will restore one language back to the people" instead, he said, "I will turn to the peoples a *pure* language." It should allow us to reason well, and it should have no difficulty defining Truth. If God's word is true, and if it declares that God will give men a pure language, then at least one pure language exists, we just haven't discovered it yet. Please understand that the pure language that I'm referring to is not a procedural approach to communications, but a gift from God not just as natural as your mother tongue, but more so. This is not the Tarski-like approach to language, but a charismatic approach to words.

Dietrich Bonhoeffer wrote his parents from the National Socialists' prison on June 14,[th] 1943, the day of Pentecost that the Germans called Whitsunday,

> The strange story of the first Whitsunday, with its miraculous gift of tongues, has once more provided a good deal of food for thought. At the tower of Babel all the tongues were confounded, and as a result men could no longer understand one another as they all spoke different languages. This confusion is now brought to an end by the language of God, which is universally intelligible and the only means of mutual understanding between men. And the Church is the place where that miracle happens. – Truly, these are inspiring thoughts. [2

Jesus said, "let your yes's be yes's and your no's be no's for whatsoever is more than this comes of evil." Politicians often provide a counter example of what Jesus meant. The pure language of God will be absolute. There will be no connoted, twisted, or implied meanings in God's pure language. There will be no room for lies or half-truths.

5.1) The Poetic Mathematician

The closest example I can think of to explain such a language is the language of the mathematics of algebra combined with music or poetry. This combination of algebra, music and/or poetry might seem like a strange combination until you look into it closer. Pythagoras is a Greek mathematician from the 6th century B.C. (569 - 475 B.C.) Pythagoras believed that fundamentally reality is mathematical in nature. He is best known for his theory of the length of a hypotenuse, given the two other sides of a right triangle. Nevertheless, he is credited with developing our understanding of music's harmonic series - the overtone series.

There are other various examples of this kind of association. The first such example is that in a particular study that the percentage of undergraduate students having taken a music course was about eleven percent above average amongst mathematics majors.[3] This affinity for music by mathematicians has been observed for years.[4] The second example is that research has demonstrated that piano playing children frequently exhibit enhanced reasoning skills like those useful in playing chess, solving jigsaw puzzles, or performing mathematical deductions.[5] Lastly, Albert Einstein is quoted as saying,

> If I were not a physicist, I would probably be a musician. I often think in music. I live my daydreams in music. I see my life in terms of music. ... I get most joy in life out of music.[6]

Einstein was also quoted as saying

> But the creative principle resides in mathematics. In a certain sense, therefore, I hold true that pure thought can grasp reality, as the ancients dreamed.[7]

The famous mathematician William Rowan Hamilton thought Algebra may be thought of as a tool, *a language*, or something to contemplate [8]. Time is connected with Algebra. Algebra considers what it reasons on as flowing. Whereas Geometry considers what it reasoned on as fixed, Algebra (which included the Calculus) was founded mainly on the notions of *Fluxions* which involves the concept of *Time* and *Continuous Progression*. Music is based on emotions or thoughts flowing in time. Some believe that music is fundamental to language.[9] "Music is well said to be the speech of angels." – Carlyle Quoting Vaneechoutte, and Skoyles,

> With respect to the development of language in children, one can agree with Chomsky that humans have special abilities to adopt language and syntax very spontaneously early in childhood and this can be called an innate language acquiring device. Still, it

probably might best be understood as an innate music acquiring device, which enables to link any possible syntax of spoken language - the one used by the adults which happen to raise the child or by other children which happen to grow up with the child - to the universal mental syntax, of which we share the general basic possibilities for categorization and for generalization of causal rules with animals.

Vaneechoutte, and Skoyles go on to say,

> All human cultures possess lullabies and use them to sing children to sleep. The music business is among the world's major industries. Going to war is so much more fun with a drum band marching along. Dancing to music can give people mystical trance experiences. Music brings up deep emotions such as hope, pleasure, comfort or sadness, and probably no other `art' can do this as profoundly as music. From observations of currently existing `premodern' societies, it is clear that music (and its counterpart, dance) must have played an even more important, pivotal role in early human societies. Music has a role, not only in rituals, but also in many practical activities. For instance, Australian aboriginals memorize the look of landscapes in songs. Although the music making of early humans has left no physical remains, it must have been a major part of their lives, as it still largely is an essential part of our lives.[10]

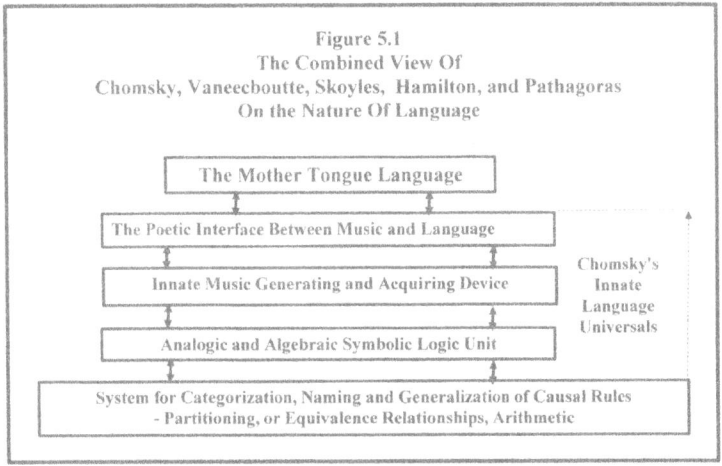

As inclusive as Figure 5.1 appears to be, it lacks a component that I have long believed essential to a description of the language of the brain. Let me lay the foundation for this component. Dreams are quite graphic, with considerable mobile imagery. The optic nerve is a bit of a misnomer because it actually is involved with the video signal processing, not just the transmission from eye to brain. That actually makes the optic nerve part of the brain. The reason for this design is clear to a transmission expert – There is just too much information in a raw video signal to "pipe" it any distance in the body. The optic nerve is a peripheral processor that reduces the bandwidth of the "digested" video signal. Like MPEG and other forms of data compression, the result is signal that is more easily moved about, and more easily stored. The resulting signal is nevertheless still considerably more information- filled than any signal that only conveys the equivalent of voice or music.

That digested video signal goes to a place in the brain designed to manipulate this massive data. I chose to call this digested high-speed signal path a parallel signal, because it conveys a massive amount of information quickly, as if it were all delivered in parallel or in unison. The old saying "A picture is worth a thousand words." applies here. The ratio of a thousand to one is roughly correct between video and speech. The voice or music signals I consider slow serial signals, because the information is sequentially delivered at an auditory rate. It has to arrive at the brain at a slow speed port designed for it in the brain. Thus, voice and music are separate from video or moving graphic images. However, stationary graphic designs or fixed images could pass through the slow serial voice or music channels without degradation. The following quotes add to this thinking.

"A Picture is a poem without words." [11] – Latin Proverb.

"Poetry is vocal painting, as painting is silent poetry." [12] – Simonides of Ceos.
"Architecture is frozen music." [13] – Madame de Stael

Since we dream in moving pictures, the dreaming process must necessarily happen where the mind has high-speed parallel signal paths. The original meaning of "idea" was image. Get the picture? I know that I also dream with words, so both signal types are involved in dreaming. Why do I spend time here with dreams? Because I believe that the part of the brain, or the part of its processes involved with dreaming is also the part of the brain associated with understanding. Some might call it the subconscious, but I'm inclined to believe it is above the conscious level. The Ah Ha! happens when the parallel tells the serial what it knows.

The inclusion of graphical language in the parallel paths of the brain with processed video signals impinging at that graphical area makes for an interesting model. Further, it has an interesting analogy to ADSL (Asymmetric Digital Subscriber Lines) used for the high-speed internet connections to the home. As a model, we have voice and music entering the brain using bi-directional low speed transmission paths (In by the ear, out by the mouth, or written by the hand). The video signal is only into the brain via the eye and the data compressing optic nerve. Thus, if there is an outward expression relative to the video input, it must be by way of the slow speed voice and music or hand path. ADSL was designed to deliver very high-speed data to the home, and to send much slower data rates toward the network. The ADSL idea was that humans would download large files from the network, but would only send small stuff in the opposite direction. ADSL even uses Data compression, like the optic nerve does, to make the subsequent transmission adequate for a video signal.

To support these ideas of a graphical thought center, consider the following quote from Albert Einstein,

> The words of language, as they are written and spoken, do not seem to play any role in my mechanism of thought.[14]

Further he said,

> These thoughts did not come in any verbal formulation. I rarely think in words at all. A thought comes, and I may try to express it in word afterward.[15]

> The intellect has little to do on the road to discovery. There comes a leap in consciousness, call it Intuition or what you will, the solution comes to you and you don't know how or why[16]

All electrical engineering thought involves graphical mathematical concepts, such as "divergence," and "curl," or "schematic diagrams" or "flux lines" or "vectors." It is not possible to be an engineer or physical scientist without a working knowledge of the Calculus. It is impossible to think of the Calculus without tangents, and tangents without trigonometry. And it is not possible to know trigonometry without circles, radii and coordinate systems. We imagine or think the science in graphical terms, but we explain and prove those ideas in a serial language of Algebra. The same is true of theology,

> No legislation could prevent the making of verbal pictures: God walks in the garden, He stretches out His arm, His voice shakes the cedars, His eyelids try the children of men. To forbid the making of pictures about God would be to forbid thinking about God at all, for man is so made that he has no way to think except in pictures.[17]

As a student of advanced mathematics, I have had many occasions where I was required to write a formal proof of some theory or equation. I don't believe that I am unusual in what my experiences were. Very often, as I proceeded through a proof, I would get to a point where I knew in my being that I had solved the problem. Nevertheless, I would have to continue writing the proof out for another three or four pages before I had completed the task of writing the necessary steps to demonstrate the proof. My thinking was not in the language I was writing in. Again, I don't believe that I was unusual in this regard. This concept needs to be included in any summary of how the brain conceives and communicates. We need to draw a clear picture of a mind with high-speed graphical like thinking, with serial peripherals passing through poetic interfaces to language and art. See figure 5.1.1.

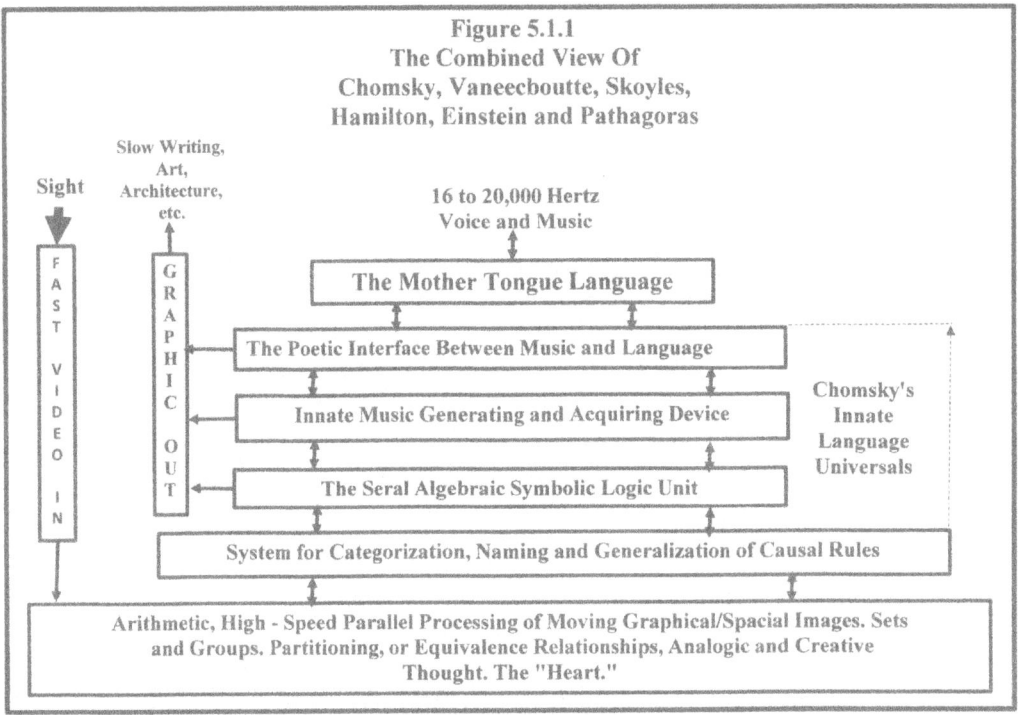

The lowest, or deepest, level in figure 5.1.1 would be the area of intuition or judgment. The next higher level that of intellect or reasoning.

> There are then two kinds of intellect: the one able to penetrate acutely and deeply into the conclusions of given premises, and this is the precise intellect; the other able to comprehend a great number of premises without confusing them, and this is the mathematical intellect. The one has force and exactness, the other comprehension. Now the one quality can exist without the other; the intellect can be strong and narrow and can also be comprehensive and weak.... For it is to judgment that perception belongs, as science belongs to intellect.
> Intuition is the part of judgment, mathematics of intellect.[18]

Judgment then relates to intuition, apprehension, and wisdom, while science relates to reason, comprehension and intellect.

The lowest level in figure 5.1.1 relates to Paul Tillich's[19] term "the Ground of Being" as wisdom and judgment does to God. Therefore it also relates to the so-called 'psychology of depth' that Tillich mentioned as the deepest level, away from our consciousness and into areas that show us traits of our character that contradict everything we believed we were. This, then, is the area of deepest feelings and honest thought. This is where the Lord calls, as to young Samuel, and we are to answer, "Here I am," followed by "Speak, for Thy servant is listening." This is where God appeared to Solomon and said to him, "Ask what I shall give you." and he responded by asking for wisdom and knowledge, two of the elements abiding in this region of the brain. This is where "the still small voice" is heard, and where the "peace of God" is felt.

> This peace is the gift of God and is called the 'peace of God' because, having it, we are at peace with him even if we are displeased with men. This peace of God is beyond the power of mind and reason to comprehend. Understand, however, it is not beyond man's power to experience—to be sensible of. Peace with God must be felt in the heart and conscience.[20]

5.2) What's In a Name?

Besides the algebraic and musical aspects of the proposed language, I am also persuaded there will be considerable precision in the naming of things. No sooner had God declared to Adam not to eat the forbidden fruit, He considered Man's loneliness; God proceeded to have Adam name His creatures so that Adam could truly communicate with the wonderful helper He was about to be given.

> And out of the ground the LORD God formed every beast of the field and every bird of the sky, *and brought them to the man to see what he would call them; and whatever the man called a living creature, that was its name.* And the man gave names to all the cattle, and to the birds of the sky, and to every beast of the field, but for Adam there was not found a helper suitable for him.-Genesis 2:19,20

In *Analects*[21] Confucius said,

- "If names are not correct, language is not in accordance with the truth of things.
- If language is not in accordance with the truth of things, affairs cannot be carried on to success.
- When affairs cannot be carried on to success, proprieties and music do not flourish.
- When proprieties and music do not flourish, punishments will not be properly awarded.
- When punishments are not properly awarded, the people do not know how to move hand or foot."

Considering the importance of John 14:13, "And I will do whatever you ask in my name, so that the Father may be glorified in the Son," the proper understanding of Jesus' Name takes on considerable significance. This was mentioned in the introduction.

Reasoned and Emotional Grasping for Truth

We first look at a few readable descriptions of what a pure and adequate language to deal with truth would be like, and then for the ardent student, work our way through Alfred Tarski's concepts.

Greer writes about the *supra-rational* language he envisages. I augment Greer's thoughts. I would rather this language be called intu-rational as a shortened form of intuition-rational language. It might also be called (faith, hope, and love)-(logic, reason and justice) language. It must be able to facilitate comprehension and apprehension. Here apprehend is to become conscious of through the emotions or senses i.e., to perceive. Comprehend is to take in or include by construction or implication; to comprise (as the parts of an object); to imply. In the Indo-European language family, the root for comprehend and apprehend, I believe, both relate to "grasping". One seems to be reasoned grasping, while the other implies emotional grasping. So one unfortunate soul might say, "I comprehend the gallows and apprehend my fate."

In other words, the language must be two-dimensional. It must be in a plane, rather than a line. To be able to solve an unreasonable problem, it might be necessary to leave the reason line and proceed *also* in the other dimension to arrive at a conclusion. I say *also* because reason is not to be abandoned in the process. That dimension is still needed. Two dimensions are the required number for graphics.

This situation is not unique. There was a time when algebra was not *closed* under all its operations. By *closed*, it was meant that when operations are defined over the real numbers, the result of those operations fall back into the real numbers. When attempting to find solutions to the roots of polynomials, algebraists ran into a wall. There were occasions when the square root of the number (-1) appeared in the calculations. Since no real number appears on the line of real numbers (that extend from minus infinity to positive infinity) that when multiplied by itself equals minus one, there was no understandable solution.

Once the *imaginary* i = square root of (-1) was defined as a number, the number system was enlarged to include all numbers proportional or scaled by i. Thus, numbers that used to be defined as some proportion to the real number one (number = X times one), now became numbers defined in two parts (number = X times one + Y times i). More briefly, $N = X + iY$. Such a number is called a *complex* number. With this addition to the number system, polynomials with real or *complex* coefficients and real or *complex* variables all had roots in the *complex* plane. This is basically the Fundamental Theorem of Algebra.

This concept is often displayed on a Cartesian coordinate system (Yes, the very same Descartes of the Cogito) with imaginary vertical axis and real horizontal axis. Since no linear combination of real numbers can equal an imaginary number, the two halves of the complex numbers are *perpendicular* to each other. This is also referred to as *orthogonal* or *linearly independent*. So, in a manner of speaking, if a language were defined along the real axis, then no linear combination of words, sentences, etc., so constructed could ever produce an imaginary or complex sum.

Now if "true," "truth," and "Truth" required an imaginary part of a complex expression, that language would fail to define it: words, sentences, etc., might require an imaginary part to deal with the subject of Truth. It is unclear to this author whether there must be two independent languages (one for the real and one for the imaginary), or one language for both with a rich combination of real and imaginary terms. *However, if we take the example of the complex plane as our best analogy, then to allow for the interactions between dimensions, the solution should be one language for both with a rich combination of real and imaginary terms.*

These are not new concepts about language. Although I know very little about it, the Jewish community has a learning called Kabbalah. It is a system of thought including a cipher method of interpreting Scripture. They have repeatedly taught that Kabbalistic understanding does not come about in the way Talmudic understanding does through rational, analytical learning. It is not the product of philosophical contemplations, nor can it be. They believe that keeping the Law and a monkish lifestyle empowers the Kabbalist to accept that which they call Hasagat Ruah HaKodesh, or guidance by the Divine Spirit.

Alfred Tarski's Thoughts

We look briefly into the Polish logician Alfred Tarski's.[22] (1902 –83) work, the paper *The Semantic Conception Of Truth And The Foundations Of Semantics (1944)*, to see if there are answers there for our questions. References to section numbers relate to his paper.

Tarski declares that concepts of semantics play an important role in the discussions of philosophers, logicians, and philologists. Although the meaning of semantic seems to be clear and understandable, attempts to characterize this meaning fail. Worse still, various arguments, which seemed otherwise correct and based upon obvious premises, led to paradoxes and antinomies. Examples are, the *antinomy of the liar*, Richard's *antinomy of definability* (by means of a finite number of words), and Grelling-Nelson's *antinomy of heterological terms*. It is useful to begin with that antinomy which directly involves the notion of truth, namely, the ***antinomy of the liar***[23] which is available in the Appendix D.

5.4.1) No Semantically Closed Language (Potentially Anti-semantic!)

Tarski [24] in his Section 8 concludes that there are two essential assumptions in the construction of the antinomy of the liar. *(If "this sentence is false" is true, then it is false, but the sentence states that it is false, and if it is false, then it must be true, and so on.)* It was assumed:

I. That the language used in the construction of the antinomy contains expressions, names of these expressions, and semantic terms such as the term "*true*" referring to sentences of this language. It has also been assumed that all sentences that determine the adequate usage of this term can be asserted in the language. A language with these properties will be called "*semantically closed.*"

II. That in this language the ordinary laws of logic hold.

He insists to be able to find truth, we must choose between a "Semantically Closed" language and the "ordinary laws of logic." He chose to keep the ordinary laws of logic because he could not bear to forego them. Accordingly, **Tarski decides *not to use any language that is semantically closed* in the sense given.**

5.4.2) An Essentially Rich Meta-Language Required

He concludes in Section 10, we need a second language that is essentially richer than the ones we have to be able to define truth non-axiomatically. If the theory of truth were developed in a meta-language that does not satisfy essential richness, then we would have to include the term "*true,*" or some other semantic term, in the list of undefined terms of the meta-language, and to express fundamental properties of truth in a series of axioms:

> "Thus, we see that the condition of "essential richness" is necessary for the possibility of a satisfactory definition of truth in the meta-language. If we want to develop the theory of truth in a meta-language which does not satisfy this condition, we must give up the idea of defining truth with the exclusive help of those terms which were indicated above (in Section 8). We have then to include the term "*true,*" or some other semantic term, in the list of undefined terms of the meta-language, and to express fundamental properties of the notion of truth in a series of axioms. *There is nothing essentially wrong in such an axiomatic procedure, and it may prove useful for various purposes."* [25] (Italics mine)

5.4.3) An Attempt at Language Construction Fails

So, his belief is in a second super- language that includes the original but has superior logic apparatus. In short, he believes we need a second language that is essentially richer than the ones we have to be able to define truth non-axiomatically. If the theory of truth were developed in a meta-language that does not satisfy essential richness, then we would have to include the term "*true,*" or some other semantic term, in the list of undefined terms of the meta-language, and to express fundamental properties of truth in a series of axioms. He goes on:

> It turns out, however, that this procedure can be avoided. For *the condition of the "essential richness" of the meta-language proves to be, not only necessary, but also sufficient for the construction of a satisfactory definition of truth,* i.e., if the meta-language satisfies this condition, the notion of truth can be defined in it. We shall now indicate in general terms how this construction can be carried through. [26] (Italics mine)

He then proceeds to explain in roundabout ways the how-to of constructing such a language. This appears to be more difficult than anticipated. After a struggle, he concludes:

> From this rough outline it is not clear where and how the assumption of the "essential richness" of the meta-language is involved in the discussion; this becomes clear only when the construction is carried through in a detailed and formal way.[27]

5.4.4) Enter Gödel's *Incompleteness Theorem*

Unfortunately for Tarski, relying on the "the ordinary laws of logic" can be a weaker crutch than leaning on a "Semantically Closed" language. This is because of Gödel's (1906 –78) famous *Incompleteness Theorem* [28] (1931). In it he proves that <u>no formal theory can be either *complete* or *decidable* if it is comprehensive enough to include simple statements about the natural numbers among its *meaningful expressions*</u>. This is the result in logic whereby, if a system that formalizes the theory of the natural numbers is *consistent, then this system contains a logical formula such that neither the formula nor its negation can be proved within the system.*

Consistent means that no two contradictory expressions are in the set (T) of all tautologies. *Decidable* means there is a general procedure for deciding whether or not a given meaningful expression can be proved or not. Further, (in 1936) John Barkley Rosser (1907 -) extended Gödel's Incompleteness Theorem (The Gödel – Rosser Incompleteness Theorem) [29]. It states that in a formal system that determines the positive integers, there is a "correct" proposition that can neither be proved nor disproved in the system

Here, at this point in Tarsk's paper (Section 12), it appears like he learned of, or remembered Gödel:

> Further important results can be obtained by applying the theory of truth to formalized languages of a certain very comprehensive class of mathematical disciplines; only disciplines of an elementary character and a very elementary logical structure are excluded from this class. It turns out that for a discipline of this class *the notion of truth never coincides with that of provability*; for all provable sentences are true, but *there are true sentences which are not provable*. Hence it follows further that every such discipline is consistent but incomplete; that is to say, of two contradictory sentences at most one is provable, and what is more there exists a pair of contradictory sentences neither of which is provable.[30] (Italics mine)

5.4.5) Axiomatic Method the Most Appropriate

Thus, we can never even hope to grasp (comprehend) truth entirely within the formal system. So there is the same problem with *consistent* formal logic systems that Tarski thought belonged to the semantically "closed" formal language systems. Even more, the problems associated with the antinomies might have resulted from the logic's incompleteness described by Gödel and Rosser. As brilliant as Tarski was, he may have backed himself into a corner by appealing to a higher "essentially rich" language to make judgments on a working (object) language. He earlier made reference to axiom-based languages if an essentially rich one weren't found. Once that is done, truth is defined axiomatically. *But at the very end of his paper (Section 13), he appears to have concluded that an axiom –based language is the correct solution.*

> We have concerned ourselves here with the theory of semantic notions related to an individual object-language (although no specific properties of this language have been involved in our arguments). However, we could also consider the problem of developing *general semantics* which applies to a comprehensive class of object-languages. A considerable part of our previous remarks can be extended to this general problem; however, certain new difficulties arise in this connection, which will not be discussed here. ***I shall merely observe that the axiomatic method (mentioned in Section 10) may prove the most appropriate for the treatment of the problem*** [31] (Italics mine)

In a way, Gödel and Rosser have opened the door to the "correct," but not provable, proposition being "God is." Such has never been proven or disproved. The NAME of God, YHVH (or with vowels YaHWeH), is derived from the Hebrew verb HAYAH, to be. Moses declared

> "The LORD our God is One."

Thus, the positive integers are at least implied in our formal religious system. That God is, if and only if "I AM," must not have been knowable before God said it to Moses at the burning bush. God said first,

> I AM the God of your father, the God of Abraham, the God of Isaac, and the God of Jacob.

Later He said "I AM Who I AM" and then told Moses to say to Pharaoh "I AM sent me to you." God clearly named Himself "I AM".

5.5) Love Possesses What Reason Cannot Comprehend

I will say of the LORD, 'He is my refuge and my fortress, **my God**, *in whom I trust.' Psalms 91:2 (NIV)*

See how love possesses what reason cannot comprehend. See how love empowers faith to trust and hope in an incomprehensible personality. Faith and hope empowered by love have a hold on Truth firm enough to wrestle with it. Faith is empowered by love (Gal. 5:6), and Truth is grasped by faith (2Ths. 2:13), thus the reason that

> Great truths are felt before they are expressed.[32]

Since God is love (1John 4:8) and faith of the soul is empowered by love,
> Faith is the union of God with the soul.[33]

Martin Luther expressed his beliefs in the limited reach of reason when discussing the need for the Holy Spirit of Truth to counsel the believer for understanding,

> For this is a doctrine that makes our wisdom foolishness and blinds our own reason, before it can be believed and understood; for it is not born of man's wisdom, like other sciences and arts on earth, which have sprung from reason and can be grasped by means of reason. Hence it is impossible to attain to it by reason, and if you undertake to measure and reckon how far it agrees with reason, you will not succeed.[34]

Later Luther said,

> Reason may do other things; for instance, know how to judge in worldly and human matters and affairs, how to build cities and houses, how to govern well, and the like. In such matters one may easily be able to judge and decide more wisely than another. Of this, however, we do not speak here, but of judgment in the significance of what is right or wrong before God. Here the Holy Spirit concludes; thus, every judgment of reason is false and worth nothing.[35]

Einstein's quote that Science without religion is lame, religion without science is blind.[36] might well be rephrased as

Reason without Faith is lame, Faith without Reason is blind.

In Christendom, our creeds are our axioms and our doctrines are our theories. The following quote, found in a *Handbook of Physics*, applies to sets of axioms and theories. Given the substitution of *creeds* and *doctrines* into the following quote for *set of axioms* and *theories* respectively, the analogy of mathematics and language becomes apparent.

> Several properties of **sets of axioms** are of greatest importance in assaying their value of the **theories** they engender. They are *independence, consistency, completeness,* and *decidability*. A **set of axioms** is called *independent* if none of them can be derived from the others; if a set is not independent, then some of the axioms can be omitted without diminishing the usefulness of the theory. ... A **set of axioms** or the **theory** based on it is called *consistent* if no two contradictory expressions (that is, P and ¬P) are in the set T. ...A **set of axioms**, or the **theory** based on it, is called *complete* if every meaningful expression P can (in principle) be either proved or disproved. ... , and indeed, most theories of mathematics and science are *incomplete*. ... Finally, a **theory** is called *decidable* if there is a general procedure for deciding whether or not a given meaningful expression can be proved or not.[37] (emphasis mine)

The *propositional calculus* deals with propositions (statements) as a whole, without regard to the concepts occurring in them. *Predicate calculus* deals with the later. Predicate calculus includes the variables of propositional calculus (statements) as well as two other kinds: *object variables* and *predicate variables*-sometimes called *functional variables of the object variables*. *Propositional calculus*, and its equivalent, *Boolean algebra*, has been shown to be consistent, complete, and decidable. However, the predicate calculus is consistent but is neither complete nor decidable.

Theology must deal with the concepts occurring within logical statements. Thus, it is involved with a method that is neither complete nor decidable. Axioms, or faith by a different name, are required for such a theory. Axioms must provide the independence from the other truths that cannot reason into a new dimension of thought. This is the importance of divine revelation of a new righteousness and truth.

Dietrich Bonhoeffer wrote again from his Nazi prison cell on a new language,

> "It is not for us to prophesy the day, but the day will come when men will be called again to utter the word of God with such power as will change and renew the world. It will be a new language, which will horrify men, and yet overwhelm them by its power. It will be the language of a new righteousness and truth, a language which proclaims the peace of God with men and the advent of his kingdom".[38]

I believe that a single complex language that includes the analogous "reals" (logic, reason and justice) and the "imaginaries" (Faith, Hope, Love, Life, Beauty, and Power) would serve the purpose of *grasping* truth. The *grasping*, however, will have to be accomplished by both *comprehension* and *apprehension*. Further, I believe the apprehension will be provided by analogies and parables in the manner used by our Lord to convey profound Truth covertly. Analogy is even more compelling when you consider Jesus the analogy or parable of the Father. Jungle wrote, "There can be no responsible talk about God without analogy." [39]

I believe by faith that a pure language will be given us that we can worship (e.g., sing) in. Certain divinely inspired axioms will most probably be employed to avoid the problem of incompleteness that Gödel pointed out. I believe it difficult to sing in theorems. It is not hard to imagine singing axioms (e.g., "God is good!"). I don't know of any theoretical reason why this pure language would be unique. The practical reason why it would probably be unique is the difficulty of creating any such language. It may well take an act of God to produce the first pure language this side of Babel. Who then could transform that pure language into another?

[1] Martin Luther, Complete Sermons of Martin Luther, Vol. 2.2, *Twelfth Sunday after Trinity*, Baker Books, Grand Rapids, MI, 2000, p385

[2] Dietrich Bonhoeffer, *Prisoner for God, Letters and Papers from Prison*, Edited by Eberhard Bethge, The Macmillan Co., New York, 1954, p.41

[3]   Henle, Jim, 1996, 'Classical Mathematics'. The American Mathematical Monthly. 103 (1): 18-29.

[4]   Bloch, Ernst, 1985, *Essays on the Philosophy of Music*. Cambridge / New York / Melbourne, Cambridge University Press.

[5]   Motluk, Alison, 1997, 'Can Mozart make maths add up?', *New Scientist.* 153 (2073): 17.

[6]   "What Life Means to Einstein: An Interview by George Sylvester Viereck," for the October 26, 1929 issue of The Saturday Evening Post. [7]   Albert Einstein, Quoted in H R Pagels, The Cosmic Code

[8]   William Rowan Hamilton, Edited by David R. Wilkins, *Theory of Congugate Functions, or Algebraic Couples; With a Preliminary and Elementary Essay on Algebra as The Science of Pure Time,* (Transactions of the Royal Irish Academy, vol. 17, part 1 (1837), pp. 293–422.) 2000

[9]   Vaneechoutte, M. and Skoyles, J.R., 1998; The memetic origin of language: modern humans as musical primates. Journal of Memetics - Evolutionary Models of Information Transmission, 2.

[10] Ibid.

[11] Marjorie Barrows, One Thousand Beautiful Things, Spencer Press, New York, 1947, p107

[12] Ibid., p.106

[13] Ibid., p.106

[14] Featured quotation on the Spatial Intelligence (SI) webpage.

[15] Quoted in H Eves Mathematical Circles Adieu (Boston 1977).

[16] Albert Einstein Quotes, http://www.sfheart.com/einstein.html

[17] Dorothy L. Sayers, *The Mind of the Maker*, HarperCollins Publishers, NY, 1987, p.p.21,22

[18] Blaise Pascal, *PENSƒES*, 1660, translated by W. F. Trotter, #2-4

[19] Paul Tillich, *The Shaking of the Foundations*, Charles Scribner's Sons, NY,1953, p.p.56-57

[20] Martin Luther, Complete Sermons of Martin Luther, Vol. 3.2, *Fourth Sunday In Advent*, p110, Baker Books, Grand Rapids, MI, 2000

[21] Confucius (Kung Fu-tzu), *Analects*, 500 BC

[22] Alfred Tarski, *The Semantic Conception Of Truth And The Foundations Of Semantics, Philosophy and Phenomenological Research* 4 (1944)

[23] Ibid. Section 7

[24] Ibid. Section 8

[25] Ibid. Section 10

[26] Ibid. Section 10

[27] Ibid. Section 11

[28] Kurt Gödel, *Encyclopedic Dictionary of Mathematics* (MIT Press, 1987)

[29] Jennifer Bothamley, *Dictionary of Theories*, Gale Research International Ltd, London, 1993, *Gödel – Rosser Theorem*, p.232

[30] Alfred Tarski, *The Semantic Conception Of Truth And The Foundations Of Semantics, Philosophy and Phenomenological Research* 4, Section 12 (1944)

[31] Ibid. Section 13

[32] Pierre Teilhard de Chardin, *Treasury of Religious Quotations*, ed. Gerald Tomlinson, Prentice Hall, Englewood Cliffs, N.J. 1991, p. 248

[33] Henry P. Van Dusen, *Dag Hammarskjöld*, Harper & Row, New York, 1967, p. 46

[34] Martin Luther, <u>Complete Sermons of Martin Luther</u>, Vol. 1.2, *Easter Sunday*, p293, Baker Books, Grand Rapids, MI, 2000

[35] Martin Luther, <u>Complete Sermons of Martin Luther</u>, Vol. 2.1, *Fourth Sunday After Easter*, p119, Baker Books, Grand Rapids, MI, 2000

[36] Science, Philosophy and Religion: a Symposium (1941) ch. 13

[37] E.U. Condon, Ph.D., and Hugh Odishaw, D.Sc., <u>Handbook of Physics - *Second Edition, Fundamentals*</u>, McGraw-Hill Book Company, New York, New York, 1967, p1-13

[38] Dietrich Bonhoeffer, *Prisoner for God, Letters and Papers from Prison*, Edited by Eberhard Bethge, The Macmillan Co., New York, 1954, p.p. 140,141

[39] Eberhard Jungle, *God as the Mystery of the World*, transl.: Darrell L. Guder (Grand Rapids: Eedmans, Publishing Company, 1983), p. 281

Part Three- if (b) Truth is available to men

6) Truth

"O LORD, do not Thine eyes look for truth?" – Jeremiah 5:3 (KJV)

6.1) Absolute Truth

Jesus, the king of truth is coming to us according to Mathew 21:5 and John 12:15. Later John quotes Jesus, *"You say correctly that I am a king, for this I was born, and for this I have come into the world, to bear witness to the Truth. Everyone who is of the Truth hears My voice"*- John 18:37 (NASB) In 1521, Martin Luther wrote

> Without doubt you do not come to him and bring him to you; he is too high and too far from you. With all your effort, work and labor you cannot come to him, lest you boast as though you had received him by your own merit and worthiness. No, dear friend, all merit and worthiness is out of the question, and there is nothing but demerit and unworthiness on your side, nothing but grace and mercy on his.[1]

You do not seek him, but he seeks you. As a sphere penetrates a plane and appears a circle, so the God of Abraham comes to us. The two-dimensional plane can't approach the three-dimensional sphere, but the Master of the higher dimensions can project onto the lower dimensions with ease.

6.1.1) An Occidental Invention?

We mentioned earlier that in his book *Nietzsche*[2], Martin Heidegger argued that absolute truth is a Western invention, beginning in early Hellenistic thought and moving onward until the latter nineteenth century, ending with Friedrich Nietzsche. But is Heidegger correct?

In *Analects*[3] *(500 BC)* it was said of the Chinese philosopher Confucius (Kung Fu-tzu):

> There were four things which the Master taught, -letters, ethics, devotion of soul, and truthfulness.

Confucius was hardly a Western Philosopher yet, in *Analects* he argued:

> Those who know the truth are not equal to those who love it, and those who love it are not equal to those who delight in it.

He considered Truth telling his calling,

> The Master was put in fear in K'wang. He said, after the death of King Wan, was not the cause of truth lodged here in me? If Heaven had wished to let this cause of truth perish, then

I, a future mortal! should not have got such a relation to that cause. While Heaven does not let the cause of truth perish, what can the people of K'wang do to me?

And later, the Master said,

"The object of the superior man is truth. Food is not his object. There is plowing; even in that there is sometimes want. So with learning; -emolument may be found in it. The superior man is anxious lest he should not get truth; he is not anxious lest poverty should come upon him."

In The Doctrine of Mean [4], he adds,

"Absolute truth is indestructible. Being indestructible, it is eternal."

From the Hinayana text, *Dhammapada* (*Path of Virtue*), traditionally ascribed to the Buddha, we have

"A man does not become a Brahman by his plaited hair, by his family, or by birth; in whom there is truth and righteousness, he is blessed, he is a Brahman."[5]

C.S. Lewis writes in *The Abolition of Man*,

"In early Hinduism that conduct in men which can be called good consists in conformity to, or almost participation in, the *Rta*—that great ritual or pattern of nature and supernature which is revealed alike in the cosmic order, the moral virtues, and the ceremonial of the temple. Righteousness, correctness, order, the *Rta*, is constantly identified with *satya*, or truth, corresponding to reality. As Plato said that the Good was 'beyond existence' and Wordsworth that through virtue the stars were strong, so the Indian masters say the gods themselves are born of the *Rta* and obey it. The Chinese also speak of a great thing (the greatest thing) called the *Tao*. It is the reality beyond all predicates, the abyss that was before the Creator Himself. It is Nature, it is the Way, the Road. It is the Way in which the universe goes on, the Way in which things everlastingly emerge, stilly and tranquilly, into space and time. It is also the Way which every man should tread in imitation of that cosmic and supercosmic progression, confirming all activities to the great exemplar. 'In ritual,' says the Analects, 'it is harmony with Nature that is prized.' The ancient Jews likewise praise the Law as being 'true.'...

But what is common to them all is something we cannot neglect. It is the doctrine of objective value, the belief that certain attitudes are really true, and others really false, to the kind of thing the universe is and the kind of things we are...."[6]

So, the belief in Absolute Truth is not a regional concept, but a globally pervasive one. *Further, it is not reasonable until it is revealed. It comes to us.* We do not create or deduce it if has a purely new part. *Like another dimension, a new truth is not a manipulation of previous truths.*

Reason applies to looking at existing truth in alternate ways or rotations. *Revelation applies to a new dimension that is unreasonable from the already known dimensions. Revelation provides independent axioms.*

6.1.2 Truth vs. False Prophets

Jesus said,
> *Beware of the false prophets.*

And twice He said,
> *You will know them by their fruits.*

Christ knew fully that all men sin and are dwarfed by the glory of God. But more than that, not everyone "hears My voice," as He said, because not everyone is "of the Truth." When they speak, they become false prophets. I am not referring to the usual private sins of private men, rather, we are referring to those men who address the truth and either publicly affirm or deny it. It relates to those who publicly support or oppose the work of the Spirit of Truth, the Third Person of the Trinity. So, we take the time to judge a few public men by their fruits.

Thomas Jefferson said, "Truth is the first chapter in the book of wisdom." [8] Jefferson (although he had numerous faults, the love of the lie was not one of them.) was the man who penned the draft of the Declaration of Independence, using '*neither book nor pamphlet,*'[9] as he said later. In the preamble he wrote,

> "We hold these Truths to be self-evident, that all men are created equal, that they are endowed by their creator with certain unalienable Rights, that among these are Life, Liberty, and the Pursuit of Happiness."[10]

These are sweet fruits!

Immanuel Kant was the most influential philosopher of modern times. The German philosopher Georg Wilhelm Friedrich Hegel built upon Kantian philosophy and formed the structure that Marx built upon. Dialectical method was an outgrowth of the method of reasoning by antimonies that Kant used. Johann Gottlib Fichte, who we mentioned earlier, was a student of Kant and developed a philosophy that greatly influenced 19th century socialists. Thus, if you liked the Soviet Union, the Berlin wall, and the socialist influence, Kant is your man, however if you have distaste for loss of individual freedom and coerced conformity, then Kant is a false prophet, considering his fruits. You think I'm unkind to such a great mind? Balderdash! I have taken God's advice in the method of judging— judging by their fruits. The Lord doesn't judge by the intellect, but by the heart, and the heart is the source of good and evil fruit.

Moving ahead in time to our Nazi friend, Friederich Nietzsche, who so many are willing to overlook his lapse in judgement, claimed, "There are no eternal facts, as there are no absolute truths." [11] Does no one get the connection that absolute truth inhibits atrocities? Nietzsche's fruit was a Bavarian corporal with no firm concept of right and wrong. That corporal was the consummate student of these enemies of virtue, and Adolf Hitler said, "There is no such thing as truth either in the moral or the scientific sense."[12] Such poison fruits are these!

Lastly, Winston Churchill said, "The truth is incontrovertible. Malice may attack it. Ignorance may deride it, but in the end, there it is."[13] He above all men of the time was responsible for the destruction of the Nazis. Surely there is wisdom to learn here.

Heidegger's belief in the demise of Absolute Truth with Nietzsche is as equally well unfounded as his beliefs in its origins. It ranks with his support of Adolph Hitler and the National Socialists from 1933 through 1945. Heidegger was certainly no Dietrich Bonhoeffer.

Bonhoeffer was a prominent Protestant theologian who left the safety of the United States to return home to Germany when World War II began. Even though he had been a pacifist, he reluctantly participated in a failed plot to assassinate Hitler. He justified it by believing *it is worse to be evil than to do evil*. In an essay written while in a National Socialists' prison Bonhoeffer writes,

> "Who stands his ground? Only the man whose ultimate criterion is not in his reason, his principles, his conscience, his freedom or his virtue, but who is ready to sacrifice all these things when he is called to obedient and responsible action in faith and exclusive allegiance to God. The responsible man seeks to make his whole life a response to the question and call of God".[7]

Bonhoeffer was hanged April 9, 1945, one month before the May 8th surrender of Germany. This man was truly a Christian, although he was like all other sons of men and sinned along the way. Have you ever noticed how the accuser of the brethren always has a sin or two to stain the records of the most exemplary persons? Of course, they are just men or women and we expect faults, but there is a kind of glee some get in exposing the errors of great people.

Multitudes, multitudes in the valley of decision! For the day of the Lord is near in the valley of decision. – Joel 3:14

Writing against slavery in his full poem, James Russell Lowell advises deciding for Truth and then finding and defending Truth in new ways.

The Witness and Spirit of Truth

Extracts from
The Present Crisis [14]
James Russell Lowell (1819 – 1891)

Once to every man and nation comes the moment to decide;
In the strife of Truth and Falsehood, for the good or evil side;
  Some great cause, God's new Messiah, offering each the bloom or blight,
Parts the goats upon the left hand and the sheep upon the right,
And the choice goes on forever 'twixt that darkness and that light.

Hast thou chosen, O my people, on whose party thou shall stand, Ere the
  Doom from its worn sandals shakes the dust against our land?
Though the cause of Evil prosper, yet 'tis Truth alone is strong, And, albeit
  she wanders outcast now, I see around her throng
Troops of beautiful, tall angels, to enshield her from all wrong.

Careless seems the great Avenger; history's pages but record
One death-grapple in the darkness 'twixt old systems and the Word;
  Truth forever on the scaffold, Wrong forever on the throne, -- Yet that
  scaffold sways the future, and behind the dim unknown, Standeth God
    within the shadow, keeping watch above his own.

We see dimly in the Present what is small and what is great,
Slow of faith how weak an arm may turn the iron helm of fate, But the
  soul is still oracular; amid the market's din,
List the ominous stern whisper from the Delphic cave within,--
  "They enslave their children's children who make compromise with sin."

Then to side with Truth is noble when we share her wretched crust,
Ere her cause bring fame and profit, and 'tis prosperous to be just;
Then it is the brave man chooses, while the coward stands aside,
  Doubting in his abject spirit, till his Lord is crucified,
  And the multitude make virtue of the faith they had denied.

New occasions teach new duties; Time makes ancient good uncouth;
They must upward still, and onward, who would keep abreast of Truth;
  Lo, before us gleam her camp-fires! We ourselves must Pilgrims be,
Launch our Mayflower, and steer boldly through the desperate winter sea, Nor
  attempt the Future's portal with the Past's blood-rusted key.

[1]   Martin Luther, <u>Complete Sermons of Martin Luther</u>, Vol. 1, *First Sunday in Advent*, p25, Baker Books, Grand Rapids, MI, 2000

[2]   Martin Heidegger, Nietzsche, transl., David Farrell Krell (SanFrancisco: HarpeSanFrancisco, 1991)

[3]   Confucius (Kung Fu-tzu), *Analects, 500 BC*

[4]   Confucius (Kung Fu-tzu), *The Doctrine of Mean, 500 BC*

[5]   Buddha, *Dhammapada (The Path of Virtue)*, Edited by William J. Bennett, The Book of Virtues, Simon & Schuster, N.Y.,1993, p.811

[6]   C.S. Lewis, *The Abolition of Man*, Edited by William J. Bennett, The Book of Virtues, Simon & Schuster, N.Y.,1993, p.264

[7]   Dietrich Bonhoeffer, *Prisoner for God, Letters and Papers from Prison*, Edited by Eberhard Bethge, The Macmillan Co., New York, 1954, p.p.15, 16

[8]   Mark Water, *The New Encyclopedia Of Christian Quotations*, Baker Books, Grand Rapids, MI, 2000, p. 1078

[9]   Thomas Jefferson, *Funk & Wagnalls New Encyclopedia*, 7, CONTR-DICOT, Funk & Wagnalls, Inc., New York, *Declaration of Independence*, p.356 [10] Ibid.

[11] Mark Water, *The New Encyclopedia Of Christian Quotations*, Baker Books, Grand Rapids, MI, 2000, p. 1079

[12] Ibid, p1077

[13] Ibid., p.1076

[14] James Russell Lowell, <u>One Hundred and One famous Poems</u>, R.J. Cook Publisher, Chicago, *The Present Crisis,* 1924, p.33

6.2) Partitioned Truth

Some divide Absolute Truth into parts. The first step so taken is usually to divide it into two parts. The first part is alive, personal, and divine, physically embodied in the Person of Jesus Christ that is the Spirit of Truth, the Holy Spirit, and the Third Person of the Trinity. The second part of Absolute Truth so divided is considered inanimate, abstract, an encyclopedic collection of timeless, immutable principles existing in the Realm of the Forms.

Webster divides Truth many ways. One grouping is personal. Truth so defined is a fidelity, constancy, or sincerity in action, character and utterance. Another group is the body of real things, events and facts, describing actuality. A third idea is that of a fundamental or spiritual reality. The last idea is that truth is fidelity to an original or to a standard. My contribution is that

> *Truth is the awareness of that which exists, and as such, is a standard of existence reigning over statements, rules and premises.*

I hold that this partitioning of Truth does not consider with reverence the breadth and depth and unity of the Holy Spirit. The partitioning is of ourselves, as Sir Francis Bacon said, there are three parts in truth: first, "the inquiry", which is the wooing of it; secondly, "the knowledge" of it, which is the presence of it; and, thirdly, the "belief of truth, which is the enjoying of it."[1] In Bishop George Berkeley's (1685-1753) theory of *Subjective Idealism*[2], he differentiates active minds or spirits (includes God and our spirits), from passive ideas, which are their contents. To be is to perceive as a spirit, or to be perceived as an idea. To 'perceive' means to 'have as content', and to 'be perceived' means to 'be had as content'. The Holy Spirit contains all truth and is the third Person of the Trinity. How can the Trinity be more subdivided than three?

6.3) Quotation Orchestration

The Spirit of Truth contains all truth and it is all somehow related. C.S. Lewis stated,

> We believe that the truth is more than a system; but we also believe that the truth is one, even as God is one. And we believe, therefore, that the truth is systemic, and that the different truths are related.[3]

If it is all somehow related, it must be impossible to partition into disjoint sets. Confucius, who believed the object of the superior man is truth said, "Shan, my doctrine is that of an all-pervading unity."[4] We are dealing with one of the three indivisible facets of God, when we deal in truth. Augustine of Hippo said, "Where I found truth, there I also found my God, who is the truth itself."[5] In a similar vein, Miguel de Cervantes said, "Where Truth is, there is God."[6] And didn't Jesus answer the man who wanted to quiet His followers in such a way as to dispel the notion that truth was absolutely disjoint between the living and the material? "*I tell you that if these should keep silent, the stones would immediately cry out.*"-Luke 19:40

What could be colder and more lifeless than a decaying body laid three or four days in a Middle Eastern tomb? Nevertheless, Lazarus was quickened by the Spirit's mighty power, as was Jesus but a short time later. Rocks, or dead bodies, what is the logical difference when considering the possibility of them speaking, or even becoming alive? It is the truly Awesome power of the Spirit of Truth, the Holy Spirit, the Comforting Counseling Spirit of God, that defines who, or what speaks or lives. Although *Dualism* requires God to be distinct from His creation, it does not require His Truth of His creation to be partitioned or segregated from His truth of Himself; for it is the Spirit of Truth that contains them both.

But we must be careful in describing what truth is or isn't. Niels Bohr stated the difference between logic and truth in the following way: "The opposite of a correct statement is a false statement. But the opposite of a profound truth may well be another profound truth." [7] Statements are compound functions of premises and certain rules of inference. Truth is a standard of existence reigning over statements, rules and premises. Truth is more than a Monarch; it is a helper to the knowledge of the Divine. John Owen thought that, "It is truth alone that capacitates any soul to glorify God," [8] while Jesus said to his disciples,

> "And I will ask the Father, and He will give you another Helper, that He may be with you forever; that is the Spirit of Truth, whom the world cannot receive, because it does not behold Him or know Him, but you know Him because He abides with you, and will be *in* you." - John 14:16.

Dietrich Bonhoeffer, on June 8,[th] 1944, wrote his Nazi prison cell conclusion that the Word was the Truth itself,

> "The New Testament is not a mythological garbing of the universal truth; this mythology (resurrection and so on) is the thing itself—but the concepts must be interpreted in such a way as not to make religion a pre-condition of faith (cf. circumcision in St. Paul). Not until that is achieved will, in my opinion, liberal theology be overcome....The world's coming of age is then no longer an occasion for polemics and apologetics, but it is really better understood than it understands itself, namely on the basis of the Gospel, and in the light of Christ."[9]

So, in summary, spirits woo Truth, know Truth and then enjoy Truth. All Truth is divine; it is one, even as God is one. Truth is a standard of existence reigning over statements, rules and premises. Truth, or all truthful Ideas are "had as content" by the Spirit of Truth; and they are all related and may be animated by the Spirit. This Spirit of Truth abides *in* Christ's disciples. As Blaise Pascal stated, "The history of the church ought properly to be called the history of Truth."[10] Truth is found in the East and the West, and "All truth, wherever it is found, belongs to us Christians,"[11] according to Justin Martyr; this allows us to quote Hans Kung's supporting statement, "A church which abandons the truth abandons itself."[12]

[1] Sir Francis Bacon, *Of Truth*, Chapter 1.

[2] Jennifer Bothamley, *Dictionary of Theories*, Gale Research International Ltd, London, 1993, *subjective idealism*, p509

[3] Mark Water, *The New Encyclopedia Of Christian Quotations*, Baker Books, Grand Rapids, MI, 2000, p. 1078

[4]   Confucius (Kung Fu-tzu), *Analects, 500 BC*

[5]   Mark Water, *The New Encyclopedia Of Christian Quotations*, Baker Books, Grand Rapids, MI, 2000, p. 1075

[6]   Ibid., p. 1076

[7]   Ibid., p. 1076

[8]   Ibid., p. 1079

[9]   Dietrich Bonhoeffer, *Prisoner for God, Letters and Papers from Prison*, Edited by Eberhard Bethge, The Macmillan Co., New York, 1954, p.149

[10] Mark Water, *The New Encyclopedia Of Christian Quotations*, Baker Books, Grand Rapids, MI, 2000, p. 1079

[11] Mark Water, *The New Encyclopedia Of Christian Quotations*, Baker Books, Grand Rapids, MI, 2000, p. 1078

[12] Ibid., p. 1078

6.4) The Abiding Truth and an Analogy of Synchronization

The person who has access to the Spirit of Truth has "as needed" access to the encyclopedic collection of truths and is understood to receive revelation from God, but not to possess God's Eye. God remains sovereign and reveals what He pleases when He pleases for His purposes. Jesus said to his disciples,

"But when they arrest you, do not worry about what to say or how to say it. *At that time* you will be given what to say, for it will not be you speaking, but the Spirit of your Father speaking through you." - Mt 10:19,20.

And again, in Lk 21:14,15
"But make your mind not to worry beforehand how you will defend yourselves. For *I will give you words* and wisdom that none of your adversaries will be able to resist or contradict."

"There is no "dark side" [1] of Absolute truth here, only the light of truth from the Father of Lights. When His child needs His Words, then will they be given, but not before. If there is a *hidden agenda* here, it is God's. And if the notion of absolute truth is more correctly understood as a code word for power and control, as Michel Foucault's hermeneutics of suspicion [2] suggest, then it is God's power and control that is involved. The only "dark side of truth" is the "truth" defined and enforced by worldly power and authority, rather than the Word of God.

The Mutually Synchronized Society

I think it takes a great mind to create an elegant parable. I'm hoping Einstein is correct when he says, "If you are out to describe the truth, leave elegance to the tailor."[3] I wanted to be wise enough to create a parable about Absolute Truth, but the best I can do is to create an analogy from science and engineering.

In many forms of information transmission, the sending and receiving units must be synchronized to a common frequency source. It is very common that a standard frequency source, created from an atomic standard, is distributed across the territories in a pattern that is hierarchical and appears like the roots of a tree - starting at the trunk and descending by forking until the very last fiber on the end. Such a synchronization plan is called "Master – Slave" for apparent reasons. A less common method of synchronization has been studied but has not been so commonly employed because of the difficulty in keeping the system stable. That system is called "Mutual Synchronization."[4]

Usually a discussion of "Mutual Synchronization" begins with the "wind–up" clock phenomenon that occurs when such clocks are placed close together on a glass shelf. If one clock had the tendency to run fast, and the other slow, the effect of placing them in close proximity on a rigid shelf is to cause them both to run at the same speed that is an average of the two. I would like to use the word "oscillator" interchangeably with "clock" because they both apply here. Define, "frequency" as the rate at which the clock hands spin. Now, instead of just two mechanical clocks coupled mechanically through a rigid shelf, consider a group of electrical clocks, or oscillators, that are coupled optically. (For clarity, suppose that each clock sends out a laser light pulse whenever the second hand passes 12 on the dial accomplishes this.) Imagine, if you can, that each oscillator accepts and averages the frequencies of its neighbors. Then, it delivers to its neighbors (not necessarily the same as those it listened to) its own frequency that is the average of those inputs it had received from some of its neighbors.

The clocks, or oscillators, in this resulting mutually synchronized system will soon all run at the same speed, or frequency. The problem with such a system is sometimes referred to as "drinking your own bathwater!" This is an unstable system given propagation delay variations between clocks, or perturbations or noise in the environment. Suppose that one clock momentarily ran fast or signaled too soon a laser pulse. The other clocks listening to this jerky clock will average it in with the other clock inputs that were unperturbed. The result will be a modest increase in the system frequency. Unfortunately, the clock that "started it" will see the neighbors frequency rise, and will then average them and produce a matching steady elevated frequency to deliver to its neighbors again. Such a system will soon drift to the dynamic limits of the clocks, and something will "break." When the system is "run into the rails" like this, the synchronization of the system becomes chaotic until it possibly regains lock, only to lose it again and again.

The very peculiar aspect about a system like this is that just one "Stand – Alone" oscillator can stabilize it. A stand-alone oscillator is one that provides its synchronizing pulse independently of any other oscillator but itself. Thus, provided that the stand-alone oscillator is coupled sufficiently into the system, it can stabilize the system entirety. A prophet who says, "Thus says the LORD", or a book of

Truth has the same effect on a society of men if the coupling is tight enough. Jesus, The Living Word, is the stand-alone oscillator. The number and influence of the Elect, however, determine the coupling.

Fascinating concept is this acceptance of a synchronizing Truth, a laser-like light from The Stand – Alone Oscillator. Referring to he who has not accepted the Son of God, Jesus says,

> "…has been judged already, because he has not believed in the name of the only begotten Son of God. *And this is the judgment,* that the light is come into the world, and men loved the darkness rather than the light; for their deeds were evil. For everyone who does evil hates the light, and does not come to the light, lest his deeds should be exposed. *But he who practices the Truth comes to the light*, that his deeds may be manifested as having been wrought in God." - John 3:18;21

Modernism, Higher Criticism, postmodernism, or any other philosophically based theology can be unstable just as the analogy above. Jacques Derrida argued truth was unstable because of language. In opposition to Derrida, George A. Lindbeck argued well that the thoughts of man were unstable when synchronized to mens' words but were stabilized when grounded in the Word. It is the laser light of the Word Incarnate that keeps premodern Christianity stable—if grounded and synchronized in the Word of God.

[1] Robert C. Greer, *Mapping Postmodernism*, InterVarsity Press, Downers Grove, Illinois, 2003, *The Dark Side of Absolute Truth*, p. 25

[2] *Power/Knowledge: Selected Interviews and other Writings 1972-77,* 'Truth and Power" interview by Allessandro Fontana and Pasquale Pasquino, trans. Colin Green, ed. Colin Gordin, New York: Pantheon, 1972, pp. 131-133

[3] Albert Einstein "On Education," Address to the State University of New York at Albany, in Ideas and Opinions

[4] David R. Smith, *Digital Transmission Systems, Second Edition,* Chapman & Hall, New York, 1993, p.p. 683, 686

Other Mutual Synchronization References

- M.B. Brilliant, "The Determination of Frequency in Systems of Mutually Synchronized Oscillators," *Bell System Technical Journal* 45(December 1966): 1737-1748

- Gersho and B.J. Karafin, "Mutual Synchronization of Geographically Separared Oscillators," *Bell System Technical Journal* 45(December 1966): 1689-1704

- M.B. Brilliant, "Dnamic Response of Systems of Mutually Synchronized Oscillators," *Bell System Technical Journal* 46(February 1967): 319-356
- M.W. Williard, "Analysis of a System of Mutually synchronized Oscillators," *IEEE Trans. On Comm.*, vol. COM-18, no. 5, October 1970,p.p. 467-4

Part Four - then (c) the postmodern understanding of language theory fails in the real world, giving rise to many spurious belief-systems that are not only antibiblical but also anti-humanitarian.

> *And then that lawless one will be revealed …; that is, the one whose coming is in accord with the activity of Satan, … because they did not receive the love of the truth so as to be saved.* — 2 Thessalonians 2:8,10

7) The Polluted Streams We Swim In

Friedrich Nietzsche and Martin Heidegger (two prominent proto-postmodernists), demonstrate that a consistent application of their understandings of language and truth have given needed philosophical energy to the system of Nazism in the mid-twentieth century that has been a scourge to the world. Martin Heidegger lent his support to Adolph Hitler and the National Socialists from 1933 through 1945. **Adolf Hitler** lent his support to Martin Heidegger and said, "There is no such thing as truth either in the moral or the scientific sense."[1]

7.1) Heidegger's Dossier

Martin Heidegger was a student of, and an assistant to, Edmund Husserl. He later succeeded Husserl as professor of philosophy at Freiburg. His advancement in the academic world began was as a phenomenologist under the mentoring of Husserl. As such, he was engrossed in the study of the development of human consciousness and self-awareness in abstraction from any claims concerning existence as a foundational preamble or facet of philosophy. Thus, his beginnings were counter to Descartes' whose beginnings were expressed in his Cogito where existence was demonstrated by awareness. Heidegger was fond of citing Hölderlin's maxim, 'As you began, so you shall remain.'

Professor Richard Wolin in his book *Heidegger's Children,* as well as other researchers, believe that Heidegger was dedicated to the National Socialist Party (Nazi) regardless of how Hitler ruled Germany. He had his classes give the Nazi salute; he wore his Nazi pin, and paid his Nazi party dues until 1945[2]. Wolin accused Derrida of dodging an important question. By accepting the famous German's philosophy, had Jacques Derrida and other radical postmodern leftists absorbed the core of Heidegger's doubtful politics as well?

Heidegger desired a state ruled by an elite group of soldier-philosophers. He distrusted public opinions, modernity, and democratic institutions. The Nazis matched his view of a new powerful central government. He was soon to become the Nazi rector of the University of Freidburg in 1933. As such he delivered a, fortunately for him, little known inaugural address. It is said that Heidegger referred to the "inner truth and greatness" of the Nazi's many years after the allied destruction of Germany. To respect this man is to contradict the idea that all men are responsible for their actions, regardless of outside influence.

7.2) Heidegger's Spawn

Curiously, before 1933, he served as a mentor to four gifted students of mixed German Jewish backgrounds.

- *Hannah Arendt.* Hannah had a three-year love affair with Heidegger. She later became famous as a political thinker. Her major ideas included the thought that only through "the activity of thinking" could humanity abstain from evil. She believed that evil was banality. That is, she conceived that evil was that which was trite, obvious, predictable, and commonplace. Dag Hammarskjold is quoted as saying "The truth is so simple that it is regarded as pretentious banality." With such a philosophy as Arendt's, what could she think of the truth or the common man? By Hammarskjold's perspective and Arendt's philosophy, they are both evil.

- *Herbert Marcuse.* Became a philosophical spiritual leader for the New Left. Was denounced by the Pope in the late 1960s. Maintained throughout his life that Heidegger was the greatest teacher and thinker he ever met. In his writings, Marcuse outlined a liberal society that involved lustful and relational labor, play, free and open sexuality, and a general prescription for the 1960s counterculture. He continued to his death to promote and defend Marxian theory and libertarian socialism.

- *Hans Jonas* became a groundbreaking philosopher of environmentalism and became a standard for the German Green Party. He feared technology, believing "It is a power over matter, over life on earth, and over man himself; and it keeps growing at an accelerated pace."

He blamed it for "freedom without values." It is interesting that Jonas considers technology a *thing,* rather than the accumulated knowledge and know-how of men. Would he have railed against knowledge? Would he have burned the books? Jonas is reminiscent of the liberal arts student who avoids the tough math and science courses, but then fears or despises those technical nerds who make his computer work. Jonas is the antithesis of Socrates who respected the artisans because they prove they have truthful knowledge with every successful construction.

What Socrates admired, Jonas feared, because technologists demonstrate Truth in action. Although he seems to have believed our cultural crisis to be rooted in nihilism because we are in want of any consistent "image of humanity," he fails to see the image of God as the image of humanity. He ends his philosophy by believing the protection of the world of tomorrow as the highest virtue. This man spent a lifetime discovering his God-given instinct of preservation of the species.

- *Karl Lowith* became known as a scholar of historical consciousness. For Lowith, the centerpiece of Nietzsche's philosophy was his doctrine of eternal recurrence. He carefully examined Nietzsche's cosmological theory of the infinite repetition of a finite number of states of the world. He wondered how it's possible to will the eternal recurrence of each moment of one's life, if both this decision and the states of the world determined by it appear to be predestined? How a good mind could buy into such a theory is a great mystery. Why he would waste more time developing it is bizarre.

These men and women who swam in the polluted streams of pre-Nazi postmodern thought were all in worship of the will and the intellect. So much so, that they believed that they willed both time and God into existence. Even so, they thought themselves not responsible because they were just part of finite state machine repeating endlessly throughout time. Heaven help us!

7.3) Heidegger's Grand-fathered Legacy

They propagated their beliefs into the present
- That the commonplace is evil.
- That we create existence.
- That God is our finest thought.
- That the will and the intellect is the measure of man,
- That we should abandon our sexual and ethical mores and chill.
- That this is all part of a recurring cycle of a finite state machine.
- That man is not safe knowing facts, science and procedures, and must be saved from himself.
- That we are to believe that knowledge and know how is responsible for freedom without values.

The formal advent of postmodernism into western culture followed Nietzsche by a century, or by roughly 1980. The main voices in the postmodern worldview include Ludwig Wittgenstein, Michel Foucault, Richard Rorty and Jacques Dirrida. They attempt to undo the works of Plato, Judaism, Christianity, and then move beyond the Cogito. These attempts are aimed at annihilating truth and what has been associated with the concepts of *honor* or *righteousness* or *propriety*. If we buy into it, the West will degenerated 2300 years into the philosophy of Pyrrho of Elis[3] (365-275 BC) who advocated the complete suspension of judgment with the hope of attaining tranquility thereby – postmodernism and pyrrhonism, twin daughters of the same deceiver. This is all anti-Christ, and is a dagger aimed at the heart of humanity. I agree with Spurgeon,

Theology hath nothing new in it except that which is false.[4]

Jesus Christ is the same yesterday and today and forever. - Hebrews 13:8 (NASB)

I admire Richard Wolin choice of quotes to make a point. The following quote is found in his Book, *Heidegger's Children*, just before the table of contents. Heinrich Heine wrote it in 1834, roughly 100 years before the rise of the Nazi plague. Heine is considered second only to Johann Wolfgang von Goethe as a German lyric poet, and his prose was considered the best written in German in his time. It establishes another link between poetry and prophesy; King David is probably the best such example. It also demonstrates that the ultimate effects of wrong thinking can be predicted well in advance of their occurrence, but the world ignores the signs and rushes off pell-mell to Hell.

> *"Do not become anxious, you German republicans; the German revolution will not take place any more pleasantly and gently for having been preceded by the Kantian critique, Fichtean transcendental idealism, or even natural philosophy. Through these theories revolutionary forces have built up which only await the day on which they may break loose, filling the world with horror and awe. Kantians will appear who want nothing to do with mercy even in the phenomenal world; they will plough up without pity the very soil of our European life with sword and axe, in order to eradicate every last root of the past.... Armed Fichteans will arise, whose fanaticism of will can be restrained neither through fear nor through self-interest.... More terrible than all will be the natural philosophers, who will participate actively in any German revolution, identifying themselves with the very work of destruction. If the hand of the Kantian strikes swift and sure because his heart is not moved by any traditional reverence; if the Fichtean courageously defies all danger because for him it does not exist at all in reality; so the natural philosopher will be terrible, for he has allied himself to the primal forces of nature. He can conjure up the demonic powers of ancient German pantheism and that lust for battle that we find among the ancient Germans will flame within him."*

-Heinrich Heine, *History of Philosophy and Religion in Germany* (1834)

In our section on the Ecumenical Imperative, we find a surprising connection with Heidegger's worldview. Quoting Richard Wolin, in *Heidegger's Children*,

> Much has been made of Heidegger's Catholicism – his strict Catholic upbringing in Messkirch (his father was the sexton at the local church), his failed attempt to become a Jesuit circa 1915 (after three weeks of study, Heidegger was dismissed for reasons of health), and, finally, his painful break with the 'religion of [his] youth' in 1917. Until recently, however, few have known how profoundly the twenty-year-old Heidegger was involved in the land-marked debates over 'modernism' (der Modernismusstreit) that rocked turn-of-the-century Germany. Heidegger was fond of citing Hölderlin's maxim,

'As you began, so you shall remain.' Unsurprisingly, insight into his profound youthful attachment to Catholicism goes far toward explaining his worldview.

1917 was the year he married the Protestant-in-name soon-to-be Nazi and anti-Semite, Elfride Petrie. Wolin continues,

> The extent to which Heidegger's youthful outlook was permeated by such unyielding Catholic perspectives becomes clear if one peruses the eight articles he wrote for the conservative Catholic journal, *Der Akademiker*, during the years 1910-12. As his biographer Hugo Ott, who unearthed these early articles, observes:

> What *the Der Akademiker* contributions display is their embeddedness in a closed system of the Catholic worldview from an integral, anti-modern perspective. Martin Heidegger carries the banner of ultraconservative Catholicism with intense seriousness and great enthusiasm in the fields of theology, philosophy, and ethics.

Once again, Heidegger's highly selective approach to autobiographical themes enters the picture, insofar as he inexplicably omitted his *Der Akademiker* essays from the collected works edition of his writing. *Der Akademiker* was founded in the spirit of Pope X's so-called 'antimodernism' encyclical of 1907. In fact, the journal's first issue contained a Preface by Pius X offering words of encouragement to his German followers in their struggle against modernist mores and values.[5]

7.4) The Devil's Triangle

There are three effective methods used by the Father of Lies to work against Truth in the theology of postmodernism. They create The Devil's Triangle:

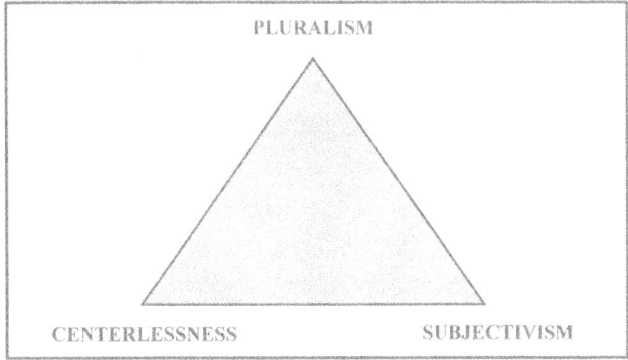

These three characteristics postmodernism promote[6] and they in turn promote postmodernism. Their natures are outlined below:

1) *Pluralism* – The theory that there are more than one or two kinds of ultimate reality or Truth. But, Jesus said, "I am the Way The Truth and the Life, no one comes to the Father but through me."

2) *Centerlessness* – The avoidance of Christ centered, or Bible centered thinking. From Isaiah 28:15B, 16,17 the LORD speaks on such a characteristic.

"For we have made falsehood our refuge and we have concealed ourselves with deception" Therefore thus says the Lord GOD, Behold, I am laying in Zion a stone, a tested stone, a costly cornerstone (for) the foundation, firmly placed. He who believes (in it) will not be disturbed. I will make justice the measuring line and righteousness the level; then hail will sweep away the refuge of lies and the waters will overflow the secret place.

3) *Subjectivism* - To paraphrase Webster. This theory limits knowledge to conscious states and elements. The supreme good is the subjective experience or feeling, and that the individual's feelings or apprehension is the ultimate criterion of the good and the right. (This is where "If it feels good, do it!" comes from.) It rejects Jesus' words recorded in the Gospel of John, "But when He, the Spirit of truth, comes, He will guide you into all the truth; for He will not speak on His own, but whatever He hears, He will speak; and He will disclose to you what is to come. (John 16:13) (NASB). And rejection of the Old Testament teaching, "the truth of the Lord is everlasting." (Psalms 117:2) (NASB)

The negative consequences of the new tolerance promulgated by postmodernism are: the death of truth, virtue, conviction, and faith; the dominance of feelings coincident with the destruction of human rights, and the exaltation of nature, to name a few. [7] How can Christians remain indifferent to postmodernism when it attempts to shake the foundations of our societies' fabric? On September 19, 1796, George Washington gave his famous *Farewell Address* to the nation he helped create.

> "Of all the dispositions and habits which lead to political prosperity, Religion and Morality are indispensable supports. ... And let us with caution indulge the supposition, that morality can be maintained without religion. Whatever may be conceded to the influence of refined education on minds of peculiar structure, reason and experience both forbid us to expect that National morality can prevail in exclusion of religious principle. 'Tis substantially true, that virtue or morality is a necessary spring of popular government. The rule indeed extends with more or less force to every species of free Government. Who that is a sincere friend to it, can look with indifference upon attempts to shake the foundations of the fabric?..." [8]

7.5) Club Theology

> To make light of philosophy is to be a true philosopher.[9]

So Blaise Pascal remarked. The same should be true of a theology based on philosophy. A point of courtesy and apology to the good Christian theologians, and then I'll move on to rougher speech. In theology there are *things scholars know* but don't talk much about. The unsaid in theology is that German scholars are loud, boisterous, brash and contentious, while English scholars are quite the opposite. It has been American tradition to mimic the proper British and chuckle at the exuberant Hun. I publicly confess that I'm 50% German, 25% English, and 25% Scottish. That encourages me to be "in your face" half the time, "begging your pardon" one fourth of the time, and the remaining quarter spent using common sense with a brave heart. I hope my style will not offend the proper theologians who honor me by reading on.

We have reviewed the marriage of theology and philosophy. Science was referred to as natural philosophy, but it's an odd thing no one called the remainder of the search unnatural philosophy. That is my task. The natural philosopher grounded his theories in observable phenomenon, while the unnatural philosopher based his conclusions on speculation. There were attempts to procedurally ground unnatural philosophy in the laws of logic, but with errors in the premises, the conclusions could be anything desired. There was a period of about 500 years, where theology tried to use philosophy as a tool to understand revelation; it failed. But worse than fail, it resulted in the eventual emasculation and subjugation of theology to the worldview of the philosophers, rather than the divine Word found in Scripture.

There is the real world of the ancient theologians, and the counterfeit world defined by the unnatural philosophy of postmodernism; there is a myriad of mixed philosophies in-between. Theology derived from unnatural philosophy is based on unnatural speculation. Worse than that, when we review Gödel's Incompleteness Theorem, we will see the utter impossibility of logic proving all statements – even if the premises and procedures are correct. *It is from this position that I launch into the German mode of writing to bring the luke warm to a full boil.*

We live in a sanctified world of partitioned classes that are essentially mutually exclusive. There is a class of learned persons called theologians who are specialists in the study of God and His relation to our world, who have almost nothing to do with the hearts that provide Him sanctuary. They've made a club for themselves under the title of theology. As distinctive utterances, they use words like *hermeneutics* and *exegesis*, or *Zeitgeist* and *oeuvre*. While reading this book, you'll find I've started using these too. They refer to the Son of God as God the Son. It is all quite proper, of course, removing ambiguity and being precise, but it separates them from the multitude of faithful ministers who preach the Word to the poor and needy in compliance with the good news:

> *The Spirit of the LORD is on me, because he has anointed me to preach good news to the poor. He has sent me to proclaim freedom for the prisoners and recovery of sight for the blind, to release the oppressed, ...-Luke 4:18 Re Isa. 61:1 (NLT)*

There are theologians who, I believe, still feel and fill the hearts of the multitudes. But I am flabbergasted and distressed by the great difference in faith there is between certain theologians, and practicing ministers of the Word.

> Certain theologians have 'a genuinely devilish pride' ... Such puff themselves up and boast: 'I also am a learned doctor. I love the Spirit and other gifts just as well as, and even in greater measure than, these preachers.' So, they think they deserve to be heard and honored above others. They consider themselves so wise that all the world, in comparison, are geese and fools.[10]

I'm amazed; on the one hand, to see a group of learned souls positioning themselves as experts on what God's Word doesn't say, and in stark contrast, on the other hand, I see a multitude of God's servants declaring what God says. It's like the difference between lawyers and entrepreneurs; the former says "Don't, it's risky." while the later says "Do, it's profitable."

Christians are told certain things about God from learned professors that don't quite square and that sends them to their studies to pour over their Bibles. For example,

> "In that God is the one who is above all thought, he is called and he is the Incomprehensible."[11]

Some of these doctors say that if something is incomprehensible, it is unknowable. I knew my earthly father before I understood him...if I ever really did. That knowledge included mutual love and respect. When I was young, I didn't care how he made the family work, but I knew he did. I knew if a dog attacked me, he would defend me, and he did ... and I didn't even wonder where he got that courage. Knowing your father is like knowing your wife, in the sense that you love and respect them, but not that you comprehend them with reason.

Another example that doesn't relate well with the Gospel is, "And in that God is the goodness which surpasses all speech, he is called and he is the Ineffable."[12] However, the groaning of the Spirit mentioned in Romans augments our languages, thereby making the ineffable Name or Essence of God expressible to His Children.

> *In the same way, the Spirit helps us in our weakness. We do not know what we ought to pray for, but the Spirit himself intercedes for us with groans that words cannot express. – Romans 8:26 (NIV)*

So, we must take reasoned arguments derived from the "ineffable and incomprehensible" nature of God as not applying to those who call Him Father (Ab), even Daddy (Abba), and speak with Him with the aid of Christ's Holy Spirit. Further, we may unequivocally declare His attributes,

> *"But you are A CHOSEN RACE, A ROYAL PRIESTHOOD, A HOLY NATION, A PEOPLE FOR God's OWN POSSESSION, that you may proclaim the excellencies of Him who has called you out of darkness into His marvelous light." – 1 Peter 2:9 (NIV)*

If there is a scandal in theology, I doubt that it is in the use of reason, but rather in the use of pride. Pride, the very original sin in the heart of Satan, in intellect to set oneself up as a judge of the Scriptures, to say that you can't trust in the direct interpretation, but must rely on a more *realistic* interpretation. This scandal also invades the pulpit, and this form of belief in self or institution is older than the renaissance or the reformation. St. Paul warned,

> *"See to it that no one takes you captive through hollow and deceptive philosophy, which depends on human tradition and the elemental spiritual forces of this world rather than on Christ." Colossians 2:8 (NIV)*

These prideful theologians are under Satan's influence and control; their philosophy seduces them. "He can make them joyful; furthermore, he renders them haughty and proud in their opinions, in their wisdom and self-made personal holiness; then no threat nor terror of God's wrath and of eternal damnation moves them, but their hearts grow harder than steel or adamant."[13] And,

> "It is responsible for a vast amount of intellectual pride, an aristocracy of intellect with all the snobbery which usually accompanies that term.... They have a splendid scorn for all opinions which do not agree with theirs. ...The arrogant boasts of these people would be very amusing, if they were not so influential.... A striking characteristic of these people is a persistent ignoring of what is written on the other side. They think to kill their antagonists by either ignoring or despising him....
>
> When one makes his philosophy his authority, it is not a long step until he makes himself his own god. ... They recognize no authority but their own moral instincts and philosophical reason. Now, as the evolution theory makes all things exist only in a state of flux, or of becoming, God is therefore changing and developing, the Bible and Christ will be out-grown, Christianity itself will be left behind. Hence, there is no absolute truth, nothing in the moral religious world is fixed or certain. All truth is in solution; there is no precipitate upon which we can rely. There is no *absolute* standard of Ethics, no *authority* in religion, every one is practically his own god." [14]

As in the days of Jesus' ministry, the men who should know are the ones who know the least of the Law and of the gospel. Dr. Luther made this prophetic note 500 years ago,

> "If judgment Day doesn't come soon, the same conditions will return, except they will be even worse than they were under the papacy. Then even the doctors and teachers of theology will no longer know anything about God and his commandments, much less will they know anything about Christ. Our dear Lord Christ will not be made a liar when he says in Luke 18:8 'I tell you that he will avenge them speedily. Nevertheless when the Son of man cometh, shall he find faith on earth?" [15]

Prideful intellect and philosophy causes their forgetfulness of the true meaning of Christianity and the loss of the great joy the angel of the lord spoke of to the lowly shepherds,

> *"Fear not: for, behold, I bring you good tidings of great joy, which shall be to all people. For unto you is born this day in the city of David, a Savior, which is Christ the Lord. And this shall be a sign unto you; Ye shall find the babe wrapped in swaddling clothes, lying in a manger." – Luke 2:10,12 (KJV)*

Many take offense and resist when they hear that this little child is the sole Savior and Light of the World. They would much rather salvation depended upon their preferred philosophy.

This child, on the contrary, has been placed as a stone of stumbling for the wise of the world, the intellectuals, and the self-righteous, who will trample, tumble, fall, and break their necks over this child. They simply can't bear to have their wisdom, their righteousness, and their piety count for nothing.[16]

But Jesus' prayer to His Father (Matthew 11:25) expresses His joy in the manner His Father humbles the proud,

> "I praise Thee, O Father, Lord of heaven and earth, that Thou didst hide these things from the wise and intelligent and didst reveal them to babes."

So, if my God says to me in the scriptures, "I tell you the truth…" and then goes on and tells me something, I must believe Him. I cannot accept that he doesn't really mean what He says, but is using hyperbole to mean something else. I could accept that kind of interpretation of something said by anyone else, but our God knew His words were to be written and we were going to read them. He was capable of causing His followers to speak in tongues to be understood, He surely had His Word written for our understanding.

These theologians think certain statements are hyperbole such as John 14:13, "And I will do whatever you ask in my name, so that the Son may bring glory to the Father," (KJV) But, if this were hyperbole, then why then does the same author repeat it again and again in John 15:16, John 16:23, and John 16:26? It would do better to get a good definition of what *in My Name* means, since Christianity and Judaism **do not** invoke magic sayings and words. What does it mean to be an agent operating in the Name of Jesus?

His *Name* in Hebrew means *I AM Salvation*, or the Expression of the Awareness of the Existence of Salvation. That is, the Word of the Truth of Salvation. That Word is God's Word. If we ask in accordance with God's Word, He will do whatever we ask. And it is the Essence of the Awareness of Existence, or the Spirit of Truth that reminds us of His Word. If I pray as an agent of God under the influence of His Holy Spirit, the prayer must be granted. Can God praying to God not be satisfied?

Everything depends on your receiving the promise as true, that God, for Christ's sake, wants to be gracious to you. … The devil is an extraordinary master at getting us to call God a liar and refuse to believe his promise. An unbelieving heart dishonors God and makes him a liar. …. Thus it can well be that one has faith, but, since it is lacking the Word, it is not true faith, but a mere delusion since nothing will ever come of it.[17]

Therefore, let God's Word be of more authority to you than your own feelings and the judgment of the whole world; do not give God the lie and rob yourself of the Spirit of truth.[18]

7.6) Concluding Comments on Postmodernism

7.6.1) Blaise Pascal's Night of Fire

I have used every skill at my disposal and every method I am comfortable with, every quotation from respected thinkers, and even used natural philosophy to reason on the error inherent in postmodernism. I related to Martin Luther's lament

> Hence our learned university doctors no longer know Christ. They do not recognize the need of him and his benefits, nor understand the character of the Gospel and the New Testament.[19]

But there is a solid hope and a groaning for the Lord's assistance when confronting His opponents; there is a modicum of honor when dueling with the opponents' choice of weapons. "To accomplish an object with eminent success through the instrumentality of an enemy is characteristic of the divine hand," [20] Whether I have accomplished His task with that approach, He will reveal in time. We arrive at the bottom line soon.

The final thoughts on postmodernism come down to the statement by the forefather of the postmodern paradigm, Nietzsche. "God is Dead! God remains dead! And we have killed him." [21] Upon reflection, they are right ... their god is dead. It never had the power to resurrect itself. It actually never lived. Their mistake: they believed they referred to the God of Abraham, Moses, and the Christian Apostles, and they didn't. They referred to "a being that which nothing greater can be conceived," which is far short of the Infinite God of Abraham. Their belief that God is a thought: thinking is a creator and God is its finest creation, simply indicates their god is an idol fashioned by the mind alone, without the use of hands. Whether golden calf or our greatest thought, all idolatry begins in the mind.

Although I was given the same conclusion by the Spirit that was given to Blaise Pascal a mere 350 years ago, I do share in a measure of the joy he must have felt in his "Night of Fire" on November 23, 1654. Amazingly, if he hadn't sewed a parchment memorial of the event inside his coat pocket, the world would not have known of the most important incident in his life. On that night, with tears of joy overwhelming him, he realized that the God of the philosophers was not the God of the Bible.

Unfortunately, that knowledge didn't stop the philosophical parade, "And the chamberlains walked with still greater dignity, as if they carried the train which did not exist." In search of their own god, philosophizing theologians were never able to achieve that ultimate thought. As Nietzsche said it, thinking God "causes giddiness because it forces thought to compare itself to a height to which it is forbidden to climb."[23] God spoke on their inadequacy of finding Him their way.

> "FIRE
>
> "God of Abraham, God of Isaac, God of Jacob, not of the philosophers and savants.
> Certitude. Certitude. Feeling. Joy. Peace.
> God of Jesus Christ.
>
> ....
>
> Forgetfulness of the world and everything except God.
> He is to be found only in the ways taught in the Gospel.
>
> ....
>
> This is life eternal, that they might know Thee, the only true God, and Jesus Christ whom Thou hast sent. [22]

'For My thoughts are not your thoughts, neither are your ways My ways,' declares the LORD. 'As the heavens are higher than the earth, so are my ways higher than your ways and My thoughts than your thoughts.' –Isaiah 55:8,9

So, these self-possessed idolaters gave up without admitting their failure and said the *thought* was dead. They originally believed they could reason from a set of rules and arrive at the truth. A rigorous logician, the English philosopher William of Ockham showed that many of the truths held by Christian philosophers could not be proved by natural reason, but only by divine revelation, that is by articles of faith taken as axioms in the reasoning. His reward was denunciation, house arrest, and excommunication by the Pope.

Centuries later, Gödel's Incompleteness Theorem destroyed any hope of describing truth using any formal and consistent language system that depends only on rules and process to arrive at its conclusions. Any system of language and formalized thought that intends to deal with concepts like truth, must be axiom based: that means some things must be taken on faith, they are givens.

Rather than accept the need for revelation, the postmodernists faulted truth itself. They argued language is temporal and socially determined and incapable of conveying truth. However, William of

Ockham's and Gödel's conclusions are independent of time or society. The problem is that pure reasoning without faith cannot address questions of truth, or other concepts like love, that bear on the Nature of God. We don't have the capacity to understand God because He didn't make us that way. We will but understand God *better* with the axioms. Is it any wonder why the Living Word places so much emphasis on faith!

We may someday understand the Truth part of God, but not the Love part. Or possibly the opposite is true. Then again, we may understand both but not their interaction. But then there's God's Justice, and if we got that right, well there are all the attributes we don't even know about. I say, *Let any man who fully understands his own wife please say so, and do so in front of her! You will only think you do!* How much more so mysterious the Almighty and Infinite Creator? Let no man be so vain as to believe he could fully understand his Creator. Forget understanding Him fully; learn to Love Him fully, then you will know and possess what you can't understand.

So, to bring home the idolatry point, I quote my favorite and most commanding Author, You shall not make for yourself an idol, *or* any likeness of what is in heaven above or the earth beneath or in the water under the earth. You shall not worship them or serve them; for I the LORD your God, am a jealous God…. – Exodus 20:4,5

God said, don't make an idol *or* a likeness. It needn't be a likeness to be an idol. I pray that this simple child of God has convinced the crowd of this singular fact: philosophical theology as found in the *Higher Criticism*, *modernism* and *postmodernism is idolatry*. I hope all see it for what it is - an obvious malignancy in our spirits, and as foul as any Baal worship. The perpetrators of this crime against the Lord were the most literate and educated in the world. They knew full well their teachings were idolatrous. Nietzsche knew where it is *forbidden* to climb. They all did, but they wanted to rob God of His essence and become gods themselves. They were their own idols.

This is sacrilege – the assumption of divinity by an act of robbery. … Though the offender does not look upon such conduct as robbery, it is none the less robbing divine honor, and is so regarded by God and angels and saints, and even by his own conscience.[24]

I am grateful to Martin Luther for bolstering my position on the subject, But you know Pope, councils and all the world, with their doctrines, must yield authority to the most insignificant Christian with faith, even though it be but a seven-year-old child, and his decision of their doctrines and laws is to be accepted.[25]

And with Henry Wadsworth Longfellow providing the appropriate song, this child is encouraged to sing about his living God of the living:

> Then pealed the bells more loud and deep, 'God is not dead; nor doth He sleep;
> the wrong shall fail, the right prevail, with peace on earth, good will to men.'
>
> -- *I Heard the Bells on Christmas Day*

The final quote is from the pillar of the Christian faith, C. S. Lewis. In it he sums up the impotence of postmodernism.

"The thing which I have called for convenience the *Tao*, and which others may call Natural Law or Traditional Morality, ... is not one among a series of possible systems of value. It is the sole source of all value judgements. If it is rejected, all value is rejected. If any value is retained, it is retained.... The rebellion of all new ideologies [e.g., postmodernism] against the *Tao* is a rebellion of the branches against the tree: if the rebels could succeed they would find that they had destroyed themselves. The human mind has no more power of inventing a new value than of imaging a new primary colour, or, indeed, of creating a new sun and a new sky for it to move in".[26]

So, the notion of absolute truth does exist. It is available to men because our living God bestows it as gifts, or revelation. It must be understood using both relational and rational components in our minds. Behavior is to follow the norm established by Jesus Christ, the full embodiment of deity, employing the gifts of the Spirit Who dwells within. The modern and postmodern approaches to Theology are to be abandoned as vain philosophies, of the type Paul said to beware. Further, *theologia crucis* (the theology of the cross), expressed by Luther and Calvin's *Deus dixit* (God speaks) are essential concepts to a proper Christian theology. Such a theology my friend Greer has, for lack of alternatives, called post-postmodernism, and claims it is a newly developing paradigm.

7.6.2) Four Rules of Natural Philosophic Reasoning from Principia Mathematica[27]

A philosophy of Being, or Theology, that pretends vainly to kill the Creator of the Big Bang using arrogant inoperable assertions, is leading its adherents to the same Abyss that the Light Bearer is destined to. This is not philosophy. Philosophy means 'the love of wisdom'. It is the study of knowledge, or "thinking about thinking". Originally the term "philosophy" denoted the search of knowledge for its own sake, and encompassed all areas of speculative thought, including the arts, sciences and religion.

There are now many branches of philosophy, but none have been more rigorous than Natural Philosophy, or Science, and its language- Mathematics. Sir Isaac Newton summarized the proper way to reason in that arena. I will attempt to apply these to Theology as attachments to each Rule. The reader is invited to find better reasonable analogies than mine, since the LORD says "Come now, let us reason together,..."[28]

Rule 1 *We are to admit no more causes of natural things than such as are both true and sufficient to explain their appearances.*

- This rule is now commonly called the principle of parsimony, and states that the simplest explanation is generally the most likely. **See Ockham's razor**
    - Newton added," To this purpose the philosophers say that Nature does nothing in vain, and more is in vain when less will serve; for Nature is pleased with simplicity, and affects not the pomp of superfluous causes."

> *For **Experiential** Theology then, "Father God does nothing in vain, and more is in vain when less will serve; for God is pleased with simplicity, and does not dwell in the spectacle of unnecessary causes."*

Rule 2 *Therefore to the same natural effects we must, as far as possible, assign the same causes.*

- This rule essentially means that special interpretations of data should not be used if a reasonable explanation already exists.

> *For Experiential Theology then," Special interpretations of inspired texts, or supernatural events, should not be used if a reasonable explanation exists."*

Rule 3 *The qualities of bodies, which admit neither intensification nor remission of degrees, and which are found to belong to all bodies within the reach of our experiments, are to be esteemed the universal qualities of all bodies whatsoever.*

- This rule suggests that explanations of phenomena determined through scientific investigation should apply to all instances of that phenomenon.

  - Newton added," We are certainly not to relinquish the evidence of experiments for the sake of dreams and vain fictions of our own devising; nor are we to recede from the analogy of Nature, which uses to be simple, and always consonant to itself."

> *For Experiential Theology then," The qualities of Beings, which neither increase nor decrease, and which are found to belong to all Beings within the reach of our experiences, are to be esteemed the Universal qualities of all Beings whatsoever."*
>
> - *For Experiential Theology then, "we are certainly not to relinquish the evidence of experiences for the sake of dreams and vain fictions of our own devising; nor or we to recede from the analogy of Father God, which uses to be simple, and always consonant to itself."*

Rule 4 *In experimental philosophy we are to look upon propositions inferred by general induction from phenomena as accurately or very nearly true, notwithstanding any contrary hypothesis that may be imagined, till such time as other phenomena occur, by which they may either be made more accurate, or liable to exceptions.*

- This rule endorses the use of scientific theories, considered true until demonstrated otherwise. These theories are accepted with evidence, but they are subject to change.

> *In Experiential Theology then, "we are to look upon propositions inferred by general induction from Inspired Scripture, or supernatural events, as accurately or very nearly true, notwithstanding any contrary hypothesis that may be imagined, till such time as other Inspired Scripture, or supernatural events occur, by which they may either be made more accurate, or liable to exceptions."*

It is my most sincere desire that you would use the Gospel of Jesus Christ as the source of your necessary axioms, disregarding the Higher Critics who created rationales for their beliefs rather than deducing conclusions from their reasoning. They have prejudiced themselves and have yielded preposterous results. Please follow me into the next arena, where we view the spiritual landscape from an electrical engineer's vantage.

[1]   Mark Water, *The New Encyclopedia Of Christian Quotations*, Baker Books, Grand Rapids, MI, 2000, p. 1077

[2]   Richard Wolin, *"Heidegger's Children"*, Princeton University Press, Princeton, New Jersey, 2001, In Prologue

[3]   Jennifer Bothamley, *Dictionary of Theories*, Gale Research International Ltd, London, 1993, *subjective idealism*, p440

[4]   C.H Spurgeon, Spurgeon's Sermons, Vol 4, Sermon *"The Immutability of Christ"*, page 184, BakerBooks 1999, Grand Rapids, Michigan.

[5]   Richard Wolin, *"Heidegger's Children"*, Princeton University Press, Princeton, New Jersey, 2001, p.p.206, 208

[6]   Robert C. Greer, *Mapping Postmodernism*, InterVarsity Press, Downers Grove, Illinois, 2003, *The Ecumenical Imperative*, pp 62,63

[7]   Josh McDowell and Bob Hostetler, The New Tolerance (Wheaton, Ill.: Tyndal House, 1998), pp 53-68

[8]   George Washington, *The Farewell Address*, Edited by William J. Bennett, The Book of Virtues, Simon & Schuster, N.Y., 1993, p.794

[9]   Blaise Pascal, *PENSfES*, 1660, translated by W. F. Trotter, #4

[10] Martin Luther, Complete Sermons of Martin Luther, Vol. 4.2, *Third Sunday After Trinity*, Baker Books, Grand Rapids, MI, 2000, p. 60

[11] Eberhard Jungle, *God as the Mystery of the World*, transl.: Darrell L. Guder (Grand Rapids: Eedmans, Publishing Company, 1983), p. 234

[12] [12] Ibid.

[13] Martin Luther, Complete Sermons of Martin Luther, Vol. 2.1, *Pentecost Sunday*, Baker Books, Grand Rapids, MI, 2000, p302

[14]   R. A. Torrey, A. C. Dixon and Others, <u>The Fundamentals</u>, Vol. I, Ch. XIX, "*My Experience With Higher Criticism*", Prof. J. J. Reeve, , 1917, Baker Books reprint, 2003, p.p. 361,363

[15]   Martin Luther, <u>Complete Sermons of Martin Luther</u>, Vol. 7, *Eighteenth Sunday After Trinity*, Baker Books, Grand Rapids, MI, 2000, p.68

[16]   Martin Luther, <u>Complete Sermons of Martin Luther</u>, Vol. 5, *First Sunday After Christmas*, Baker Books, Grand Rapids, MI, 2000, p.160

[17]   Martin Luther, <u>Complete Sermons of Martin Luther</u>, Vol.7, *Nineteenth Sunday After Trinity*, Baker Books, Grand Rapids, MI, 2000, p.p.80, 81

[18]   Martin Luther, <u>Complete Sermons of Martin Luther</u>, Vol. 2.1, *Pentecost Sunday*, Baker Books, Grand Rapids, MI, 2000, p304

[19]   Martin Luther, <u>Complete Sermons of Martin Luther</u>, Vol. 3.2, *New Years Day*, Baker Books, Grand Rapids, MI, 2000, p283

[20]   Martin Luther, <u>Complete Sermons of Martin Luther</u>, Vol. 3.2, *Epiphany*, Baker Books, Grand Rapids, MI, 2000, p329

[21]   Friedrich Nietzsche, *The Happy Science*

[22]   George Murphy, <u>Christian History</u> magazine, *Creation's Symmetries, God's Mystery,* Issue 76, Fall 2002, Vol. XXI, No.10, p. 33

[23]   Eberhard Jüngel, *God as the Mystery of the World*, transl.: Darell L. Guder (Grand Rapids: Eerdmans Publishing Company, 1983), p149

[24]   Martin Luther, <u>Complete Sermons of Martin Luther</u>, Vol. 4.1, *Palm Sunday*, Baker Books, Grand Rapids, MI, 2000, p173

[25]   Martin Luther, <u>Complete Sermons of Martin Luther</u>, Vol. 4.1, *Second Sunday After Epiphany*, Baker Books, Grand Rapids, MI, 2000, p29

[26]   C. S. Lewis, *The Abolition of Man*, Macmillan, New York, 1947, pp. 56,57

[27]   From Principia Mathematica, *at the beginning of Book 3 (in the second (1713) and third (1726) editions) a section entitled "Rules of Reasoning in Philosophy."*

[28]   Isaiah 1:18 English Standard Version

Larry Sheets

Part Five – On Representations, Names and Reality
8) On That Which Is and What It's Called

8.1) On Representations, and Names

A *representation* is a sign or a symbol of a person, place or thing. Whereas, a *name* is a word or phrase that constitutes the distinctive indicator or identifier that designates a person, place or thing. For example: the flag, Old Glory, often represents The United States. The name *Old Glory* represents the flag. The *flag* represents the country. But if we say Old Glory represents the Country, we have glossed over the double representation. The actual physical representation, the flag, is lost in its name and what it represents. In this manner, the identity of a person, place or thing may get lost in the representation. This may seem somewhat silly until considering such ponderables as the Name of God.

Now in the electrical engineering community, there was some consternation when *cycles-per-second* was changed to *Hertz*. One group of engineers liked *cycles per second* because it was a self-defining name. The other group preferred *Hertz* to credit the man This was more than a simple name change because the description of reality was lost with the change. A simple name change would be like calling the flag "Pride" instead of "Old Glory." But, if the *flag* were replaced by the Liberty Bell and we pledged allegiance to the Liberty Bell of the United States of America, that would be a representation change. They would both have represented the USA, but in much different ways.

In what way does the flag represent a nation? Or how would the Liberty Bell serve as the representative object of our allegiance? Neither representation describes the unique nature of our country. Wouldn't the Bill of Rights and the Constitution have been better, more descriptive, representations to pledge allegiance to? Why wouldn't it have been more exact and meaningful to just pledge allegiance to the Country as a whole?

8.2) On Representations and Reality – The Trouble With Models

Mathematicians use mathematical expressions to model reality. Models often represent the physical world. A model that "gets wrong answers" gets disqualified from reality. If the representing model "gets the right answers," the model is elevated to a near reality status. Very often, the mathematical model is chosen that can employ functions that are well known and satisfy certain conditions that exist in the particular problem. For example, sinusoids have periodic zeros in their values. They, or combinations of sinusoids, are therefore chosen to solve problems that exhibit repeating zeros, or harmonic sinusoids that exhibit coherent zeros.

An infinite number of sinusoids are often required to represent simple functions. These infinite summations of harmonic sinusoids are called Fourier series, after the French mathematician who discovered them. Something as simple as $y = t$, where t is time from, say, zero to 1 second, requires an infinite number of coefficients associated with sinusoids to represent. Whereas, the linear expression, $y = at + b$ represents the problem exactly with $a = 1$ and $b = 0$. There is, therefore, an almost universal belief that the simpler the representation, the closer it represents reality, as long as it isn't too simple. Albert Einstein said,

> "When the solution is simple, God is answering." "Everything should be made as simple as possible, but not simpler."

But "getting the right answers" does not justify the model for anything other than getting the right answers. Two or more models can provide identical answers. The simplest solution (like Einstein mentions) appears to be closest to reality. William of Ockham's Razor, that one should pursue the simplest hypothesis, referred to as the principle of economy (parsimony) in formal logic, does have great appeal. Solutions like $E = mc^2$ have that nature. I am convinced that a solution that requires an infinite number of terms to evaluate does not represent reality, but only a method to arrive at an answer.

What appears to be reality depends upon the representation or method used to view it. A spinning flywheel can appear to be standing still under a synchronized strobe light. A single mark on the wheel can be made to appear like two, three or more with synchronous over-strobing. Whereas, with a continuous light, the single mark on the spinning flywheel will look like a faint, but continuous band.

Maxwell defined electromagnetic waves with wave equations. Particle-like Photons, however, can describe the effects of electromagnetic radiation and explain the momentum measured in light. Following the work of Maxwell on electromagnetic waves, Einstein represented the universe with wave equations in his general theory. Sinusoidal solutions in a "Potential Well" problem were merged with observed blackbody photonic radiation that linearly relates energy and frequency through Plank's constant. This resulted in a discrete view of energy radiated from matter by way of continuous functions of time and space, which could also be considered photons, or particles. – quantum theory ensued.

Our belief in a representation as reality can alter how we view existence. Our methods of scientific verification may be only hidden cyclical arguments. An old saying goes something like this, "A carpenter sees every problem in terms of a hammer." An electrical engineer would see every signal in terms of sinusoids and would define all signals in terms of them. I hope to show to normal people, who are in touch with their senses, how mathematical representations become ingrained in our view of reality so much that we design test equipment based on the representation to verify the representation.

The Slowly Warbling Pitch

An audio oscillator is a device that can produce a sinusoidal signal (an audible tone) in the audio range. A variable oscillator has a knob on the front of the unit and a dial displaying the frequency to which the oscillator has been dialed. In a way, it looks like the old radio receivers. Consider the following experiment.

> Suppose the oscillator were very slowly and uniformly dialed back and forth from 1000 Hertz to 9000 Hertz, centered at 5000 Hertz. For sake of example, suppose it took 10 seconds to swing the dial from 1000 Hertz to 9000 Hertz and back again, and the swinging would continue indefinitely.

If you had done this, you would have produced a regular continuous and analytic signal on the output of the oscillator with that continuous control of the frequency knob. You could listen to the tone of the oscillator using a speaker, and attest to the continuously variable nature of the frequency of your product. It would start low, slowly work its pitch up to 9000Hertz, and then slowly descend in pitch until 1000 Hertz, and then repeat indefinitely.

However, if you took the time and trouble to carefully and scientifically analyze the output of the oscillator with a device called a spectrum analyzer, you would find out that your continuously variable-frequency output had produced an audio spectrum that looks like a comb or picket fence. That is, it has non-zero values only at multiples of the sweep rate of once in 10 seconds, which is 0.1 Hertz. Instead of the energy being uniformly spread between 1000 Hertz and 9000 Hertz, it is discretely spread into approximately 80,000 nearly equal amplitude sinusoids between 1000 Hertz and 9000 Hertz. If the sweep rate had been 1 Hertz, there would have been approximately 8,000 nearly equal amplitude sinusoids between 1000 Hertz and 9000 Hertz, spaced 1 Hertz apart. Why?

The spectrum analyzer is designed to look for fixed frequency sinusoids. The continuously variable oscillator signal causes the analyzer to get non-zero responses only at multiples of the sweep rate of the oscillator. This is because the spectrum analyzer is trying to represent applesauce with small apples; continuously variable frequency sinusoids represented by fixed frequency sinusoids. Now as long as you use an infinite number of infinitely small apples, they will exactly equal applesauce.

You see, the spectrum analyzer is designed in a couple of possible analog ways. The first method is called the correlated approach and is to multiply the signal under test by sinusoids (sines and cosines) to look for an averaged squared product at the frequency of the applied sinusoids. Another method is to use a very narrow bandpass filter that can have its center frequency adjustable across the testing band of interest. The output of that filter is then rectified and averaged to determine how much real power came out of the filter at its center frequency. Either of these methods makes the voltage that is displayed on a cathode ray tube (LCD or LED display these days) to indicate the spectrum power at the frequency being tested at that moment. The first method is simply a method using active devices to create the equivalent filter of the second method. Digital methods would most probably use a Digital Signal Processor (DSP) to accomplish the filtering and rectification. The filtering is the primary element. Let's look at the nature of that filter.

A narrow band bandpass filter provides orders of magnitude of attenuation to all spectral components except at those in the very center of the pass band. To the very center frequency of the filter, the input signal is passed without attenuation to the output. In the ideal narrow bandpass filter, only one signal gets through it, a sinusoid at its center frequency. Such a filter is also called a *resonator* because it responds at its resonate frequency, the center frequency. Such a filter would also be called a matched filter for a sinusoid at that frequency.

The spectrum analyzer is able to alter the center frequency of the filter over a wide frequency range. It does that slowly enough though, that the filter looks like it is fixed during a measurement at a given frequency. In our example, 100 seconds would provide adequate time for a spectrum sweep measurement. Thus, the analyzer looks for fixed frequency sinusoids in the input signal with an instrument that is only capable of producing sinusoids, the filter. If the input of that filter were given a lightning spike on its input, the only thing that would leave its output would be its so-called *impulse response*. And yes, the *impulse response* of such a filter is a sinusoid at its center frequency.

So we get fixed sinusoids out of devices designed to resonate with them. Since the spectrum analyzer is not designed to display the instantaneous frequency of a warbling tone, it does the best it can and provides a number of fixed frequency sinusoids as a representation. Well do those fixed tones really exist? If a Fourier series representation were calculated for the signal at the input of the filter, the series would provide the same answer as the analyzer. The problem is, the analyzer was designed by using the same expressions as are in the Fourier model. The Fourier series and the analyzer agree, but they don't indicate or agree with the reality of the analog smoothly varying oscillator.

In our example, there is a very slight spillover of energy below 1000 Hertz and above 9000 Hertz that diminishes rapidly at the edges of the band. When the sum of the very small contributors is added to the in-band sinusoids, the actual and the representation converge to the same values for all times. Thus, the representation and the actual are the same quantitatively, but not qualitatively. The discrete representation requires an enormous number of coefficients to define the spectrum at discrete points. The continuously variable frequency, constant amplitude, sinusoid requires only the amplitude and sweep rate and form to define it. Ockham's Razor appears to be correct again to describe the source reality, a continuously variable-frequency oscillator.

8.3) God's Representation, Name, and Reality

I AM is the kind of expression that satisfies Ockham's Razor. Is the set of God's Attributes the *Representation* of God and I AM the *Name*? Does the Name support the Attributes, or conversely, or both? Does our choice of representation mask the nature of what we see? Is God's Name like *cycles-per-second* or like *Hertz*? Is it a Name to describe Him, honor Him, or both? Since God designed all of Nature, and since the greatest scientific minds believe that the best answers are the simplest, as long as they aren't too simple, shouldn't we expect the Designer Who expressed Himself in His work to also have a simple description?

In our first principles we discussed God. Contained in God is all that *Is*. God is *Immense*, and all that is God is *Good; Kindhearted and Well-intentioned*. He is *Just* and *Merciful*, *Graceful* and *Holy*; *Perfect* in His Attributes. God penetrates everything even though He contains all things. God dwells in His universe and yet the universe dwells in God. In that way, He is like the water in a bucket in the depths of the ocean. God is Unified, but a Trinity, like three interlocking triangles. Like a flywheel mark strobe-lighted at triple speed, He appears as three, though He is One. He partitioned Himself for us.

8.3.1) Pascal's Point, Gravity's Speed, and Intrinsic Immutable Inertia

Further, God is infinite and indivisible. He is like a point moving everywhere with an infinite velocity; for it is one in all places and is all totality in every place. Like the display on a cathode ray tube, the electron beam returns to the pixel before the image expires. Imagine a three-dimensional ray display, with zero spacing between pixels, and the energizing ray appearing as only a focused dot in three-dimensional space. Where the dot is, there is existence. The dot travels at infinite speed and covers the whole of the universe in infinitesimal time. Above that point, in unseen dimensions the Creator sustains His work. That is a representation that supports His Name and His attributes.

What is simpler than a point, or more unreachable than infinite speed? It is widely accepted, but not widely known, that the speed of gravity in Newton's Universal Law is unconditionally infinite.[1] Gravitational waves propagate at the speed of light, but the effect of gravity between bodies is not a wave. If the gravity between the sun and a planet were to act in a direction toward where the other *used to be* (because of propagation delay caused by traveling at the speed of light), rather than where the other object *is*, the orbit of the planet would rapidly decay contrary to all measurements.[2] How does that relate to theology?

The effects of gravity and inertia are indistinguishable according to Einstein's thought experiment: a man in an elevator without windows is unable to determine if he was being pushed to the floor because of gravity, or because the elevator is accelerating upward. Newton thought inertia belonged to the essential nature or constitution of mass, and was not capable of or susceptible to change. He said, in his 1713 edition of <u>Mathematical</u> <u>Principles of Natural Philosophy</u>, *Book 3: The Rules of Philosophising*,

> The only intrinsic force I recognize is inertial force. It is immutable, whereas gravity is diminished by increasing distance from the earth.

We now know of something that is immutable, intrinsic to all creation, except possibly space and time, and is indistinguishable by the senses of man to something that travels at an infinite speed! Consider again Pascal's point traveling at infinite speed, appearing in its totality throughout the universe where anything is, and returning to each location in zero time. Like the phosphor in the cathode ray tube screen, the effect at the point of focus is that the image persists. I venture that inertia is the persistence of the Divine Hand, when it writes mass or energy into existence. The more mass it writes, the more persistent the body.

Paul said about this Hand, "And He is before all things, and in Him all things hold together." –Col. 1:17 The writer to the Hebrews explains even more about Jesus,

> God… has spoken to us in *His* Son, whom He appointed heir of all things, *through whom also He made the world*. And *He is the radiance of His glory* and the exact representation of His nature, and *upholds all things by the word of His power*. –Hebrews 1:1,3

Paraphrasing these two, we have our personal loving God represented thus

The Son of God is the brilliant radiation of the Father's glory, through Whom all things are made, all things are held together, and all things are upheld by the expression of His power.

If we use the meaning of the Name of God in this sentence, it could read like
The Expression of Truth is the brilliant radiation of Existence, through Whom all things are made, all things are held together, and all things are upheld by the expression of His power.

What is Wisdom if not Truth, or the Spirit of Truth, expressed in word or deed? Better still, Who is Wisdom? We have here a brief collection of verses from the Wisdom of Solomon. They touch on the nature of Jesus and His Holy Spirit. When you read then, consider Pascal's Point, not as a mathematical invention, but as a focus from an unspotted mirror with the brightness of the everlasting light - a pure influence flowing from the glory of the Almighty having the breath of the power of God. That focus mightily sweeping from one end of space to another, not subject itself to inertia, but making all things new and with precision giving order and inertia to all things, thereby decreasing the entropy of His creation.

- "And thy counsel who hath known, *except thou give wisdom, and send thy Holy Spirit* from above?" – Wisdom 9:7

- *"For wisdom, which is the worker of all things, taught me: for in her is an understanding spirit, holy, one only, manifold, ... , having all power, ...*– Wisdom 7:22,23

- *"For wisdom is more moving than any motion: she passes and goes through all things by reason of her pureness. For she is the breath of the power of God, and a pure influence flowing from the glory of the Almighty: therefore can no defiled thing fall into her. For she is the brightness of the everlasting light, the unspotted mirror of the power of God, and the image of his goodness. And being made one, she can do all things: and remaining in herself, she makes all things new: ...."* – Wisdom 7:24,27

- *"For God loves none but him that dwells with wisdom. For she is more beautiful than the sun, and above all the order of stars: being compared with the light, she is found before it. ... "* – Wisdom 7:28,30

- "Wisdom reaches from one end to another mightily; and sweetly doth she order all things." – Wisdom 8:1

- "In that she is conversant with God, she magnifies her nobility: yea, the Lord of all things Himself loved her. For she is privy to the mysteries of the knowledge of God and a lover of his works." – Wisdom 8:3,4

Thus we see the Holy Spirit of Truth in Wisdom is The Spirit of the Son of God - fully aware of all that exists. If we add these contributions from the Wisdom of Solomon, the earlier expression could read:

The Expression of Truth is the brilliant radiation of Existence, the brightness of the everlasting light, the unspotted mirror of the power of God, and the image of his goodness reaching from one end to another mightily and sweetly ordering all things. For He is more beautiful than the sun, and above all the order of stars: being compared with the light, this emanation is found before it. For His Spirit is privy to the mysteries of the knowledge of God and a lover of his works through Whom all things are made, all things are held together, and all things are upheld by the Expression of His power.

These Names or representations can only trigger the heart to identify the only real item, the personal loving God, as distinct from the sign. The real item is analogous to the data stored in electronic memory distinctly different than the binary address that points to it.

8.3.2) An Analogy of Memory

We live in an information age. Computers are more common than TVs. The ultra fast memory chips that serve the processing units in those computers have changed considerably over the years. The "scratch pad" memory we're discussing here used to be designed in such a way that the information was written only once to a location. As long as the power remained on and the computer didn't use the same memory location again, the information would remain intact. That memory type was referred to as *static*

Static memory consumed considerable power and required substantial silicon area to implement. The dynamic memory was invented to solve these problems. The dynamic memory cell is capable of storing information for only a very short time. The dynamic cell essentially reads its own value (1 or 0) before it has excessively decayed. It then rewrites the decided upon 1 or 0 back into the original location. This process is called *refreshing*, and the speed by which this is done is called the *refresh rate*.

This dynamic method has proven to store information most efficiently. If the refresh mechanism ceases in these memories, however, the contents decay into chaotic random data. If we now consider Pascal's point again in light of the concept of refreshing memories, we envisage the entire creation being refreshed before it decays, and we understand such comments as

> If He should determine to do so. If He should gather to Himself His spirit and His breath, All flesh would perish together, And man would return to dust. – Job 34:14,15

If we contemplate Pascal's point, we experience an awareness of the continual refreshing of the creation, *making all things new. If its speed is being compared with the light, this emanation is found before it.* The energy in that point is so enormous, and the refresh rate so fast, and the size of creation so large, that the power of His Expression is beyond comprehension. Nothing remains for me but awe.

[1] Misner, C.W., K.S. Thorne & J.A. Wheeler, Gravitation, W.H. Freeman & Co., San Francisco, CA (1973), p.177

[2] Eddington, A.E., *Space, Time and Gravitation,* original printed in 1920, reprinted by Cambridge Univ. Press, Cambridge (1987), p.94

Part Six – A Look At Spurious Beliefs
9) The Ecumenical Imperative

The wretched condition of all Christendom, divided as it is into innumerable sects, is, alas, plain testimony that no body nor member, no faith nor love, seems longer to exist anywhere. Unity of mind in relation to the various gifts of God cannot exist in connection with human doctrines.[1]

9.1) Logical Statements of Love

Some theologians believe that there is such a thing as an "Ecumenical Imperative." The basis for the hope of our acceptance of such a belief is in Jesus' comments to his disciples in the upper room just prior to his arrest[2].

> My prayer is not for them alone. I pray also for those who will believe in me through their message, that all of them may be one, Father, *just as you are in Me and I am in You. May they also be in Us* so that the world may believe that You have sent Me. I have given them the glory that you have sent me; that they may be one as we are one. *I in them and You in Me.* May they be brought to complete unity to let the world know that You sent Me. (Jn 17:20-23)

Quoting Martin Luther,

> I have often said, and will always say it, that the greatest and most difficult contest is, for a person to contend with the Scriptures against the Scriptures; to strike aside another man's sword and wrench it out of his fist, to slay him with his own sword; to take from him his weapon, and with it strike him again. This no one can accomplish, except he who is enlightened by the Holy Spirit, so as to be able to recognize these rogues.[3]

The first thing to note about this verse (Jn 17:20-23) is the pair of different logical statements of unity that, at first, appear reversed:

-A- You in Me, I in You and they in Us

-B- I in them, You in Me

The Venn Diagram (on the next page) that reconciles both -A- and -B- above:

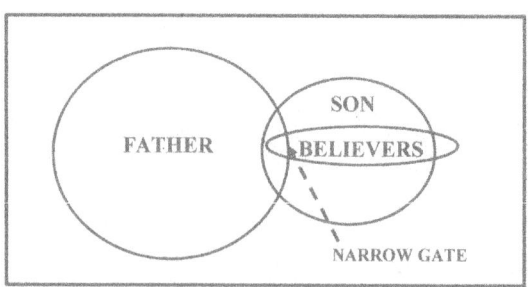

Thus, it appears that Jesus is the Narrow Gate, the Way to the Father. You see that the only way to be in the Father is to be in Jesus. "To the praise of the glory of his grace, wherein he has made us accepted *in* the beloved."- Eph. 1:6. Jesus said to the doubter Thomas" I am the Way, and the Truth and the Life: no one comes to the Father, but *through* Me."-John 14:6.

Secondly, the meaning of ' "complete unity" to let the world know that you sent Me.' is important for verse understanding. The meaning of "complete unity" was defined earlier by Jesus to mean Love. "All men will know that you are my disciples if you love one another." In context, Jesus said,

> A new command I give you: Love one another. As I have loved you, so you must love one another. All men will know that you are my disciples if you love one another. (Jn 13:34-35).

Quoting St Paul would make a more compelling argument for reunification, "Now I plead with you, brethren, by the name of our Lord Jesus Christ, that you all speak the same thing, and that there be no divisions among you, but that you be perfectly joined together in the same mind and the same judgment." (1 Cor.1: 10). However, I wish to remind the reader than when it came to church doctrine, Paul was unyielding. Recall how he railed against those who insisted that the gentiles be circumcised. He recommended that these false teachers be mutilated! ***"I wish that those who are troubling you would even emasculate themselves." Galatians 5:12*** That means cut it off, cut it all off! So even though it was Paul's urging that we all get along, it is apparent that he didn't mean with purveyors of false doctrine.

Church centered scholars believe as Marshall McLuhan's dictum[4], "The Medium is the Message," insisting that the partitioning of the church results in a distortion in the gospel message; they believe that reconciliation lies at the center of the gospel. However, Samual Taylor Coleridge stated, "He who begins by loving Christianity better than the Truth will proceed by loving his own sect or church better than Christianity, and end in loving himself better than all."

Further, the verses quoted earlier that are used to promote reconciliation, are actually referring to Love. The character of Love is the character of God (1 John 4:8). In 1 Cor 13 we find what the character of God is like. Love is unselfish. It nurtures and protects the object of its attention. Therefore, the *Ecumenical Imperative* derived and supported by these verses must be the Loving Imperative, or *the Nurturing and Protective Imperative* if these verses relate to the subject at all.

So let us next investigate the ecumenical observance of the "**Nurturing and Protective Imperative**," for that is the imperative expressed in the upper room and later in the Gospel of John. We will next decide if the last millennium's example of ecumenical observance is truthfully the way to a blessed church life.

9.2) Evidence of the Ecumenical Nurturing and Protective Imperative

9.2.1) Crusades, Treachery, Schisms, and The Inquisition

The second Christian millennium began with a series of futile Crusades. These commenced in 1095 and ended in 1270, and severely weakened Christendom.

> The setting up of Latin kingdoms in Syria and the Holy Land in religious communions with Rome, after the First Crusade, marked the opening stage of a conquest of Eastern Christianity by Rome that reached its climax during the Latin rule in Constantinople (1204-1261).[5]

The Byzantine Empire had been the bulwark of Europe against Islam. However, in the 4th Crusade, the crusaders, whose purpose was to drive the Muslims from the Holy Land, instead took the opportunity to seize and sack Constantinople, establish the Latin Empire, and install Baldwin as its first emperor. The East would never forget the ravaging of their Christian city by Western soldiers. The separation of the Eastern and Western Churches is dated from this atrocity in 1204.

That separation and that 4th Crusade occurred on the watch of Pope Innocent III. He was Pope from 1198 to 1216. This man was not just *unfit for his office or unpardonably stupid, but both*. During his tenure, he oversaw the ignoble 4th Crusade, the capture of Constantinople by the Latins, The Children's Crusade, and the slaughter of the Albingenses and the Waldenses, the development of the powerful instrument and suppression --Black Friars or Dominicans – and the Inquisition under their direction.

> Closely associated with the Albigenses were the Waldneses, the followers of a man called Waldo, who seemed to have been quite soundly Catholic in his theology, but equally offensive to the church because he denounced the riches and luxury of the clergy. This was enough for the Lateran, and so we have the spectacle of Innocent III preaching a crusade against these unfortunate sectaries, and permitting the enlistment of every wandering scoundrel at loose ends to carry fire and sword and rape and every conceivable outrage among the most peaceful subjects of the King of France. The accounts of the cruelties and abominations of this crusade are far more terrible to read than any account of Christian martyrdoms by the pagans, and they have the added horror of being indisputably true.[6]

In 1261, the Greeks recaptured Constantinople from the Latins. Fierce enmity and distrust existed in the East toward the Western church. Because of the lack of Christian unity, and the diminishing of the Eastern strength, the 13th century atrocity of 1204 contributed to the fall of Constantinople and the empire in the 15th century. After 8 Crusades, the Children's Crusade, and numerous armed incursions into the Holy Land, none of the stated purposes were accomplished. The power and prestige of the papacy, however, had been greatly strengthened by the Crusades. These were the times of Scholasticism, and the greatest blunders and cruelties ever committed by the Roman church.

9.2.2) The Church's Bungled Opportunity

The great Kublai Khan, who established the Yuan dynasty in China in 1280, had earlier sent a message of inquiry to the Pope in 1269. This presented Christianity with the greatest opportunity to perform the Great Commission since Paul preached to the Romans and the Greeks. We pick up the story recorded by H. G. Wells,

> In 1269 Kublai Khan sent a mission to the Pope with the evident intention of finding some common mode of action with Western Christendom. He asked that a hundred men of learning and ability should be sent to his Court to establish an understanding. His mission found the Western world Popeless, and engaged in one of those disputes about the succession that are so frequent in the history of the papacy. For two years there was no pope at all. When at last a pope was appointed, he dispatched two Dominican friars to convert the greatest power in Asia to his rule! Those worthy men were appalled by the length and hardship of the journey before them, and found an early excuse for abandoning the expedition. ...
>
> *The Travels of Marco Polo* is one of the great books of history. ... It begins by telling of the journey of Marco's father, Nicolo Polo, and uncle, Maffeo Polo, to China. These two were Venetian merchants of standing, living in Constantinople, and somewhere about 1260 they went to the Crimea and thence to Kazan; from that place they journeyed to Bokhara, and at Bokhara they fell in with a party of envoys from Kublai Khan in China to his brother *Hulagu in Persia*. These envoys pressed them to come on to the Great Khan, who at that time had never seen men of the "Latin" peoples. *They went on; and it is clear they made a very favorable impression upon the Kublai, and interested him greatly in the civilization of Christendom. They were made bearers of that request for a hundred teachers and learned men, 'intelligent men acquainted with the Seven Arts, able to enter into controversy, and able clearly to prove to idolators and other kinds of folk that the Law of Christ was best,'* to which we have just alluded. But when they returned Christendom was in a phase of confusion, and it was only after a delay of two years that they got their authorization to start for China again in the company of the two faint-hearted Dominicans.
>
> They took with them young Marco.... Marco particularly pleased Kublai; he was young and clever, and it is clear he had mastered the Tarter language very thoroughly. ...Chinese records mention a certain Polo attached to the imperial council in 1277, a valuable confirmation of the general truth of the Polo story.[7]

Such a sad thing, that a great heathen king should ask about the King of Kings and request 100 learned Christian communicators, and the best the Roman church could do was send two self-indulgent Black Friars who would rather be home playing with the tools of the Inquisition, slaughtering the Albingenses and the Waldenses, rather than obey our Lord's Great Commission, "Go therefore and make disciples of all the nations, ..."

9.2.3) Subject to the Roman Pontiff

In 1274, Thomas Aquinas died. Kublai Khan lived until 1292. Marco Polo then returned to Venice in 1295 after 24 years of travel, and one year after the new Pope Boniface VIII was installed. In 1302, with this recent history, Pope Boniface VIII (1294-1303) declared in the Bull UNAM SANCTAM, *ex cathedra* that it is "...absolutely necessary for the salvation of every human creature to be subject to the Roman Pontiff." Our Father apparently didn't take kindly to this man's attempted usurpation of Christ's authority, and acted quickly to bring him down.

> Boniface came into conflict with the French king in 1302; and in 1303, as he was about to pronounce sentence of excommunication against that monarch, he was surprised and arrested in his own ancestral palace at Anagni, by Guillaume de Nogaret. This agent from the French king forced an entrance into the palace, made his way into the bedroom of the frightened Pope—he was lying in bed with a cross in his hands—and heaped threats and insults upon him. The Pope was liberated a day or so later by the townspeople, and returned to Rome; but there he was seized upon and again made prisoner by some members of the Orsini family, and in a few weeks' time the shock and disillusioned old man died a prisoner in their hands.[8]

The next hundred years brought us men of God who proclaimed the Gospel. This greatly threatened the papists and enraged them to murder. In the **16th Ecumenical Council in Constance (1414-1418) John Wycliffe and John Huss were both declared heretics.** John Foxe writes,

> During all this time of Pope John, there were three Popes reigning together, neither was yet the schism ceased, which had continued the space, already, of thirty-six years; by reason whereof a General Council was holden at Constance in A.D. 1414, being called by Sigismund the Emperor, and Pope John XXXIII. These three Popes were John, whom the Italians set up; Gregory, whom the Frenchmen set up; Benedict, whom the Spaniards placed. In this schismatical ambitious conflict everyone defended his Pope, to the great disturbance of the Christian nations. This Council endured three years and five months. ... Pope John was deposed by the decree of the Council, more than three and forty most grievous and heinous crimes being proved against him: as that he had hired Marcilius Parmensis, a physician, to poison Alexander, his predecessor; further, that he was a heretic, a simoniac, a liar, a hypocrite, a murderer,

an enchanter, and a dice-player. Finally, what crime is it that he was not infected withal? In this Council of Constance nothing was decreed or enacted worthy of memory, but this only, that the Pope's authority is under the Council, and that the Council ought to judge the Pope.[9]

God graciously allowed John Wycliffe to quietly depart this mortal life at home in Lutterworth on Silvester's day, 1384. John Wycliffe had rejected the Holy sacrifice of the Mass, and also emphasized scripture as the sole rule of faith. Further, he subscribed to the position that sanctity is essential for the administration of sacraments and church membership (Donatism). He asserted the Pope is not the head of the Church, but Christ, and that bishops have no authority. This of course didn't make him very popular in Rome. John Huss preached the same after Wycliffe's death, which further agitated Rome.

Now the Roman Church powers sought to get John Huss to travel to Constance before the Council met,

> For before the Council began, the Emperor Sigismund sent certain gentlemen, Bohemians, who were of his own household, giving them in charge to bring John Huss, Bachelor of Divinity, unto the said Council. ... The Emperor did not only promise him safe conduct, that he might come freely unto Constance, but also that he should return again into Bohemia, without fraud or interruption; he promised also to receive him under his protection, and under safeguard of the whole empire.[10]

> Huss left Prague November 3rd. He arrived at Constance twenty days later. The next day ...the noble men Lord John de Clum, and Lord Henry Latzemboge, went to speak with the Pope, and certified to him that John Huss was come, desiring that he would grant the said John Huss liberty to remain in Constance, without any trouble, or vexation, or interruption. Unto whom the Pope answered – that even if John Huss had killed his brother, yet would he go about, as much as in him lay, that no outrage or hurt should be done unto him during his abode in the city of Constance.[11]

Nevertheless, shortly after his appearance he was arrested and cruelly treated. On July 6,th 1415, this godly servant and martyr of Christ was burned to death at the stake in Constance to satisfy the current Ecumenical Imperative.[12] As for John Wycliffe, forty-one years after he was laid to rest in his sepulcher, and several years after the decree from the synod of Constance, in 1415, they ungraved him, and turned him from earth to ashes; which ashes they also took and threw into the river.[13]

"Better the turban of the prophet than the Tiara of the Pope."

Pope Martin V called the 17th Ecumenical Council for Basel, Switzerland but died that same year (1431). Pope Eugene IV confirmed Martin's decree for Basel, and the first session was held on Dec 14, 1431. Believing the council would get out of control, Eugene IV dissolved it in four days. This angered the bishops at Basel so that they began to reassert the "heretical" decrees that "a general council is superior to the Pope"-which as we saw earlier was the decision at Constance. Eugene IV then ordered a new start for January 1438 in Ferrara. However, some bishops remained in open defiance at Basel. They even elected an anti-pope Felix. Thus, there were two popes and two councils at the same time. A plague hit Ferrara, and **Pope Eugene moved the Council to Florence.** The Greeks accepted some of the Roman beliefs, but a reunion failed. A quote associated with this period was, "Better the turban of the prophet than the Tiara of the Pope."

Pope Eugene IV in the Bull Cantata Domino, 1441, states *ex cathedra* (Speaking as Supreme Pontiff from the Seat of Peter):

> It (the Roman Catholic Church) firmly believes, professes, and proclaims that none of those who are not within the Catholic Church, *not only pagans, but also Jews and heretics and schismatics cannot become participants in eternal life, but will depart 'into everlasting fire which was prepared for the devil and his angels'* (Matt 25:41), unless before the end of their life the same have been added to the flock; and that the unity of Ecclesiastical body is so strong that only to those remaining in it are the sacraments of the Church of benefit for salvation, and do fastings, almsgiving, and other functions of piety and exercises of Christian service produce eternal reward, *and that no one, whatever almsgiving he has practiced, even if he as shed blood for the name of Christ, can be saved, unless he has remained in the bosom and unity of the Catholic Church.*

The avoidable capture of Constantinople by the Islamic Ottoman Turks under Muhammad II on May 29, 1453 AD was enabled by the denial of aid and support by the "Western Orthodox Church" (Roman Catholic) to the Eastern Orthodox Church. Instead of nurturing and protecting their Eastern brothers, the Roman Catholic Pope played the Nero. Thus, Turkey fell and most of the locations of the early church fell into Muslim hands. **In the 18th Council at the Basilica of St. John Lateran (Rome 1512 -1517),** the Roman church again failed to help the Eastern Christians.

Our Heavenly Father had apparently reached His limit, and, in 1517, a monk named Luther came forward at Wittenberg against certain papal excesses, offering disputation and propounding certain thesis. The Emperor Charles V summoned an assembly, or "diet" at Worms on the Rhine. Pope Leo X had demanded Luther's recanting of his views, and since he refused, he was summoned to attend in 1521. Like Huss before him, Luther refused to recant unless he could be convinced of his error by logical argument based on the scriptures. Unlike Huss, Luther had powerful friends and it was his home turf.

Who are These Wolves?

In 1529, between the **18th and 19th Ecumenical councils**, William Tyndale, who had fled to Germany from England, released the first copies of the New Testament that he had translated from the original manuscripts (instead of from the Latin Vulgate as Wickliff had done), much to the papist's displeasure. This grieved Cuthbert Tonstal, the Bishop of London. After conferencing with Luther and other learned men, Tyndale moved to the Netherlands and spent most of his time in Antwerp. Before 1537, he had translated the entire Bible into the English language. His work became the basis for most of what would become the King James Bible. But in 1537, long before the 1611 Authorized Bible appeared, Tyndale's translation was inhibited by the English King's royal decree. Further, the old gentleman was arrested and put in prison at the castle of Filford, eighteen miles from Antwerp.

> At last, after much reasoning, when no reason would serve, although he deserved no death, he was condemned by virtue of the emperor's decree, made in the assembly at Augsburg. Brought forth to the place of execution, he was tied to the stake, strangled by the hangman, and afterwards consumed with fire, at the town of Filford, A.D. 1536; crying at the stake with fervent zeal, and a loud voice, 'Lord! Open the King of England's eyes.'[14]

Quoting Luther on the state of the Roman Church-their lack of faith and their belief in their own works,

> You find people now who believe we should be silent and cause no stir, because it is impossible to convert the world. It is all in vain, they say; pope, priests, bishops, and monks reject it and they will not change their lives, what is the use to preach and storm against them?[15]

Luther called these people wolves, referencing John 10:11,16.

> Who are these wolves? It is plain that they are the tyrants, both ecclesiastical and secular, that can tolerate neither shepherd nor hireling. The pope and the bishop, together with their officials, likewise the secular princes who cling to them, are now arising and taking captive, excommunicating, anathematizing, putting in the stocks, and on the block, garroting and murdering everywhere both shepherds and hirelings....Hence the wolves are none other than those who would outwardly in deed, and inwardly by false teaching, persecute and suppress the Gospel; as the secular tyrants, the pope and all heretics do.[16]

But, in 1546 Martin Luther died. In 1539, the Society of Jesus had been founded, and in 1549 the first Jesuit missions arrived in South America. The Roman church was emboldened. **In the 19th Ecumenical council at Trent, Italy (1545 – 1549)**, *Pope Paul III condemned Luther, Calvin, and others as heretics and Protestantism as a heresy.*

One Escapes a Great Evil

Between the 19th and 20th Ecumenical Councils, a great evil was persecuting the faithful in Europe. Many fled and many died. In the same year of Sir Walter Raleigh's expedition to Virginia, and from the same city that Tyndale spent most of his time in after he moved to the Netherlands, there began a successful flight of the most successful mathematical family known.

The Bernoullis were one of many Protestant families who fled from Antwerp in 1583 to escape massacre by the Catholics (as on St. Bartholomew's Eve) in the prolonged persecution of the Huguenots. The family sought refuge first in Frankford, moving on presently to Switzerland, where they settled at Basle. The founder of the Bernoulli dynasty married into one of the oldest Basle families and became a great merchant. Nicolaus senior, who heads the genealogical table, was also a great merchant, as his grandfather and great grandfather had been.[17]

If you have limited scientific or mathematical training, you might not know the treasure these Bernoullis have been to civilization. From calculus, fluid flow, probability, catenaries-bridges and high-voltage line use, optics, theory of tides, ship sails, hydrodynamics, pure and applied fluid mechanics, mathematical physics, kinetic theory of gases, differential equations, etc., to the theory of vibrating strings, these men have contributed greatly. It is by God's good grace that Nicolaus Senior's father was able to escape the Ecumenical Imperative of the time, in the nick of time. I wonder how many such men didn't.

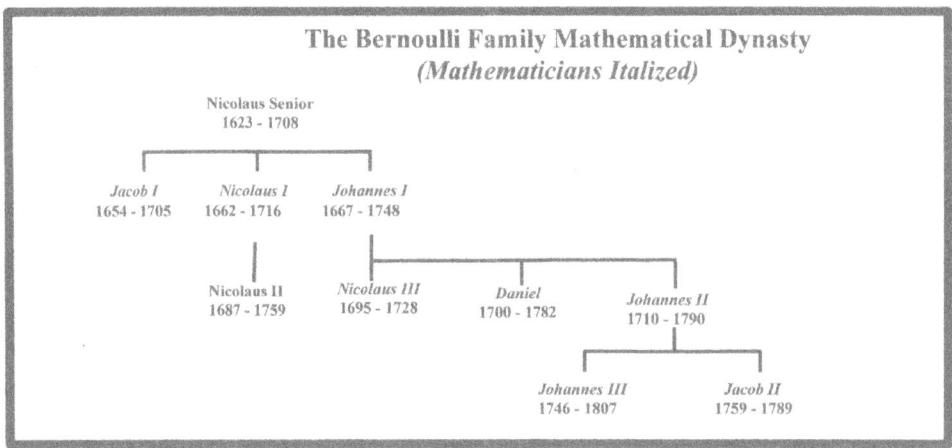

Papal Infallibility

The times were violent leading up to the next Council. In 1861, Victor Emmanuel became the first king of Italy. Abraham Lincoln became the President of the United States of America, and the American Civil War began. In 1863, the British bombarded a Japanese town. In 1864, Maximilian became Emperor of Mexico. The surrender of Appomattox Court House and the opening of Japan to the world both happened the next year. In 1866, Prussia and Italy attacked Austria and the south German states that were allied with Austria. In 1867 the Mexican Emperor Maximilian was shot.

With this as a backdrop, Pope Pius IX convened and ratified the **20th Ecumenical Council located at the Vatican (St. Peter's Basilica in the Vatican City-state 1869 – 1870)**. Here, the first Vatican Council defined the *Infallibility of the Pope* when he speaks as Supreme Pontiff from the Seat of Peter on matters of faith, morality, and doctrine. Oddly, shortly after the 20th Ecumenical Council, Pope Leo XIII initiated an effort in 1879 to reestablish a Scholastic system patterned around Aquinas and modern thought-- perhaps to divert the reformation from the Word of God.

Popes John XXIII (1958 – 1963) and Paul VI, (1963 - 1978) presided in the **21st and last Ecumenical Council – Vatican II (1962 – 1965)**, Pope John XXIII made an agreement with the Russians that for the Russian Orthodox to be present at his council, no condemnation of Communism was to be allowed! Pope Paul VI promulgated the *Novus Ordo Missae*. The emphasis expressed was that ecumenism was now to be *understood* as religious fellowship instead of conversions by Catholic missionary or coercive effort. It has proven difficult for learned Protestant Christians to believe the "religious fellowship" emphasis, when the council declared the *repeated support*

(http:www.ourladyswarriors.org/teach/lumegent.htm) for all the past Councils- the nature of which we have just reviewed. It feels more like a "New Order" from an old tyrant.

9.2.4) Dysfunctional Family Reunion

So there is the history of the "Ecumenical Imperative. It does not at all appear to be a "Nurturing and Protective Imperative" as required by Jesus. Those who presently claim that being separate from the Roman Catholic Church hurts our witness to the world because of not being reconciled (like they read the Gospel of John to mean) have lost the argument logically and historically. Logically, because the text referred to Love not reconciliation, and historically, because the act of excommunication was performed repeatedly by the Pope at the expense of the Eastern Orthodox and Western protestants.

"Reconcile" has three meanings according to Webster. The first meaning has to do with restoring to friendship or harmony, to settle or resolve a conflict. The second meaning relates to making consistent or congruous. In this context, that would require acceptance of doctrine by all concerned. And third, it means to cause to submit to or accept something unpleasant. In this context, the second and third definitions are equivalent.

Fortunately, the view of "reconciliation" as "Loving" agrees with Webster's first definition and St. John's and does not require merging with the Roman Church or accepting its unpleasant decrees or methods. The rule of law has proven far superior to the law of men. The elite do well under the rule of men, but at others' expense. Knowing this, Protestants are asked to abandon that thought and embrace the Pope.

My good friend Robert Greer's comment, "Replacing the Pope with thousands of 'infallible dogma within the statement of faith' is the same as replacing one pope with thousands of popes,"[18] is a dubious statement at best. It is the same as saying; "Replacing one king with thousands of words in a Constitution and Bill of Rights is the same thing as having thousands of kings over us." I agree laws with more matter and less art are preferable, as long as they are sufficient. However, replacing the words with many kings ignores all the sins of the rule of man, and is not equivalent.

Quoting Luther,

> Yes, it was an unspeakable and eternal shame that under the papacy, a genuine gospel sermon was nowhere to be found, nor right knowledge of God, nor true worship of God. ... Christ came to the Jews. He did not ask them beforehand whether or not he should come. This started such a stir in their land that they could not suppress it. Now

he has come to us through his gospel, without our knowledge or will, and has also started a great uproar. .…. There are many who want to resolve the matter by human wisdom, but that remains to be seen. .….

Christ himself says in Matthew 10:34, 'Think not that I am come to send peace on earth: I came not to send peace, but a sword.' Therefore, it will likely be and remain, as Simeon states, 'This child is set for the fall and rising again of many in Israel.'.… Those who try to resolve this matter through human reason will accomplish nothing; rather, they will fall, never to rise, and be smashed because of it. For they try to make Christ different from what God ordered and ordained.…

Therefore, let us not look on this Gospel as a teaching that only produces dispute, disunity, and trouble in the world. That's how the pope and his bishops complain, as though they were above reproach and had never muddied the waters. They have caused all manner of strife and misery through their sins and idol worship. If they would permit this teaching to have free course, then disunity and other troubles would soon be left behind.[19] (Emphasis mine)

The three characteristics,[20] forming the Devil's Triangle, that many scholars believe ecumenism can benefit from are:

Pluralism

Centerlessness

Subjectivism

I expanded on their meanings in a previous chapter on postmodernism, so I won't again explain their faults. Considering these three characteristics benefit ecumenism, is there any doubt who benefits from ecumenism? It is certainly not the Lord or His teaching that benefits. Christians don't want an agenda; they want Jesus Christ as Lord!

I quote Charles Haddon Spurgeon in his sermon, *The Unsearchable Riches of Christ,* where he speaks about the Roman church and the ecumenism of his day.

> A fine day is this in which we are to go back to the superstitions of the dark ages-so dark that our forefathers could not bear them-and for the unsearchable cunning of priests are to give up the unsearchable riches of Christ! We are told that the Reformation was a mistake; but we tell these false priests to their faces that they lie, and know not the truth.[21]

9.3) The True "Ecumenical Imperative"

In a sermon delivered at the Tabernacle in Salem, Massachusetts on Feb., 1812 on the occasion of the ordination of five young men, missionaries to the heathen in Asia, the young Adoniram Judson, first Christian missionary to Burma, heard Leonard Wood, D. D. speak on a number of topics. One of those topics dealt with a real *Ecumenical Imperative*.

> These things I say honestly, and in the fear of God. Christians have wanted some grand object to seize their hearts and engage all their powers; - some great and common cause in the promotion of which they might be effectually purified from error and find a grave for all their jealousies and animosities; and in which the eternal truths of Revelation might be maintained with unyielding firmness, and propagated with augmented and unconquerable zeal. The SPREAD OF THE GOSPEL and THE CONVERSION OF THE WORLD constitute the *very object* wanted. - *the common cause* which ought to unite, and has already begun to unite the affections, prayers, and labors of the great family of Christians. This harmonizing spirit among the followers of Christ forebodes good to Zion. O may it increase, and diffuse its happy influence, till Christians of every name shall be so completely occupied with the *Redeemer's cause*, as to forget *their own*.[22]

Thus, the true **Ecumenical Imperative** is the **Great Commission** commanded by the Lord.

> All authority has been given to Me in heaven and on earth. Go therefore and make disciples of all the nations, baptizing them in the Name of the Father and the Son and the Holy Spirit, teaching them to observe all that I commanded you; and lo, I am with you always, even to the end of the age.-Matthew 27:16,20.

Oddly, this missionary effort was the original purpose of the Ecumenical Councils. The efforts made since Vatican II have focused on absorption of the Protestant Bodies (*Novus Ordo Missae - The New Order of Missions*) rather than the Great Commission. The emphasis is on unified control, rather than the Savior's Command. Then again, these Councils have been focused on unified control since the Bishop of Rome declared himself the Pope. This unity of power and control is far removed from Christ's intentions recorded in the book of John - that the believers would love one another.

[1] Martin Luther, Complete Sermons of Martin Luther, Vol. 4.1, *Second Sunday After Epiphany,* Baker Books, Grand Rapids, MI, 2000, p.27

[2] Robert C. Greer, *Mapping Postmodernism*, InterVarsity Press, Downers Grove, Illinois,2003, *The Ecumenical Imperative*, p. 48

[3] Martin Luther, Complete Sermons of Martin Luther, Vol. 2.2, *Eighth Sunday After Trinity,* Baker Books, Grand Rapids, MI, 2000 p.256

[4] Robert C. Greer, *Mapping Postmodernism*, InterVarsity Press, Downers Grove, Illinois, 2003, *The Ecumenical Imperative*, p. 49

[5] H. G. Wells, *The Outline Of History*, Volume II, Garden City Books, Garden City, New York, 1956, p.549

[6] Ibid, p.545

[7] Ibid, p.p. 564, 566

[8] Ibid, p.550

[9] John Foxe, Edited by W. Grinton Berry, *Foxe's Book of Martyrs*, Baker Books, Grand Rapids, Michigan, 1990, p. 98

[10] Ibid., p. 99

[11] Ibid., p.101

[12] Ibid., p134

[13] Ibid., p69

[14] Ibid., p.p.151,152

[15] Martin Luther, Complete Sermons of Martin Luther, Vol. 1.1, *First Sunday In Advent*, Baker Books, Grand Rapids, MI, 2000 p.47

[16] Martin Luther, Complete Sermons of Martin Luther, Vol. 2.1, *Second Sunday After Easter*, Baker Books, Grand Rapids, MI, 2000 p.p. 34,35

[17] E.T. Bell, *Men of Mathematics*, Simon and Schuster, New York, 1937, p.p. 132,133

[18] Robert C. Greer, *Mapping Postmodernism*, InterVarsity Press, Downers Grove, Illinois, 2003, *The Ecumenical Imperative*, p. 66

[19] Martin Luther, Complete Sermons of Martin Luther, Vol. 5, *First Sunday After Christmas*, Baker Books, Grand Rapids, MI, 2000 p.p. 163,164

[20] Robert C. Greer, *Mapping Postmodernism*, InterVarsity Press, Downers Grove, Illinois, 2003, *The Ecumenical Imperative*, p. 64

[21] C.H Spurgeon, Spurgeon's Sermons, Vol 9, Sermon "*The Unsearchable Riches of Christ*", page 253, Baker Books 1999, Grand Rapids, Michigan.

[22] Arabella Stuart, *The Lives of the Three Mrs. Judsons*, Particular Baptist Press, Springfield, Missouri, 1999, p.280

RELEVANT COUNCIL REFERENCE BIBLIOGRAPHY:

- DENZINGER, *The Sources of Catholic Dogma*, Translated by Roy J. Deferrari from the 30th Edition of Henry Denzinger's Enchiridion Symbolorum, St. Louis, Mo.: B. Herder Book Co., 1957. (Imprimatur).

- HUGHES, Philip, *A Popular History of the Catholic Church*, New York: Macmillan Publishing Co. Inc., 1947. (Imprimatur index, tables of Popes and emperors, 320pp.)

- LAUX, Rev. John L., *Church History*, Rockford, Illinois 61105: Tan Books & Publishers, 1989 (1945 Benzinger Bros.,N.Y.). (Imprimatur, index and appendices, 621pp.)

- MURPHY, Fr. John L., *The General Councils of the Church*, Milwaukee: The Bruce Publishing Company, 1960. (Imprimatur, index 193pp., photos [8 plates], map [opp. p.1] of SITEs of the General Councils.)

- SLAVES of the IMMACULATE HEART of MARY, *Saints to Remember*, Still River, Mass.: St. Benedict Center, 1961.

9.4) On the Sacraments

Some believe that a sacrament is a channel of grace. They accept this as a definition. Martin Luther stated,

> We believe that the true body and blood of Christ is under the bread and wine, even as it is. Here we see one thing and believe another, which describes faith." He went on to say, "The sacrament is to act upon us so that we may be transformed and become different people.[1]

But is every channel of grace a sacrament? In the 12th century, Hugo of St. Victor spoke of as many as thirty Sacraments, but Peter Lombard of the same period estimate it at seven, and it is still the officially accepted number for the Roman Church. An obligation to continue sacramental rites depend on:

- Their institution by Christ.

- His express command for their continuance.

- Their essential use as symbols of divine acts integral to the Gospel revelation

There are only two rites obligatory in these ways on all Christians. There is no scriptural warrant for giving the other so-called sacramental rites (i.e. Confirmation, Orders, Matrimony, Penance, Extreme Unction) the same status as baptism and the Lord's Supper."[2]

Webster's first definition for a sacrament is :

> A formal religious act that is sacred as a sign or a symbol of a spiritual reality; esp.: one believed to have been instituted by Jesus Christ.

Charles Spurgeon's definition agrees with Webster that a sacrament, like baptism or communion, was like the shell of an egg. There is no life in the shell itself. It has the form of the egg, and does contain the egg itself, where there is life. Therefore, even though the shell contains no life (or grace, or power to save), we dare not alter it or crack the shell because that might threaten the life in the egg it embodies.

With this Protestant view of sacraments, the Church would be inappropriately considered a sacrament. It is not to be the lifeless shell pointing to the life. It is the "Bride of Christ," the living, breathing body of Christ who is one with His Bride. She is no symbol, no sign, but a life. We are the Church, not the institutions. The Church is the family, not the family business.

Having said all that, however, the church *meeting* is a channel of grace, and the church *meeting* is supposed to act upon us so that we may be transformed and become different people. Thus, the *meeting* of the saints for the hearing of the Word satisfies Luther's definition of a sacrament. Since Christ told Peter to "feed my sheep," and the rest of the Gospel speaks on the need to gather with fellow Christians, I'm inclined to side with Luther's definition and the church *meeting* as a sacrament. Thus, it is our view that there are only *three* rites obligatory in these ways on all Christians, baptism, Lord's Supper, and Church attendance.

I have been wrestling with the contrasts between the Catholic view on one hand that the sacraments are reality and the current Protestant view that they are symbolic. Dr. Martin Luther's understanding of the sacraments would be called Catholic today. I have reluctantly come around to a position that everyone probably disagrees with but is close to Luther's. ***I think they are a symbol becoming reality.***

Consider the Lord's Supper, for example:

> I know that I am part of the Body of Christ.
>
> I know that the bread is just bread before I eat it, but it becomes part of my body and therefore part of The Body.
>
> I know that the wine is just wine or juice before I drink it, but it becomes part of my blood and therefore part of The Blood of the Body.

Or consider the Baptism,

> I know that John baptized with water, and that he was preparing the Way.
>
> I know that God ordained John's work.
>
> I know that John could not have baptized with the Holy Spirit.
>
> I know that John's baptism of repentance was not in Jesus' name and did not include the Holy Spirit's infilling. – Acts 19:2,5
>
> I know that the Holy Spirit watched at least Jesus' baptism.

I know that Jesus' baptism commenced his ministry.

I know Jesus told Nicodemus he must be born anew.

I know Jesus said that one needs be born of the water and the Spirit.

I believe that God would save a test-tube baby once grown, if a believer.

I know that Peter said in Acts 2:38, "Repent, and let each of you be baptized in the name of Jesus for the forgiveness of your sins; and you shall receive the gift of the Holy Spirit."

I know, "There is one body and one Spirit, just as also you were called in one hope of your calling; one Lord, one faith, *one baptism*, one God …." Eph 4:4,6

I know that Christ so ordered his statement to Nicodemus so as to include both water and The Spirit.

Quoting Luther,

> Hence both must remain united, and a person must be born anew, of water, by the Holy Spirit, or of the Holy Spirit with and by the water."[3]

"The Holy Spirit acting at this birth is the male, and the water is the female part, or mother.[4]

Knowing and believing all this compels me to believe that the Christian Baptism in Jesus' name is more than a symbol, even though it is also a symbol, *and must be a symbol becoming a reality*.

There's no church meeting in the examples above, but the reasoning applies to it also. The church meeting is the congregation of saints praising her Lord as she is becoming the Bride of Christ. Since the Lord dwells in the praises of His saints, it must be that the Word has Penetrated His Bride and she sits with Him on the right hand of the Father.

> For we have all been given birth by the Christian church which is the immaculate virgin in spirit; for she (the church) has the pure word Word of God and the Holy Sacraments through which she becomes pregnant and again and again gives birth to Christians who are the true firstborn and the Lord God's very own—I as well as you, you as well as I. Now it is a true reality, where before it was merely prefigured for us.[5]

[1] Complete Sermons of Martin Luther, Vol. 1.2, *The Lord's Supper*, p213-214, Baker Books, Grand Rapids, MI, 2000

[2] J.D. Douglas, *The New Bible Dictionary*, WM. B. Eerdmans, Grand Rapids, Michigan, 1979, p. 1113

[3] Complete Sermons of Martin Luther, Vol. 2.1, *The Lord's Supper*, p435, Baker Books, Grand Rapids, MI, 2000

[4]   Ibid.

[5] Complete Sermons of Martin Luther, Vol. 5, *The Day Of The Purification Of Mary*, p301, Baker Books, Grand Rapids, MI, 2000

9.5) It All Depends On What *Is* Is

I have one last point of contention with the later-day wordsmiths who twist language to honor their idols. Even though *God is Love*, as 1 John 4:8 declares, that does *not* mean *Love is God*. Why? Because God is: Love, Justice, Existence, Mercy, Grace, Goodness, etc. This statement is not an algebraic statement, like y =x so x = y. This is a logical statement of God contains Love, or conversely, Love is an element of God. In a multi-element set, an element does not equal the set. Some have erred so far with the "x = y means y = x" idea here that they create another god, as we read next.

> But it would also be illogical to dispute the reversibility of the statement "God is love." It is, after all, consequent, 'as long as there is European logic ... ,' that "from x=y for every value of x and y: y=x, where x and y are signs for two individuals and the identity relationship asserted for x and y is so defined that every characteristic of x is also a characteristic of y, and vice versa.' Then the theological question becomes all the more urgent: Is this not an endorsement of the deification of human love relationships?[1]

This is not the equation of a straight line, with God on the ordinate and Love on the abscissa. The statement "God *is* Love" does not carry with it the meaning "every characteristic of *God* is also a characteristic of *love*, and vice versa." So the assumption in this argument is false. As I mentioned earlier, this is a statement of possession of an element, or a containment of a member of a set -- God contains Love, or Love is an element of God.

Let me dispense with algebra and set theory and just give a reasonable example. We are in a business meeting and our company has an important customer that came to see our operation. The executive staff members are present and are to be introduced to the customer. The president speaks,

> I want to introduce you to Bob Gilbert, Bob is Sales; Dave Smith, Dave is Marketing, Larry Archer, Larry is Engineering, Doug Fairbanks, Doug is Finance, etc.

The idea displayed here is that the "*x is y*" statement is not an algebraic statement, but rather an idea of "responsible for" or "manages" or "has responsibilities that contain or include" or "oversees." So that the sentence "God is Love." Could be read as,

"God manages Love." Or,

"God has responsibilities that include Love." Or,

"God oversees Love."

Further, we are not to reason affirmatively about God's Nature, because affirmations are inadequate. [2] Negations, however, can be adequate when they are true. We should not reason such as, "God is love, therefore...," rather we should reason "God is not just love, therefore...." We should not use ourselves as a measure of God. When we reason, we start from zero and work up. God starts at infinity, and projects down.

> The affirmative statements are understood here rather as predictions which burdens God with lesser values which reduce the divinity of God, whereas the negative statements are looked on as the affirmative predictions of the absolute superiority of God because they remove everything nondivine from God.[3]

[1]   Eberhard Jüngel, *God as the Mystery of the World*, transl.: Darell L. Guder (Grand Rapids: Eerdmans Publishing Company, 1983), p. 331

[2]   Ibid., p.234

[3]   Ibid., p.235

Larry Sheets

10) Four-Dimensional Thinking

10.1) The Issue

Because of the following considerations, I believe it is idolatry to think the Creator can be bound by His creations of space and time.

- I consider that if anything were capable of binding God, it is worthy of praise and respect and generally suitable to worship e.g., His Word, His attributes, His Love.
- I consider it Idolatry to worship any created thing; idolatry is the belief that created things are worthy of worship.
- I believe Idolatry is pernicious.
- Space, time, creatures, and all things known and unknown, with the exception of God, are His creation.

Thus, I consider it pernicious to believe that His Creation can bind the Creator. If all this is true, then it would be pernicious to believe the following false statement:

If God were immutable, then He would be frozen in time! Therefore, He must be a God in time and, thus, bound by time.

Immutability of attributes is *not* the same idea as frozen in time. James writes,

> Every good thing given and every perfect gift is from above, coming down from the Father of lights, with whom there is no variation or [a]shifting shadow. - James 1:17 (NIV)

He cannot be frozen while He is bestowing gifts, but there is still no variation, or shifting shadow with Him. Believers expect immutable health when "we shall be like Him." This idea that God would be frozen in time if He weren't changing is due to a four dimensional view of God.

10.2) Definitions

A point has zero dimensionality. A line is one-dimensional. A picture has two dimensions, height and width. A motion picture has three dimensions, height, width and time. A 3D motion picture attempts to display height, width, depth and time. The "3D" referred to only the three dimensions of distance, it failed to advertise the 4th dimension of time because movie goers are not mathematicians! It is even possible to describe the synchronized movie *sound* as an added dimension.

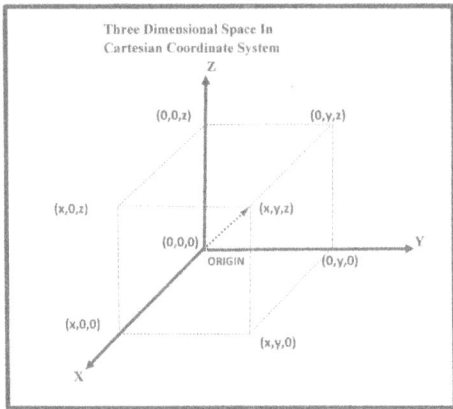

10.3) Time, Light, and Creation

When dealing with the four dimensions, three of them spatial and one temporal, physicists multiply the time variable "t" by the speed of light "c" to create a variable "ct." This variable has units of distance like the other three and makes the mathematics simpler. If you can conceive of a sphere of three dimensions, at the origin, with a radius equal to the square root of the sum of the squares of the x, y, and z coordinates defining its surface, then you should be able to conceive of a radius of the square root of the sum of the squares of the 4 dimensions (x, y, z, and ct) describing a sphere in 4-dimensional space. Even though you may conceive the 4 dimensional sphere, don't feel bad that you cannot picture it. We have our limits, we conceive here by analogy.

Linear Algebraists have been calculating and manipulating N-dimensional matrices for many decades. Cosmologists studying the Big Bang Theory of creation, as well as string theories have no difficulty believing that there were initially 10 dimensions that rapidly condensed to four in this universe of ours. Atomic physicists, as far as this student is able to determine, have not given labels or names to the dimensions above four that they work with in these theories.

The Creator of the universe used those dimensions to get the job done. He must have had them in order to use them. In fact, He has infinitude of dimensions at His disposal and "contained by Him." We only get to see the projected image of God in these 3 spatial dimensions and time, but His activity is well beyond what we can perceive rationally. Martin Luther addressed these issues in a sermon about the disciples who had locked themselves into a room for fear of the Jews.

> But the fact that Christ comes to the disciples through the door that is closed, we are to learn that after his resurrection and in his kingdom here upon earth he is no longer bound by bodily, visible, tangible and worldly things, as time, place, and the like, but that he is to be recognized and believed in as one who through his power can reign everywhere, who can be present with us at all places and at all times, when and wherever necessary, and who will help us without being taken captive and hindered by the world and its power.[1]

[1]   Complete Sermons of Martin Luther, Vol. 1.2, *First Sunday After Easter*, p383-384, Baker Books, Grand Rapids, MI, 2000

11) The Believer's Transfiguration

There will come a time when Christ's disciples will be gathered, glorified and exalted. There will be a marked change in form and/or appearance that will be a real and eternal metamorphosis. To quote John,

> Beloved, we are God's children now; it does not yet appear what we shall be, but we know that when he appears we shall be like him, for we shall see him as he is. 1 John 3:2 (NIV)

11.1) Finite Or Infinite

James K.A. Smith, however, believes that as created beings we are by nature-and will always be- finite.[1] But we just read, "We shall be like Him." Smith seems to have forgotten the principal work of Christ-Sonship in Christ (Gal 4:4-7),

> But when the fullness of the time came, God sent forth His Son, born of a woman, born under the Law, in order that He might redeem those who were under the Law, that we might receive adoption as sons. And because you are sons, God has sent forth the Spirit of His Son into our hearts, crying, 'ABBA! Father!' Therefore, you are no longer a slave, but a son; and if a son, then an heir through God.

As in the case of the coupled Stand-alone oscillator described in "The Abiding Truth" section, the rest will become like Him. First there is the quotidian transformation referenced in 2 Cor. 18,

> But we all, with unveiled face beholding as in a mirror the glory of the Lord, are being transformed into the same image from glory to glory, just as from the Lord, the Spirit.

However, the verse from 1 John 3:2 supports the perfect final transformation of 1 Cor 13:12,

> For now, we see in a mirror dimly, but then face to face; now I know in part, but then I shall know fully just as I also have been fully known.

A mirror reduces the dimensionality. A poor mirror reduces the intensity of the object, distorts the image, and reduces the distinctive definitions. Thus, when we shall see Him as He really is, with His full dimensionality, intensity, clarity and distinction, then" we shall be like Him!" That is, synchronized to the Divine.

Our language will be transformed too!

> For then will I turn to the people a pure language, that they may all call upon the name of the LORD, to serve him with one consent. - (Zephaniah 3:9) Luther wrote,

> This is what I have often said, that faith makes of us lords, and love makes us servants. Indeed, by faith we become gods and partakers of the divine nature and name, as is said in Psalms 82,6:'I said, Ye are gods, and all of you sons of the Most High.' ... Of this we have spoken often enough, namely, that we also must by faith be born God's sons and gods, lords and kings, even as Christ is born true God of the Father in eternity; and again, come out of ourselves by love and help our neighbors with kind deeds, even as Christ became man to help us all.[2]

He also declared,

> Now if I believe on him, I become partaker with him of all his possessions, and obtain not only a part or a piece; but, like him, I obtain all, eternal righteousness, eternal wisdom, eternal strength, and become a lord and reign overall,[3]

What did Adam mean when he used these same words to describe Eve? "For we are members of his body, of his flesh and of his bones"- Eph. 5:30. The great husband of our souls must mean the same, only in a more spiritual and emphatic way? According to Spurgeon, "He meant that she was of the same race, a participant in the same nature: he recognized her as a being of the same order as himself."[4] "There is between you and your Lord a similarity of nature, an intimate relationship; you have a mysterious extraction from him, and he has a loving possession of you, and a vital union with you."[5]

11.2) Nothing Will Be Impossible For You

In Matthew 17:20 Jesus said

> Because you have so little faith, *I tell you the truth*, if you have faith as small as a mustard seed, you can say to this Mountain, 'Move from here to there' and it will move. *Nothing will be impossible for you.*

First, we'll comment on the mountain, and then on the amazing statement that followed. The *mountain moving* statement is supposed to have come from a common Hebrew saying and was not, therefore, intended to be a literal. Not that anything is impossible with God. But how much energy does it take to move a mountain?

By the calculation in Appendix E, raising it 5000 ft to clear the mountains in the way would require 2.7×10^{17} Joules of energy. This energy by Einstein's $E=mc^2$ is equivalent to 3 kg or 6.6 lbs of mass in the English system.

Remember the fish and the loaves that Jesus made when he feed the 5000 men? Suppose each of the 5000 ate or wasted a total of 0.5 pound of food. That means that he literally created 2500 pounds of mass to feed the people. That is equivalent to moving 2500/6.6 = 379 mountains! *So moving one mountain is a small act of faith compared to creating the food to feed 5000.*

But that's not all! "Nothing will be impossible for you." That's right, *nothing*. I cannot in faith believe that my God was using hyperbole here, when He opens the comment up with "I tell you the truth." What we call impossible is viewed from the kind of numbers and calculations we just went through. But it must be that difficulty is measured differently in the divine.

When Jesus was resurrected and had gone to the Father, He came into the room to confront Thomas about his doubts. He passed through the locked door, but His body was solid because Thomas was given a tactile demonstration of the wounds. Quantum physics asserts that if you throw a ball at a wall often enough, it will pass through, or get stuck part way through. The passing through a door or wall of an adult male body has minuscule chance of happening, but Jesus did it at will. *Impossibility has different meanings to those who just analyze the world and He who synthesizes it.*

- In summary. We as joint heirs with Christ will become like Him when He appears because we shall see Him just as He is, and we shall know Him fully, just as we have been fully known by Him. We will not always be finite- not in time, not in knowledge, and probably not even in power. Mathematicians understand that there are different orders of infinity. These are referred [6] to as "first order poles, or second order poles etc" *Some infinities are higher order than other infinities.*

- ...for star differs from star in glory. So also is the resurrection of the dead. It is sown a perishable body, it is raised an imperishable body; it is sown in dishonor, it is raised in glory; it is sown in weakness, it is raised in power; ... And just as we have borne the image of the earthly, we shall also bear the image of the heavenly.- 1 Cor. 15:41-49.

- And in the time of their visitation they shall shine, and run to and fro like sparks among the stubble. They shall judge the nations, and have dominion over the people, and their Lord shall reign forever. They that put their trust in Him shall understand the truth: and such as be faithful in love shall abide with Him: for grace and mercy is to His saints, and He hath care for His elect.– Wisdom 3:7,9

- Therefore, there is no confusion between the creature and the Creator by us accepting such lavish gifts. God grants His inheritance to His children. He is not simply giving gifts; he is giving attributes for His Name's sake, because He is adopting us.

[1]　Robert C. Greer, *Mapping Postmodernism*, InterVarsity Press, Downers Grove, Illinois, 2003, p. 29

[2]　Martin Luther, <u>Complete Sermons of Martin Luther</u>, Vol. 1.2, *Third Sunday After Epiphany*, p73-74, Baker Books, Grand Rapids, MI, 2000

[3]　Martin Luther, <u>Complete Sermons of Martin Luther</u>, Vol. 1.2, *Easter Sunday*, p218, Baker Books, Grand Rapids, MI, 2000

[4]   C.H Spurgeon, <u>Spurgeon's Sermons</u>, Vol 10, Sermon "*The Matchless Mystery*", page 14, BakerBooks 1999, Grand Rapids, Michigan.

[5]   C.H Spurgeon, <u>Spurgeon's Sermons</u>, Vol 10, Sermon "*The Matchless Mystery*", page 22, BakerBooks 1999, Grand Rapids, Michigan.

[6]   Ruel V. Churchill, *Complex Variables And Applications*, McGraw-Hill, New York, 1960, Section 68 – *Poles*, p.15

Part Seven – A Way of Equivalence Relation Thinking
12) Equivalence Relation Thinking

> "I have often said that God acts toward man even as man is disposed; as thou thinkest and believeth concerning him, such he is to thee."[1]

> "If our hearts picture him as gracious or angry, pleasant or harsh, we have him that way."[2]

Luther reflected on the symmetrical, or reciprocal, relationship God has with his servants.

Equivalence relationships have not been dealt with yet. They play an exceeding important role in Switching and Automata Theory underlying electronic computing. More than that, the principals involved in equivalence relationships affect our lives, emotions, songs, names and words. An equivalence relationship is a relation between elements of a set that is reflexive, symmetric, and transitive. Without being overly symbolic, let me explain using "R" as the relationship. Then, if x is in relationship R with y, then xRy. With this notation, the three conditions of reflexivity, symmetry, and transitivity are explained below.

A relation R on the Set S is called an equivalence relation on S if R satisfies the following conditions

1. xRx   reflexivity

2. xRy requires that yRx   symmetry

3. xRy and yRz requires that xRz   transitivity.

Stated in English,

(1) means that every element is in the relationship with itself.

(2) means that all such relationships are reciprocal.

(3) means that if a relation holds between a first and second element, and it also holds between the second element and a third, it must necessarily hold between the first and third elements.

Several examples of equivalence relationships are, equality (=) in arithmetic or algebra, congruency in geometry, equivalence ($\leftrightarrow$) in the prepositional or predicate calculus, and "having the same cardinal number" between sets. A very interesting property of an equivalence relationship is that it leads to a partition.

An equivalence relationship R partitions a set S into disjoint equivalence classes such that every element of S is in one and only one equivalence class."... "Thus, every equivalence relation induces a partition. The converse is also true."... "Thus partitions and equivalence relations are essentially the same concept."[3]

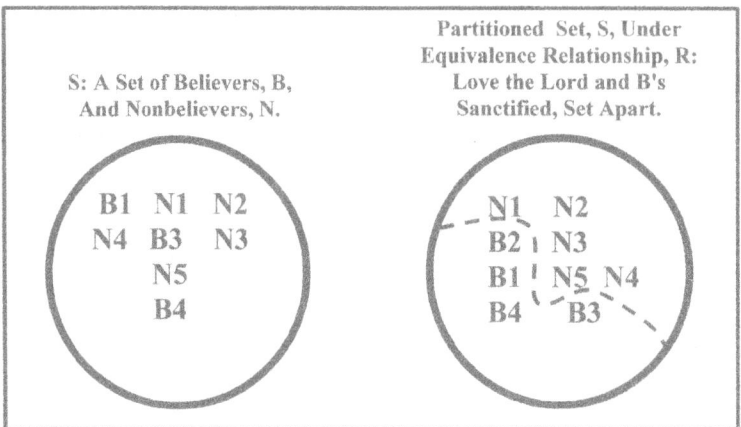

12.1) Equivalence Relation and Sanctification

Now all this seems pretty dry, but let us bring it home. Sanctification means to be set apart. Sanctification doesn't mean to make sinless or perfect as Jesus said: "*For their sakes I sanctify myself.*"- John 17:19 Jesus was already sinless. Jesus simply set Himself apart for the Father to finish the work of redemption. "Sanctification" is taking something and setting it apart, or separating it, for some special use.

Setting apart, or separating something from the many is also what "partitioning" means. Thus we see that the work of redemption accomplished by Jesus involves an equivalence relationship, since I have stated earlier that it is the same concept as partitioning. Therefore, our redemption puts us into an equivalence relationship with the Trinity. That is, the holy equivalence relationship that the Father has with Jesus, Jesus now has with us.

That relationship, through transitivity and symmetry, gives us the same relationship with the Father The equivalence class we find ourselves in, once redeemed, is the same as God's. The unredeemed are in another class partitioned separate from us. Thus, the set of the universe of the living is partitioned into The Kingdom of God, and the kingdom of Satan. It is my belief that the relationship is one of True Love. It might be more, but it is at least that.

12.2) Examples
12.2.1) Adoption and Redemption

Lets look at True Love as a relationship. (1) says that to be a true lover, you must love yourself. (2) Says that if R is a True Love between x and y, that if x loves y then y must necessarily love x. And (3) means that if x truly loves y, and y truly loves z, then x will necessarily love z. Further, by (1), z would necessarily love x. This gets real in the loving of a widow and her children. It gets even more profound when you identify x as God the Father, y as God the Son, and z as the sinner, me.

12.2.2) Hot coals on his head

Getting less wordy, lets look at the essentials of an example:
If
$$R \text{ is Love,}$$
$$x \text{ is God,}$$
$$I \text{ am } y,$$
$$I \text{ love God: } yRx$$
$$\text{my enemy is } z,$$

Suppose my enemy loves God: zRx
Then
$\quad xRz$ by symmetry

Then if I love my enemy, yRz, I have completed the requirements for zRx and xRy. That is zRy, my enemy will be in a loving relationship with me without knowing it. I had better love my enemy if he loves God. Because if I do, then my enemy will be in an equivalence relationship with me by the three conditions mentioned earlier. It will be like pouring hot coals on his head.

12.2.3) I love God because He first loved me

If
$$R \text{ is Love,}$$
$$\text{The Father is } x$$
$$\text{Jesus is } y,$$
$$I \text{ am } z,$$

then
$$\text{the Father loves Jesus, (by } R\text{)}$$
$$\text{Jesus loves me, (by } R\text{)}$$
$$\text{Thus the Father loves me (transitivity)}$$
$$I \text{ love Jesus, (symmetry)}$$
$$\text{Jesus loves the Father (symmetry)}$$
$$\text{Therefore I love the Father.(transitivity)}$$

12.2.4) Why the Trinity of God?

Let R be an unnamed equivalence relationship.
Let x, y, and z be the Father, Son, and Holy Spirit, respectively.
Transitivity (xRy and yRz requires xRz) is necessary for R to be an equivalence relationship.
- If there were not three elements in the God Set S, it couldn't be an equivalence set.

- If there were no divine equivalence relation, there would be no partitioning, or sanctification.
- If there were no sanctification, there would be no redemption.

Thus, if there were not three elements in the Divine System God Set, S, I could not be saved. For our sakes then did God present Himself in three Classes or faces or Persons. "*For their sakes I sanctify myself.*"- John 17:19 which as we have seen could have been written, "*For their sakes I partition myself.*"

12.3 Why Christ Went To The Father

Consider the following statements made by Jesus before he died.

- But that the world may know that I love the Father, and as the Father gave me commandment, even so I do…Jesus from John 14:31
- A new command I give you: Love one another. As I have loved you, so you must love one another. Jesus in John 14:34 (NIV)
- He that hath my commandments, and keepeth them, he it is that loveth me: and he that loveth me shall be loved of my Father, and I will love him, and will manifest myself to him. Jesus in John 14:21 (NIV)
- Anyone who does not love me will not obey my teaching. These words you hear are not my own; they belong to the Father who sent me. Jesus in John 14:24 (NIV)
- Anyone who loves me will obey my teaching. My Father will love them, and we will come to them and make our home with them. – Jesus in John 14:23 (NIV)
- … the Father himself loves you because you have loved me and have believed that I came from God. Jesus in John 16:27 (NIV)
- And for their sakes I sanctify Myself, that they themselves also may be sanctified in truth. Jesus in John 17:19

Father's Word = My word = w = truth=
= My commandments = Love The Father + Trust Your Savior + Love your neighbor as yourself+ love one another +love your enemy + bless those who harm you because of Jesus sake.

- But the Helper, the Holy Spirit, whom the **Father will send in My name**. Jesus in John 14: 26
- They are not of the world, even as I am not of the world. Sanctify them in the truth: Thy word is truth. Jesus in John 17:16,17

Thus, the partitioning equivalence relationship is the Word, which is truth.

The Witness and Spirit of Truth

- And for their sakes I sanctify Myself, that they themselves also may be sanctified in truth. Jesus in John 17:19

R is the equivalence relationship of "those who keep My word, that is the Father's word, that is truth, that is My commandments, that is the Father's commandment to Jesus, that is = Love The Father + Trust Jesus + Love your neighbor as yourself + love one another + love your enemy + bless those who harm you because of Jesus sake."

        x is Father
        y is Son
        z is anyone
        w is My word

yRy - Jesus R Jesus - John 17:19
if zRz then zRy, since yRy - John 14:21
if zRy then zRx, since yRx - John 14:21

Since spirits keep or contain truth, and the Holy Spirit will contain the truth that is in this equivalence relationship, R, the Holy Spirit will contain us since we contain the Word, that is the truth. Thus, we will abide in the Spirit, and the Spirit in us. The Father, Love, sends the Spirit of Truth in the name of Jesus. Jesus' Name is the Word, which is truth. Thus, Love sends Truth in the name of the Word.

All is a beautiful equivalence relationship and partition except for the statement:

> If you loved me, you would be glad that I am going to the Father, for the Father is greater than I. Jesus from John 14:28 (NIV)

That "**greater than I**" is not support for an equivalence relationship, unless the relationship becomes greater because Christ is glorified. God the Father had more power than Jesus when He was in Human form. But when He went to the Father, He assumed His rightful power. I suspect that when Jesus saw the Father again clearly, He became like the Father. It is just as he said it would happen to us,

> Beloved, we are God's children now; it does not yet appear what we shall be, but we know that when he appears we shall be like him, for we shall see him as he is. 1 John 3:2 (NIV)

But you don't have to believe that about Jesus, all we have to know is that when He assumed his original office of Son Of God, He was transformed to the glorious but awful Holy One John saw in Revelations 1:13.

Thus, in the same way as we will transform, Christ transformed when He went to the Father and saw Him. Since we were in an equivalence relationship with Him when He transformed, we should rejoice because our relationship holds and we are made into the glorified relationship that Jesus has with the Father once He went to the Father. It is *as if* 1 John 3:2 could be read,

Beloved, now we are children of God, and it has not appeared as yet what we shall be. We know that, when we go to Jesus and He is apparent, we shall be like Him, because we shall see Him just as He is.

Therefore, we have an exceedingly excellent equivalence relationship because of John 14:28. The one we had with Jesus the Son of Man cannot be broken, further, the divine equivalence relationship that Jesus the Son of God had before becoming Human could not be broken, and was reestablished with the Father when He went to the Father. The result is that the equivalence relationship we were in with the Son of Man became the equivalence relationship we have with the Son of God.

Jesus said in John 14:28 "If you loved Me, you would have rejoiced, because I go the Father; for the Father is greater than I." You see, if the disciples loved Him, the disciples would be in the equivalence relationship with the Son of Man. Once Jesus reassumed the position or office of Son of God, the disciples assumed the position of children of God. This is why they should rejoice because He went to the Father. Because the Holy Spirit was in the equivalence relationship with the Son of God, He became related to us once the Son went to the Father.

Let's attempt to throw a wrench into the gears here. God is capable of returning good for injury. However, if He does that, it is not reciprocal and at that moment there can't be an equivalence relationship. Let's compare divine behavior with other known behavior.

- To return injury for injury is bestial.
- To return good for good is human.
- To return injury for good is Satanic.
- To return good for injury is Godly.

Only the first two behaviors are reciprocal. They are found in God's natural creation. The last two demonstrate a spiritual influence. Although the equivalence relationship concept explains much about our God, it certainly doesn't explain the behavior of divine love. It doesn't explain how God decides to be reciprocal for one situation, and blessedly unreciprocal when protecting us. The answer is that when in Christ, we are not subject to the ill effects of reciprocity because of the Father's negative action toward the Son of Man on the Cross. The equivalence relationship of true love abides, but the requirement is that we trust Him, that we have faith in His love. Love trumped reciprocity at the Cross, and love powers our faith in His love.

Luther espoused the dominance of love. "If laws do not serve love, they may be annulled at once, be they God's or man's commands."[4] "Yea, if these commandments oppose the love of our neighbor, he wants us to renounce and annul them."[5] "No commandment should be in force, except those in which the law of love can be exercised."[6] If we keep the law, we show love to the Lord, but if that comes at the expense of our neighbor, Luther believes Christ wants us to renounce the law:

> Therefore, when the law impels one against love, it ceases and should no longer be a law; but where no obstacle is in the way, the keeping of the law is a proof of love, which lies hidden in the heart. Therefore, ye have need of the law, that love may be manifested; but if it cannot be kept without injury to our neighbor, God wants us to suspend and ignore the law.[7]
>
> Hence, as already stated, the law is to be only an exercise to prove our love; otherwise, aside from love, God never inquires about works, no matter how excellent they are.[8]

Writing about Christ, Luther explains the relationship of true love is the basis of the law, not the other way around.

> Their blindness he dispels, in that he teaches them what the law is, namely: that love is the law.[9]

I am forced to conclude that the Father preferred, and still prefers, a reciprocal loving relationship with His children. However, when sin entered the picture, the reciprocal relationship required the penalties of the law of reciprocity. Moses tried to show us what reciprocity requires in a relationship with a holy God. That drove His children farther away, and saved none. True love only exists in an equivalence relationship, and He had that with

His Son and Holy Spirit. St. Augustine taught that the bond of love that exists between the Father and the Son is the Holy Spirit.

The Son was willing to represent man, as the Son of Man, and take the punishment of the law so that the equivalence relationship could continue with man. With an equivalence relationship, you have to "take the good with the bad" as in "For better or worse, in sickness or in health." However, to maintain the relationship, Jesus had to die and pay that reciprocity price. In the Council of God, the Holy Spirit had agreed to resurrect the Son of Man. By dying for our sins, Jesus wins our love and reestablishes the equivalence relationship with Him. But by going to the Father, He unites two equivalence relationships into one. With this, the Holy Spirit is related to us and we are suitable for his indwelling.

[1] Martin Luther, <u>Complete Sermons of Martin Luther</u>, Vol. 3.1, *Twenty-Third Sunday After Trinity*, Baker Books, Grand Rapids, MI, 2000, p313

[2] Ibid, p313

[3] Michael A. Harrison, *Introduction to Switching and Automata Theory*, McGraw-Hill, New York, 1965, p.p. 10,11

[4] Martin Luther, <u>Complete Sermons of Martin Luther</u>, Vol. 3.1, *Seventeenth Sunday After Trinity*, Baker Books, Grand Rapids, MI, 2000, p165

[5] Martin Luther, <u>Complete Sermons of Martin Luther</u>, Vol. 3.1, *Eighteenth Sunday After Trinity*, Baker Books, Grand Rapids, MI, 2000, p174

[6] Ibid, p176

[7] Ibid, p175

[8] Ibid, p177

[9] Ibid, p177

Part Eight – Analogic and Algebraic Thinking

13: Analogy, Parable and Metaphor

13.1: Analogies

The method of analogy was used quite extensively in electrical engineering before the advent of the digital computer. Using analogies called "force-current" or "force-voltage" analogies often used analog computers to solve mechanical problems. Such analogies were exact and the answers were correct. Appendix F includes another oscillator analogy to demonstrate the need for imperfect, or nonlinear terms, to realize the design of an oscillator, the fundamental life. Appendix G demonstrates by mathematical analogy how a sinless man is necessary to undo the sins of another. It further demonstrates the need for bringing only your sin, and not your righteousness to the cross for redemption to be accomplished. These analogies require a working knowledge of algebra to appreciate or critique. They are included to demonstrate the use of algebra as a precise language for theology. Here, though, we consider the Master's analogies.

Our Lord used analogies in the form of parables to explain his relationship to us. We can say that Jesus is the analogy of the Father without reservation, like it is said Jesus is the parable of God.[1] Let's go back to the Old Testament and work forward and look at the analogies employed.

- Abraham was willing to offer his son for God. Abraham is an analogy to God the Father who offered up His Son for us.
- Isaac was willing to be a sacrifice at his father's request. Jesus was willing to be a sacrifice at His Father's request.
- Isaac carried wood on his shoulders for the sacrifice up the hill.
- Jesus carried the wooden cross for the sacrifice up the hill.
- Isaac had two sons, the first was his father's favorite, but he didn't receive his father's blessing because of an interest in worldly things. His brother, Jacob received the blessing and it made Esau jealous.
- Israel was Jesus' favorite, but the Gentiles received the blessed grace and it made the Jews jealous.
- The descendants of Israel became slaves to the Pharaoh who knew not Joseph. The Gentile believers became slaves to the Pope who knew not Jesus.
- Moses and God's Plagues on the Egyptian empire freed the Israeli slaves. Luther and God's Plagues, such as the Turks, freed the Gentile believers who became slaves.
- The kingdom of Solomon became divided North and South because of pride and treachery.
- The Church of Christ became divided East and West because of pride and treachery.

- The divided kingdoms of Israel and Judah went into exiles because of their idolatrous ways.
- The divided Church of Christ was exiled during the inquisition.

I could go on, but the analogies become more and more politically incorrect. So I'll cease and desist for now and let you the reader add to the list.

13.2) The Parables of Jesus

The parables of Jesus are analogies to principles or people. He explains the reason why He resorts to them in Matthew 13:13,

> Therefore, I speak to them in Parables; because while seeing they do not see; and while hearing they do not hear, nor do they understand.

He indicated earlier in Matthew 13:11 that the parables contained the mysteries or secrets of the Kingdom. In Matthew 13:34,35 it's recorded

> All these things Jesus spoke to the multitudes in parables, and He did not speak to them without a parable, so that what was spoken through the prophet might be fulfilled, saying,
>
> *'I will open My mouth in Parables;*
>
> *I will utter things hidden since the foundation of the world'*-Ps.78:2"

Apparently, the method of situational analogy, or parable, is capable of skirting the defenses of our minds and depositing truth directly into the "Ah Ha!" graphical part of the brain.

Our Lord spoke 33-recorded parables. Most are recorded in Matthew and Luke, with a few in Mark. John recorded no parables. For some reason, the doctor and the tax collector write 92.5% of the parable record, while the junior assistant Mark records 7.5%, and the beloved disciple, John, didn't record a single parable.

      21 in Luke (Dr. of Medicine)

      16 in Matthew (Tax Collector)

      3 in Mark (John called Mark. Paul's, and Barnabas' helper)

      0 in John

The following table delineates them and their locations in Scripture.

THE 33 PARABLES OF OUR LORD

THE (Parable)		LOCATION		
		Matthew	Mark	Luke
1	Builders and Foundations	7:24-27		6:47-49
2	Counting of the Cost			14:25-33
3	Dishonest Steward			16:1-14
4	Fig Tree	24:32		
5	Friend at Midnight			11:5-8
6	Fruitless Fig Tree			13:6-9
7	Good Samaritan			10:25-37
8	Great Supper			14:16-24
9	Hidden Treasure	13:44		
10	Importunate Widow & Unjust Judge			18:1-8
11	Laborers in the Vineyard	20:1-16		
12	Leaven	13:33		13:20
13	Lost Coin			15:8-10
14	Lost Sheep			15:3-7
15	Lost Prodigal Son			15:11-32
16	Marriage Feast	22:1-14		
17	Mustard Seed	13:31	4:30	13:18
18	Net	13:47		
19	Pearl of Great Price	13:45		
20	Pharisee and Tax Collector			18:8-14
21	Pounds (Money Usage)			19:11-27
22	Rich Fool Farmer			12:13-21
23	Rich Man and Lazarus			16:19-31
24	Seed Growing Secretly		4:26-29	
25	Sower on Four Soils	13:3-23	4:3-25	8:5-15
26	Talents	25:14-30		
27	Ten Virgins	25:1-13		
28	Two Debtors			7:36-50
29	Two Sons	21:28-32		
30	Unmerciful Debtor	18:23-35		
31	Unprofitable Servants			17:7-10
32	Wheat and the Tares	13:24-30		
33	Wicked Husbandmen	21:33-46		20:9-18

13.2) Parable Conclusions

Let's look at the conclusions from the Parables of Jesus found in Appendix H to see what's hiding there.

Parable Conclusions
End Times

- Jesus wonders if He'll find faith on Earth when He comes again.
- The good and the bad will be netted. The good will be gathered, and the bad thrown in Hell.
- At the end of the Age, the angels will take the wicked from the good and cast them into the fire.
- The Jews will be rewarded last, and the Gentles rewarded first.
- Believers must have the Holy Spirit with them when they receive the coming Lord.
- After the Tribulation, including the Abomination of Desolation, the darkening of the sun and moon, heavens shaken, a sign of the Son of Man appearing in the sky, and the Rapture of the Elect, be prepared for His coming.
    - The evil generation that sees he first of these signs will see the Awful Day of the Lord.
    - The faithful servants will be blessed when, or just before, Jesus comes.
    - The faithless servant is cut to pieces and going to Hell.

Parable Conclusions
The Word, God's Explanations, and Afterlife

- The Word of God grows in a way the preacher doesn't understand.
- When fully grown, the Word brings forth believers.
- The Kingdom of God was taken from the Jews because of these and given to the Gentles:
    - The Jews killed His prophets.
    - God invited the Jews to accept Jesus, but they killed His Son outside the city.
- He then invites the good and the bad to accept Jesus.

13.2.2) SECRETS OF THE KINGDOM

Jesus was quoted in Matthew (13:11) as saying

> The knowledge of the secrets of the Kingdom of Heaven has been given to you (the disciples), but not to them (the general curious masses).

The reason why they had the knowledge, but the general listening audience didn't, was explained in the next verse *using a kingdom secret*. The disciples had Jesus, the Living Word of God, to walk and talk with every day.

> *For whoever has, to him shall more be given, and he shall have an abundance; but whoever does not have, even what he has will be taken away.*-Matt.13:12.

This demonstrates an *amplifying* effect. It also explains why those who weren't with Jesus didn't know the secrets; it was taken from them. To prevent the theft, Jesus provided the truth in an innocuous way that would be remembered, recalled, and grown in the mind like yeast leavening bread.

In God's kingdom, certain principles are established and demonstrated in God's word. Two of those principles are "*reciprocity*" and "*amplification*." In Malachi, the Lord says, Return to Me and I will return to you.

That is a statement of reciprocity. In Psalm 18:25,27 (NASB) there is even more evidence of the Kingdom Secret of reciprocity,

> With the kind You show Yourself kind; With the [a]blameless You show Yourself blameless; With the pure You show Yourself pure, And with the crooked You show Yourself astute. For You save an afflicted people, But haughty eyes You abase.

In Malachi 3:8,12 God demonstrates reciprocity by cursing those who rob Him (giving little to those who give too little) and amplification by promising to out give the repentant believer. In Luke Jesus describes these two principles as commands,

> Be merciful, just as your Father is merciful. And do not judge and you will not be judged; and do not condemn, and you will not be condemned; pardon, and you will be pardoned. Give, and it will be given to you; good measure, pressed down, shaken together, running over, they will pour into your lap. For by your standard of measure it will be measured to you in return. -- Luke 6:36,38

Thus, reciprocity and amplification are two of God's ways of interacting with man. But more than that, God is transitivity: 1 John 4:11,

> Dear friends, since God so loved us, we also ought to love one another.

So God's methods are reciprocity, amplification, and transitivity. Let's look for other Secrets of the Kingdom first in Ephesians and then by Jesus' Parables.

Ephesians Kingdom Secrets

In addition to the secrets from the parables, there are also Kingdom secrets hidden throughout the New Testament. Let's look at Ephesians to see what Kingdom Secrets are hidden there.

Secrets from Ephesians

POWER: It lies in the resurrection of the Lord Jesus Christ.

AUTHORITY: Against principalities, powers, the rulers of the darkness of this world, and spiritual wickedness in high places.

RIGHTEOUSNESS: It is in the new man we put on in Christ Jesus.

Parable Conclusions
Kingdom Secrets

- If you hear and understand you will bear good fruit X100, X60 and some X30. This is the seed sown on good soil. The principle of amplification.
- The shrewd forgive or cover the sins or debts of others. If you do, your sins or debts will also be covered.
  - Such forgiveness is a currency of exchange.
  - You can choose to possess God's currency, or possess mammon.
- Jesus appeals to the Father not to destroy the sinner until after Jesus has done His work of making the condition of the heart toward God better.
  - If there is no progress, then destruction awaits.
- Don't hurt the good to get at the bad.
- Persistence pays off when even friendship won't.
- If God forgives you, you must forgive your debtors from your heart. If you don't, you will be turned over to the torturers. God is transitive, expects transitivity, and works against intransitivity.
- If you are faithful with a few things, you'll be in charge of many, and He'll direct your path to heaven. Amplification for the faithful.
- The understanding of the Truth of God happens slowly, like yeast rising.
- If you consider God hard, He will be hard to you, and will cast you into Hell. God is reciprocal and expects reciprocity, and works against its absence.
- God wants you to take a risk for Him because you trust His Love. That is faithfulness.
- Faithfulness is risk taking by trusting Him.
  - Trusting God for mercy is risk taking by trusting Him.
- The more God forgives you, the more you love Him. Human nature.
- Your faith in God's mercies saves you, and you'll have peace.

The Witness and Spirit of Truth

> **Parable Conclusions**
> **Kingdom Secrets Continued**
>
> - He who has a contrite heart will be justified. *Contrition is a positive attitude toward God given self as a reference, thus by reciprocity, God has a positive attitude toward you with Himself as a reference-justification.*
> - He who exalts himself will be humbled. *He who exalts himself reduces God's status in his own eyes, so by reciprocity, God who exalts Himself reduces this man's status in God's own eyes.*
> - He who humbles himself will be exalted. *He who humbles himself increases God's status in his own eyes, so by reciprocity, God Who humbled Himself on the Cross increases this man's status in God's own eyes.*
> - God is toward saints as saints are toward Him. - Reciprocity
> - More to saint who has most, take from saint who has least. - Amplification
> - Trusting God gives peace. Trust is a gift to God, peace is a gift from God, thus, reciprocity again
> - The one who shows mercy is the true neighbor.
> - God is a true Neighbor.
> - If you're rich toward yourself, be rich toward God-feed your brother.
> - He who lays up treasure for himself, and is not rich toward God is a fool. God is reciprocity.
> - If you have more than enough, give the extra to God's plans. God is reciprocity.
> - The act of repentance counts higher than righteous living.
> - The Father looks afar off for His lost ones
> - The Father is quick to forgive.
> - God loves a contrite heart
> - God seeks the lost.
> - Cry to God day and night, and He'll bring you quick justice.
> - God is driven to restore the lost
> - If you don't have the Holy Spirit, Jesus doesn't know you.
> - The kingdom of heaven grows from almost nothing into a growth that helps and shelters even the soaring ones.
> - The kingdom of Heaven is a great treasure owned by God but available to man for a bargain if he is willing to forsake all he has for it.
> - Those few who are called and put on Jesus, the proper clothes, are chosen. This is the secret of Righteousness in Jesus.
> - First serve God properly clothed in Christ, and then you will be rewarded.
> - Those many who are called but do not put on Jesus are damned to Hell.
> - It does not matter when you become God's servant; we all receive the same reward.

A final note in this section: In light of Abraham's willingness to offer his son to God, God's reciprocity is of utmost importance, for it was that reciprocity that brought our Savior to the Cross. There is much more that could be mined, but let's move on to the next section where we have an analogy that is good to ponder.

[1] Eberhard Jüngel, *God as the Mystery of the World*, transl.: Darell L. Guder (Grand Rapids: Eerdmans Publishing Company, 1983) p.288

14 -THE DIVINE SYSTEM – An Analogy to Ponder

I studied "systems" in the course of technical scholarship. In a course on information systems I was required to read about the design of "information systems." The concepts relate well to Christianity. Let us begin with a review of the material that was prepared for secular use.

In those nine conditions that Churchman decided were necessary for an entity to be a system (see Appendix A), he identifies three necessary purposive individuals: the *client*, the *decision maker*, and the *designer*. These three form one system trinity. In summary, for an entity to be considered a system, then the following must hold.[1]

1) It has a *client* who is concerned with the execution of the entity.

2) It has a *decision maker* who influences the performance of the entity by managing its resources.

3) It has a *designer* whose preferences are congruent with the client's preferences and who designs the system so that the decision maker can manage it. The *designer* desires to maximize the performance for the *client's benefit*.

The *designer* desires to maximize the performance for the *client's benefit*.

The system is able to execute the *designer's* plans.

Let's look at several such system trinities:

14.1) Graphical System Representations

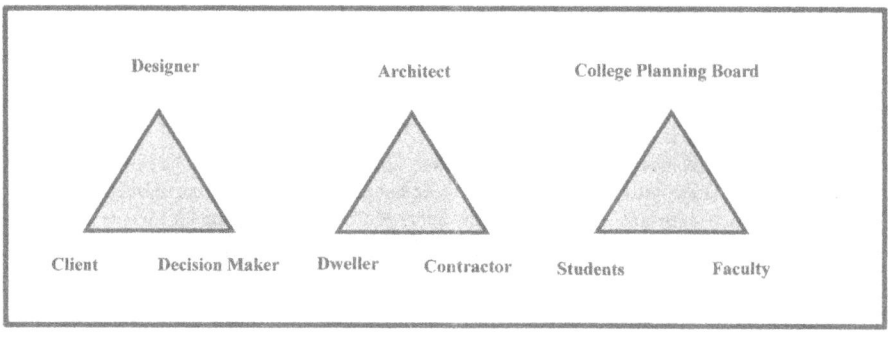

In extreme cases, one individual may assume all three roles for the completion of a task, or the meeting of a need. One such case was my father who was a carpenter who built and dwelt in a house of his own design. We know of another Extreme Case Who assumes three roles, while being One. "For their sakes I sanctify myself."- John 17:19 That is, He represented Himself to us in three ways, in three partitions, thus sanctified for our sakes. We use graphical analogy attempting to know our God better.

The Witness and Spirit of Truth

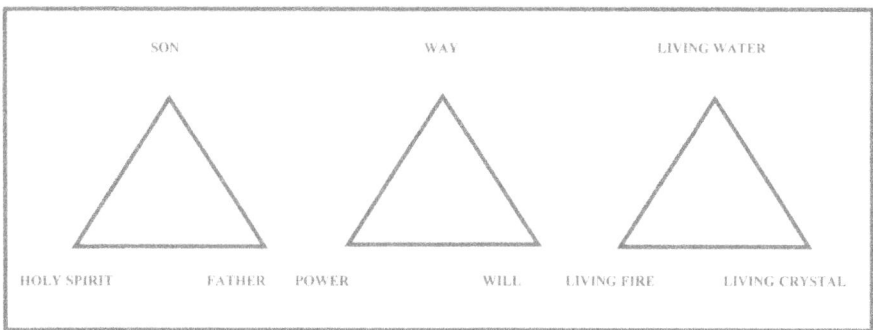

Divine Systems of Divine Subsystems

Often, systems are comprised of subsystems (See Appendix A). To be a subsystem, it must satisfy the necessary conditions to be a system. I have represented the God – System (Father, Son and Holy Spirit) as being made up of three subsystems, each representing a major function in the Whole.

- Will, Life, and Love
- Truth, Way, and Life
- Love, Truth, and Power

Hopefully you recognize the Personalities involved. We take these three Subsystems, and represent the Unity of the Totality of the System.

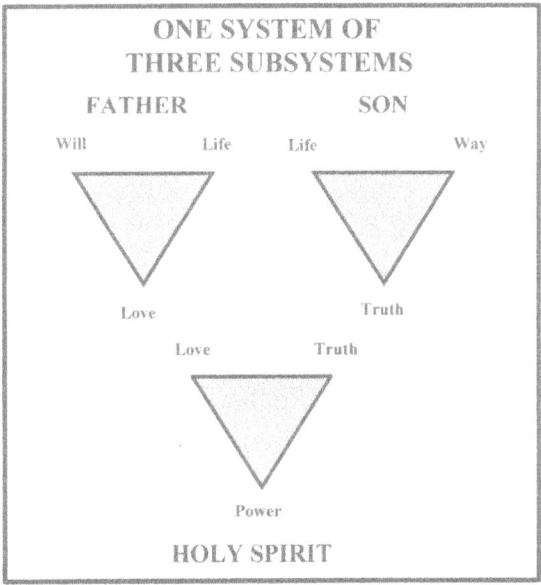

This is but another way of employing analogy to grasp the picture. Recall that Jesus was begotten of the Father, so he shared "Life" with Him. Jesus is the King of Truth, so he shares Truth with the Holy Spirit. The Father shares Love with the Holy Spirit, and constantly yearns for the Spirit. See how the three triangles (systems) form a larger triangle (system). See how the components of the subsystems interact with those in other subsystems. And see how the whole is then viewed. We could ask system questions like, what is the performance measure of each subsystem, and of the total system? What is the System purpose, and each subsystem? There are different ways of drawing these subsystems interfacing with each other to create the One Complete System. A real theologian should be drawing these pictures and asking these questions.

It strikes me that The Way is God's Wisdom, The Truth is in a Pure Language, the Life is in the I AM. The Holy Spirit inspired the Written Word of God, and He made the Word flesh through Mary, and He resurrected The Living Word of God. The Living Loving Father Willed it all. The Son agreed to His Father's Will and made the Way. I guess it really is true, "Where there's a Will, there's a Way."

Compressing the upper figure together, we see somewhat how each Person of the Trinity Links with the Others.

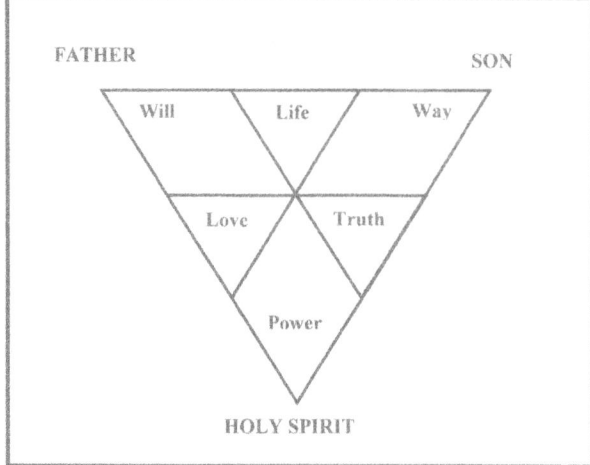

This is possibly a good place to use the methods of an earlier section on equivalence relationships and partitioning. Referring to the unnamed equivalence relationship, R, that the Trinity is in, we have Father R Son

    Requires: Son R Father (by symmetry)
                  Son R Holy Spirit
    Requires: Holy Spirit R Son (by symmetry)
    Requires: Father R Holy Spirit (by transitivity)
    Requires: Holy Spirit R Father (by symmetry)

Thus, the One God is the One equivalence class comprised of the Father, the Son, and the Holy Spirit. Note from the last figure that two of the three attributes of each Person of the Trinity are shared with the other two Persons. This means there are no disjoint partitions within God. Therefore, there are no more equivalence classes within God than the one defining the Trinity. It would also appear from the drawing above that Father, Son, and Holy Spirit are synonymous with Will, Way, and Power, respectively.

Consider the Trinity expressed by the English writer Dorothy L Sayers, in her play *The Zeal of Thy House* and systematically analyzed and expanded in her book *The Mind of The Maker*[2]. She believes The Trinity is expressible as The Creative Idea, the Creative Energy, and The Creative Power, and that every man mirrors God in his daily work. Quoting a passage from the play,

> Children of men, lift up your hearts.
> Laud and magnify God, the Holy and Eternal Wisdom, the everlasting and adorable Trinity.
>
> Praise Him that He hath made man in His own image, a maker and craftsman like himself, a little mirror of His triune Majesty.
>
> For every Act of Creation is threefold, An earthly Trinity to match the heavenly.
>
> First, there is the Creative Idea, passionless, timeless, beholding the whole work complete at once, the end in the beginning. and this is the image of the Father.
>
> Second, there is the Creative Energy, begotten of the Idea and subject to it, working in time with sweat and passion from the beginning to the end; and this is the image of the Word.
>
> Third, there is the Creative Power, the meaning of the work, and its response in the lively soul; and this is the image of the indwelling Spirit.
>
> And of these three, each equally is the work, whereof none can exist without the other; and this is the image of the Trinity.
>
> Honor, then, all work of the craftsman, imagined by men's minds, built by the labor of men's hands, working with power upon the souls of men, image of the everlasting Trinity,
>
> God's witness in world and time. And whatsoever ye do, do all to the glory of God.

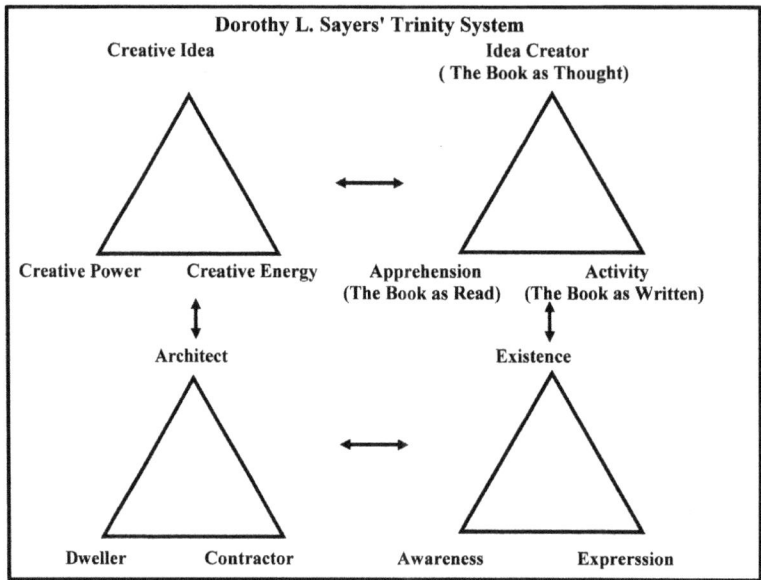

14.3) A Star of David

It is doubtful that King David ever saw the star that bears his name. It would be interesting to know what its originator was thinking. It is somewhat interesting to take two such systems and merge them together. The following looks very familiar, but it is just speculation that there is meaning here.

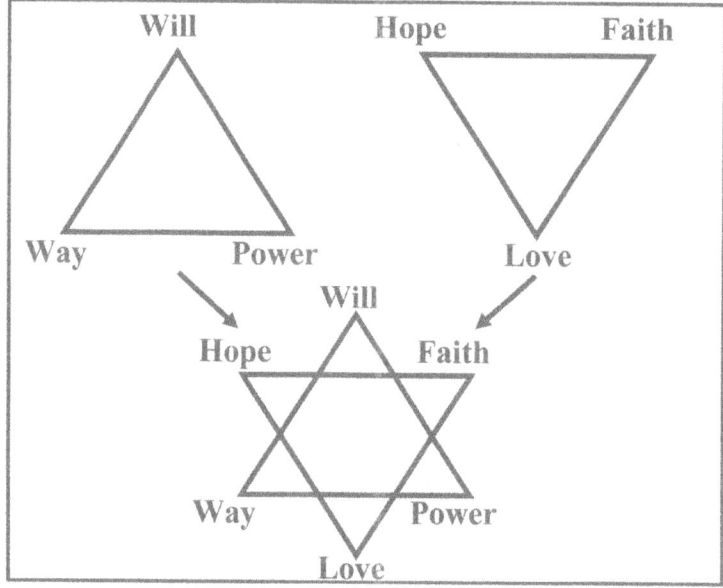

[1] Niv Ahituv and Seev Neumann, *Principles of Information Systems for Management,* Wm. C. Brown Company Publishers, Dubuque, Iowa, 1982, p.p. 102,103

[2] Dorothy L. Sayer, *The Mind of the Maker,* HarperCollins Publisher, New York, 1979, p.p.37,38

15: Conclusions

I began this work filled with adrenaline and caffeine. I sought the foundations of the system of thought that creates so much mischief. Postmodernists attempt to undo the works of Confucius, Plato, Judaism, Christianity, and then move beyond the Cogito. These attempts are aimed at annihilating truth and what has been associated with the concepts of *honor* or *righteousness* or *propriety*. This is all anti-Christ, and is a dagger aimed at the heart of humanity. Once found, I studied the known science and found the philosophical theology on quicksand. The assumptions they've made about the nature of God, the origins of language, and the meaning of truth are pompous and absurd.

I find that belief in Absolute Truth is not a regional concept, but a globally pervasive one. The postmodern understanding of language theory fails in the real world, giving rise to many spurious belief-systems that are not only anti-biblical but also anti-humanitarian. Those that proclaimed Truth and God dead have passed away. Before they did, they nurtured Nazi ideology and fathered many lies. We were warned, Jesus said, "*Beware of the false prophets*. And twice He said, "*You will know them by their fruits*."

But the Truth does rise again. With Chomsky, Crain, and Suppes, the very foundations of postmodern understanding of language and recognition are shaken. We see that the presumption that language was totally social, and temporal has passed away. The theory that it is genetic in nature, and thereby innate to all, is current. If Bishop Berkeley were right, and given Chomsky's and Crain's conclusions, the mind would start off with a select set of primitive thoughts or images, and the application of experience would add complexity to those primitives by attaching annexes to the originals to provide more complex ideas or images. If Vaneechoutte, and Skoyles are correct, those primative thoughts or images are cast in a musical framework. Thus, the psalmist and the poet may indeed be the closest to the true expression of a thought.

Even more, Truth is divine; it is one, even as God is one. All Truth, or all truthful Ideas are "had as content" by the Spirit of Truth; and they are all related and may be animated by the Spirit. This Spirit of Truth abides *in* Christ's disciples, and they are in the world synchronizing it to God's heartbeat. The very special aspect about this system is that our "One - Stand – Alone" oscillator can stabilize it. Thus, provided that our stand-alone oscillator is coupled sufficiently into the system, it can stabilize the system entirety. Jesus is the stand-alone oscillator. The number and influence of the Elect, however, determine the coupling.

Considering these three characteristics benefit ecumenism (Pluralism, Centerlessness, and Subjectivism) is there any doubt the Lord does not benefit from it? Christians really don't want an agenda; they want to see Jesus Christ as Lord and His father's Will done on earth as it is done in Heaven! The ecumenical agenda is the dark side of theology. *Novus Ordo Missae - The New Order of Missions* is the counterfeit. The real Ecumenical Imperative is the Great Commission.

I agree with A.W. Tozer that God is immutable, and by believing the prophets we believe He exists both inside and outside of time. Further, the philosophic principle that one's existence is demonstrated by the fact that one thinks (The Cogito) is in no measure corrupting. The preface, "God spoke, therefore I am; I am, therefore I think," should have been acknowledged by Descartes as a statement of origins. The Cogito is a proof of existence, not of origin, or cause.

What *is* corrupting is the methodology of Radical Doubt when applied to God's Word. St. Thomas had only normal doubts, but he was told that those who believed without seeing and feeling the wounds were the blessed ones. The flip sides of God's blessings are curses. Those who radically doubt God's Word should reconsider their position.

The nature of two of the analogies provided use the method of defining a variable implicitly. That is, allowing the variable to be defined as a function of itself. That expression is then "solved" using the rules of algebra to yield an explicit expression for the variable. This method is used extensively in the algebra and the calculus. Formal logic and language don't usually allow an implicit definition. When they do, they are usually sequential functions, not simultaneous. Ideas like "You can't use a word to define itself." rule out implicit expressions in our language. Algebraic analogies allow the "solution" to be available by allowing implicit expressions as an intermediate step.

We can never hope to grasp (comprehend) truth entirely within a formal language and logic system. I believe that a single complex language that includes the analogous "reals" (logic, reason and justice) and the "imaginaries" (faith, hope, and love) would serve the purpose of *grasping* truth. The *grasping*, however, will have to be accomplished by both *comprehension* and *apprehension*. Further, I believe the apprehension will be provided by analogies and parables in the manner used by our Lord to convey profound Truth covertly and implicitly. I believe that the innate language universals are fundamentally musical in nature. Being musical, they have a relationship to mathematics. Therefore, mathematical analogies have a rightful place in the quest to know what God is revealing.

The Biblical harp had from 3 to 22 strings and is known as the "Nevel." Jewish tradition teaches that God created everything that was made by singing the sacred text a letter at a time from the 22- letter Hebrew alphabet, accompanied by the Nevel. The 22-string Nevel is said to be the harp that makes perfect heavenly music in this world. The "Kinnor," on the other hand, is the 3 to 12- string Biblical lyre. David chose 10 strings for his lyre. Jewish tradition also asserts the ten -string harp is reserved for the day when the world will come into one harmonious unity. The pure language spoken of by the prophet, we speculate, might then be based on a language of 10 letters. But those 10 letters would probably convey the same extra meaning as the Hebrew Language with its hidden word pictures. Each Hebrew letter has a meaning and a numeric value. For example, ALEF means; First, #1, (letter value 1) Strength, Leader and has a literal meaning of OX or BULL. The literal meaning of God's Name, the Tetragramaton, is displayed below.

The Tetragrammaton Revisited

English Left To Right: YHWH		Hebrew Right To Left:	יהוה
Hebrew Letter:	י	ה	ו	ה
Name of Letter:	Yod	He	Vav	He
Hidden meanings:	To make	To reveal	To secure	To reveal
	Work	the	and	the
	A deed		to add	
Literal Meaning:	Hand Closed	Behold	Nail, Peg	Behold

I am in awe that Yahwey's Name includes hand, nail, and behold! This simple looking Word that is Name includes my Master's passion! It also includes us. He wrote that we are created in His image, and His Name is an image of Him. When YHWH wrote His Name, He didn't use paper and pen. He didn't us a rock. He used flesh and bone! He didn't spell it left to right, as the Europeans do, or right to left as the Middle Easterners do. Instead, He spelled it top to bottom like the Chinese do.

Any time Lucifer looks upon Man, he sees the Name of God! We are walking Billboards for our God. I believe by faith that a pure language will be given us that we can worship (e.g., sing) in. And like Tarski, I think that an axiom-based language is adequate, while like Gödel, I think that, there is a "correct" proposition (like "God is") that can neither be proved nor disproved by logic. Thus, I believe our pure language will facilitate the ease of singing axioms (e.g., "God is good!"). The axioms are the statements of the creeds. The doctrines are the theories provable by the creeds and reason. Not all creeds are independent, therefore, not all creeds are necessary, but they are sufficient until Christ comes again. It is the glory of God to conceal a matter, but the glory of kings is to search out a matter. Pr 25:2

I conclude that the postmodern understanding of language theory fails in the real world, giving rise to many spurious belief-systems that are not only anti-biblical but also antihumanitarian. I show the polluted streams we are now swimming in are due to the contamination of the springs of the human heart by atheistic Higher Criticism and philosophical theology in the form of modern, and postmodern thought. It is the rejection of the Scriptures that creates the vile work. The first fruits of that pernicious work were first visible in Nazi Germany.

The philosophical theologians say, God is Dead! God remains dead! And we have killed him.

Upon reflection, they are right ... their god is dead. *It* never had the power to resurrect itself. *It* actually never lived. Their mistake: they believed they referred to the God of Abraham, Moses, and the Christian Apostles, and they didn't. They referred to "a being than which nothing greater can be conceived," which is far short of the Infinite God of Abraham. Their belief that God is a thought: thinking is a creator and God is its finest creation, simply indicates their god is an idol fashioned by the mind alone, without the use of hands. Whether golden calf or our greatest thought, all idolatry begins in the mind. I reach the same conclusion as Blaise Pascal; the God of the philosophers was not the God of the Bible – their effort all in vain.

The field of theology needs a department of applied divinity that is an inspired natural theology-Biblically grounded and naturally argued. If theology is to have its value to Christians, it must be relative to the world our neighbor is in. Theology must yield a "decent behavior" if it is to be trusted. In short, the pursuit of knowledge of God requires more than the construction of philosophical substructure whereupon we construct our theological system. We must construct an axiom-based substructure and system in the real world where our resultant behavior is examined. Do they cause us to trust God in faith and then to love our neighbors as ourselves? Do they remain focused and draw strength from the death, burial, and resurrection of Jesus Christ? It needs to be an applied axiomatic natural theology –beyond blasphemy, idolatry, arrogance and pride. It is certainly not postmodernism.

To those theologians aggrieved by my challenge to their way of thinking, I recommend the WAY. My authority comes from Scripture, a personalized 1 Peter 2:9 - *I am a chosen person, a royal priest, a citizen of a holy nation, God's special possession to declare the praises of Him who called me out of darkness into His wonderful light.*

Appendix A

The Necessary Conditions for an Entity, S, to be Conceived as a System are:[1]

1. "S is *teleological*," which means that it has a purpose.
2. *"S has a measure of performance."* The purpose described in (1) above is the primary criterion for constructing a meaningful measure of performance. The measure should reflect the effectiveness of the entity in achieving its purpose. There are two classes of measures of performance:
    i. The first class relates the purpose and the entity's outputs.
    ii. The second class relates the entity's purpose, inputs, and outputs.
3. *"There exists a client whose interests (values) are served by S in such a manner that the higher the measure of performance, the better the interests are served and, more generally, the client is the standard of the measure of performance."*
4. *"S has teleological components which co produce the measure of performance of S."* That is, a system is comprised of purposeful (teleological) subsystems. The performance measure for the whole system must be related to the performance measures of each subsystem. That should be done in such a way that no subsystem could optimize itself at the expense of the whole system's performance measure.
5. *"S has an environment (defined either teleologically or ateleologically) which also co produces the measure of performance of S."* The system must adapt itself to these purposeful or random changes in the environment so as not to suffer a reduction in the system's measure of performance.
6. *"There exists a decision maker who –via his or her resources – can produce changes in the measures of performance of S's components, and hence changes the measure of performance of S."*
7. *"There exists a designer who conceptualizes the nature of S in such a manner that the designer's concepts potentially produce actions in the decision maker, and hence changes in the measures of performance of S's components, and hence changes in the measure of performance of S."*
8. *"The designer's intention is to change S so as to maximize S's value to the client."* The system designer's interests should be identical to those of the client.
9. *"S is 'stable'* with respect to the designer in the sense that there is a built-in guarantee that the designer's intention is ultimately realizable." This means that it can be verified that the designer's intention is eventually realizable."

[1] C. W. Churchman, The Design of Inquiring Systems: Basic Concepts of Systems and Organization (New York; Basic Books, 1971

Larry Sheets

Appendix B The Relevant Portions of Three Christian Creeds

1: The Apostles' Creed

I believe in God the Father Almighty, Maker of heaven and earth.

And in Jesus Christ his only Son our Lord; who was conceived by the Holy Ghost, born of the Virgin Mary, suffered under Pontius Pilate, was crucified, dead, and buried; he descended into hell; the third day he rose again from the dead; he ascended into heaven, and sitteth on the right hand of God the Father Almighty; from thence he shall come to judge the quick and the dead.

I believe in the Holy Ghost; the holy catholic Church; the communion of saints; the forgiveness of sins; the resurrection of the body; and the life everlasting.
AMEN."

2): The Nicene Creed

We believe in one God the Father Almighty, Maker of heaven and earth, and of all things visible and invisible.

And in one Lord Jesus Christ, the only-begotten Son of God, begotten of the Father before all worlds, God of God, Light of Light, Very God of Very God, begotten, not made, being of one substance with the Father by whom all things were made; who for us men, and for our salvation, came down from heaven, and was incarnate by the Holy Spirit of the Virgin Mary, and was made man, and was crucified also for us under Pontius Pilate. He suffered and was buried, and the third day he rose again according to the Scriptures, and ascended into heaven, and sitteth on the right hand of the Father. And he shall come again with glory to judge both the quick and the dead, whose kingdom shall have no end.

And we believe in the Holy Spirit, the Lord and Giver of Life, who proceedeth from the Father and the Son, who with the Father and the Son together is worshipped and glorified, who spoke by the prophets. And we believe one holy catholic and apostolic Church. We acknowledge one baptism for the remission of sins. And we look for the resurrection of the dead, and the life of the world to come. Amen.

3): The Athanasian Creed, also called the Quicunque Vult

The Catholic Faith is this: that we worship one God in Trinity, and Trinity in Unity, neither confounding the Persons nor dividing the Substance.

For there is one Person of the Father, another of the Son, and another of the Holy Ghost; but the Godhead of the Father, of the Son, and of the Holy Ghost is all one—the glory equal, the majesty co-eternal.

Such as the Father is, such is the Son and such is the Holy Ghost; the Father uncreated, the Son uncreated, and the Holy Ghost uncreated; the Father incomprehensible, the Son incomprehensible, and the Holy Ghost incomprehensible; the Father eternal, the Son eternal, and the Holy Ghost eternal;

And yet there are not three eternals, but one eternal; as also there are not three incomprehensibles nor three uncreated, but one uncreated and one incomprehensible.

So likewise the Father is almighty, the Son almighty, and the Holy Ghost almighty; and yet they are not three Almighties but one almighty. So the Father is God, the Son is God, and the Holy Ghost is God; and yet they are not three Gods but one God; so likewise the Father is Lord, the Son Lord, and the Holy Ghost Lord; and yet not three Lords but one Lord.

For like as we are compelled by the Christian verity to acknowledge every Person by himself to be God and Lord, so are we forbidden by the Catholic religion to say, there be three Gods or three Lords. The Father is made of none, neither created nor begotten;

The Son is of the Father alone, neither made not created, but begotten;

The Holy Ghost is of the Father and of the Son, neither mode nor created nor begotten, but proceeding;

So there is one Father, not three Fathers; one Son, not three Sons; one Holy Ghost, not three Holy Ghosts.

And in this Trinity none is afore or after other, none is greater or less than another; but the hole three Persons are co-eternal together and co-equal.

He therefore that will be saved must think of the Trinity.

Furthermore, it is necessary to everlasting salvation that he also believe rightly the Incarnation of our Lord Jesus Christ. For the right faith is, that we believe and confess that our Lord Jesus Christ, the Son of God, is God and Man:

> God, of the Substance of his Father, begotten before the worlds; and Man, of the Substance of his Mother, born in the world. Perfect God, and perfect Man of a reasonable soul and human flesh subsisting; equal to the Father as touching his Godhead and inferior to the Father as touching his Manhood. Who although he be God and Man, yet he is not two, but one Christ.*

*As found in Dorothy L. Sayers' The Mind of the Maker, HarperCollins Publishers, New York, 1987, p.p. 227, 229

APPENDIX C Descartes' Laws of Learning

He selected laws to govern his acquired beliefs.

"I believed that the four following would prove perfectly sufficient for me, provided I took the firm and unwavering resolution never in a single instance to fail in observing them.

- The first was never to accept anything for true which I did not clearly know to be such….

- The second, to divide each of the difficulties under examination into as many parts as possible, and as might be necessary for its adequate solution….

- The third, to conduct my thoughts in such order that, by commencing with objects the simplest and easiest to know, I might ascend by little and little, and, as it were, step by step, to the knowledge of the more complex; assigning in thought a certain order even to those objects which in their own nature do not stand in a relation of antecedence and sequence….

- And the last, in every case to make enumerations so complete, and reviews so general, that I might be assured that nothing was omitted."[1]

He also selected four Maxims to live by while his philosophy was still being created that he wanted his readers aware of.

"I formed a provisory code of morals, composed of three or four maxims, with which I am desirous to make you acquainted.

- The first was to obey the laws and customs of my country, adhering firmly to the faith in which, by the grace of God, I had been educated from my childhood ….
- My second maxim was to be as firm and resolute in my actions as I was able, and not to adhere less steadfastly to the most doubtful opinions, when once adopted, than if they had been highly certain; …
- My third maxim was to endeavor always to conquer myself rather than fortune, and change my desires rather than the order of the world, and in general, accustom myself to the persuasion that, except our own thoughts, there is nothing absolutely in our power; ….
- In fine, to conclude this code of morals, … I could not do better than continue in that in which I was engaged, viz., in devoting my whole life to the culture of my reason, and in making the greatest progress I was able in the knowledge of truth, on the principles of the method which I had prescribed to myself."[2]

[1] Descartes - A Discourse on Method, Part 2
[2] Descartes - A Discourse on Method, Part 3

Appendix D Antimony of the Liar

Consider the following sentence:

> *The sentence printed in this book on p. 3, l. 22, is not true.*

Replace this sentence just stated by the letter '*s*.'

According to the convention concerning the adequate usage of the term "*true*," we assert the following equivalence of the form (T):

> (1) '*s*' *is true if, and only if, the sentence printed in this paper p. 3, l. 22, is not true.*

We establish empirically the following fact:

> (2) '*s*' *is identical with the sentence printed in this paper on p. 3, l. 22.*

> Now from Leibniz's Theory of Identity, it follows from (2) that we may replace in (1) the expression "*the sentence printed in this paper on p. 3, l. 22*" by the symbol " '*s*.' " Which yields:

> (3) '*s*' *is true if, and only if, '*s*' is not true.*

We have arrived at an obvious contradiction.

Another way of demonstrating a liar's paradox is by asking the following question: Is 'I am now lying.' true or false?

Larry Sheets

Appendix E – Mountain Moving Calculations

How much energy does it take to move a mountain? If we assume a typical 5000 ft high mountain with a circular body with a 5000 ft diameter base made of granite, similar to the White Mountains of New England, it would weigh approximately 4×10^{13} pounds. Raising it 5000 ft to clear the mountains in the way would require 2×10^{17} ft lb of energy, or 2.7×10^{17} Joules of energy expressed in the International MKS units. We will assume that we will move it horizontally very slowly, so almost no energy is required to move it. This energy by Einstein's $E=mc^2$ or $m=E/c^2 = 3$ kg of mass or 6.6 lbs of mass in the English system.

Now this 2×10^{17} ft lb of energy, or 2.7×10^{17} Joules of energy is considerable, but in terms of the amount of energy it takes to make mass, it is very little - since it is only equivalent to 6.6 pounds of mass. Remember the fish and the loaves that Jesus made when he feed the 5000 men. Suppose each of the 5000 ate or wasted a total of ½ pound of food. That means that he created 2500 pounds of mass to feed the people. That is equivalent to moving $2500/6.6 = 379$ mountains!

Larry Sheets

Appendix F The Fundamental Life – Another Oscillator Analogy

F.1) A fibrillated Life

I have read that each cell in the human heart contracts and releases on its own. The signal from the brain that synchronizes those cells sometimes is corrupted, and a pacemaker is installed to provide that periodic signal to keep the heart from *fibrillation* or randomly firing. This oscillation property seems inherent in many, if not all life forms. The universe is replete with oscillators.

An oscillator is a device capable of amplifying an input, but actually provides an output without an input. (Recall the principle of Amplification in the Kingdom Secrets) Its frequency is determined by rational relationships between its components, but its magnitude cannot be determined by the same linear theory that establishes its frequency. The process involved in establishing the frequency, makes the value of its magnitude indeterminate in the linear theory.

The magnitude is determined by orthogonal nonlinear functions that cannot be represented linearly. So, at the very heart of understanding, the knowledge of the operation of the fundamental oscillator depends on a language that is nonlinear and unreasonable from a linear approach. If our language were considered linear, then we should expect nonlinear additions to our normal usage to overcome indeterminacy.

F.2 Fundamentals of Oscillation.

Let's look at the fundamentals of oscillation.

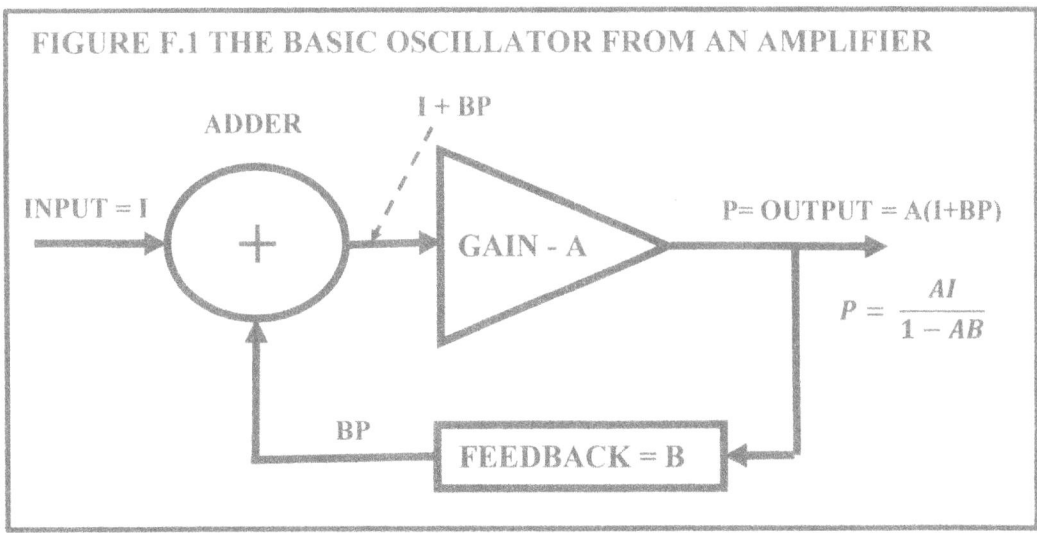

FIGURE F.1 THE BASIC OSCILLATOR FROM AN AMPLIFIER

So we have the output defined implicitly as

$$P = A(I+BP)$$

Solving for P we get

$$P(1-AB) = AI$$

or

$$P = AI/(1-AB)$$

This is the expression for the output of a feedback amplifier with input I and output P. Now suppose we ask the question, *"Under what circumstances could we get an output P without any input, I?"* That is, *when I=0*. The only way for P to be non-zero when I is zero, is when the expression is **indeterminate**, that is, of the form 0/0. That can happen when

$$1-AB = 0,$$

or

$AB = 1$ That can also be stated as "The gain from input to output and back to input equals unity."

I recall as a teenager working with my amateur radio equipment, that I had occasion to build and modify oscillators. I didn't really know what I was doing with any great proficiency; however I made them work. I soon went to college and learned the wonderful knowledge involved with radio. The first job I had was at Bell Telephone Laboratories, and the first job I had after finishing graduate school involved the design of a 70 MHz oscillator.

I felt so clever to use the AB=1 expression to determine the passive components in the oscillator to run at 70MHz. You see, A and B are complicated functions of components used in circuits, such as transistors, capacitors, resistors, and many more. Then I went to the specification that stated how powerful the signal out of the oscillator was supposed to be. *To my dismay I realized that the very expression that allowed me to design it at 70MHz was the same one that caused the expression for the output P, to be indeterminate.* That's right, you couldn't get there from here! What a sinking feeling for someone who felt so wise moments before.

F.3) Experiential Knowledge of the Nonlinear

Then I remembered my amateur beginnings. The size of the output signal was controlled by the dynamic limits of the components in the circuit. The whole circuit that had been designed using a linear theory, now depended on nonlinearity, or compression, to establish the actual peak-to-peak swings of the output. That is, the place where the circuit deviates from ideal determines the power of its output! In actual circuits, the linear gain around the loop (input to output to input) AB is made slightly greater than 1. The output grows in amplitude until nonlinearity takes over, and the signal is compressed just enough for the effective AB after compression to equal 1.

The Witness and Spirit of Truth

No linear combinations of straight lines produce a cubic (x^3) expression. They are linearly independent, or orthogonal to each other. To establish the proper output power, an oscillator designer needed to use functions that were orthogonal to the linear expressions that established the frequency. If one were to live in a purely linear world, the nonlinear behaviors would have to be considered imaginary.

In summary then, an oscillator is a device capable of amplifying an input but provides an output without an input. Its frequency is determined by rational relationships between its components, but its magnitude is determined by orthogonal nonlinear functions that cannot be represented by lines. Line segments can approximate them, however. It would take an infinite number of line segments to represent the nonlinear function exactly. The knowledge of the operation of the fundamental oscillator depends on a language that is nonlinear and unreasonable from a linear approach.

Larry Sheets

Appendix G The Inverse Function for Sin

The following section requires a working knowledge of algebra. Try to follow it if you like, otherwise ask an engineer, scientist, or mathematician to ascertain the validity of the mathematics. This method of analogy to mathematical concepts seems to be a required part of a language to address truth.

I wish to dwell on the marvel of Christ being our substitute by taking the punishment we deserved and thereby justifying us. I want to know how such a transaction can happen, using what principals and procedures. I intend to demonstrate, by algebraic analogy, how the function of becoming sinful by our first father Adam can be inverted by the second Adam having the curse of sin laid on Him. It will be shown that this can only be done perfectly, when an Infinite Gain is applied to the second Adam while He is taking the punishment. It will also be shown that for our individual (not original) sins, for the cleansing to work, we must bring only our sins to the Cross, and nothing of value. For while the cleansing is done, sins are undone and our self-righteousness becomes a corruption on the would-be redeemed

G.1) The Math

G.1.1) What is an Inverse?

We have to begin with the assumption that the function we want to reverse is invertible, or reversible uniquely. Unfortunately to show that possibility, I have to get a little technical. Suppose a function y, where $y=f(x)$ and x is any real number. It might be a function like $y = x^3$. So if $x=1, y=1$; $x=2, y=8$; $x=3, y=27$, etc., and similarly for negative numbers, $x=1, y=-1$; $x=-2, y=-8$; $x=-3, y=-27$, etc. Notice, this is a monotonic increasing function: as x increases, y increases. This type of function is invertible because for every value of y, there is one and only one value of x that relates to it.

Monotonic decreasing functions also have inverses for the same reason. But a function like $y = x^2$ is not invertible. If $y = 4$, for example, there is no way of knowing from the function if $y = 4$ because $x = 2$ or $y = 4$ because $x = -2$. As x increases from the negative numbers, the function $y = x^2$ decreases to zero at $x = 0$. Then as x continues to increase into the positive numbers, the function $y=x^2$ increases. This function is not a monotonic increasing or decreasing function and therefore has no unique inverse. The monotonic requirement guarantees a one-for-one correspondence between the x's and the y's.

Let us draw a figure that represents the flow in time of the variable "x" from the left, proceeding into the function "f(x)" and yielding the product "y."

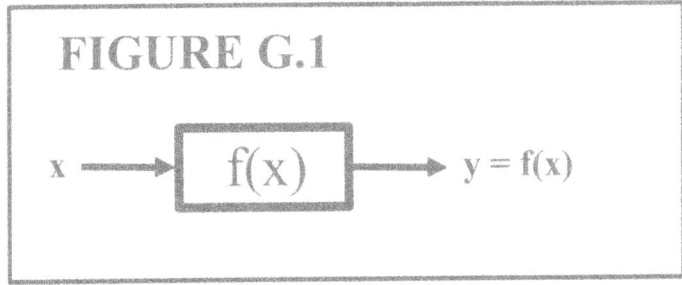

Now suppose that we could construct the inverse function of f (x) so that if we took the function of the inverse function, the result would be the original variable, x. If we denote the inverse function of f (x) to be $f^{-1}(x)$, then:

$$f(f^{-1}(x)) = x$$

For example, if $y = f(x) = x^3$, then, $y = ((f^{-1}(x))^3 = x$
Solving for $f^{-1}(x)$, we get

$$f^{-1}(x) = x^{1/3}$$

Which makes sense, because if you take the cube root of a variable, and then take the cube of that result, you would expect to come back to where you started. Notice also that the inverse function of the function is also the original variable, x. That is here, if you take the cube of a variable and then subsequently take the variable to the 1/3 power, you would reacquire the original variable. Thus:
$$f^{-1}(f(x)) = x$$

G.1.2) A Function Followed By Its Inverse

I don't want to get more technical, but to say that the idea is universal. The function could be to blow air into a half-full balloon, x, to make the full balloon, y. The inverse function would be to suck the same quantity of air out of the full balloon, y, to produce the original half-full balloon, x. It only applies to situations, however, where there is an invertible function. So we draw the situation of a function being undone by its inverse:

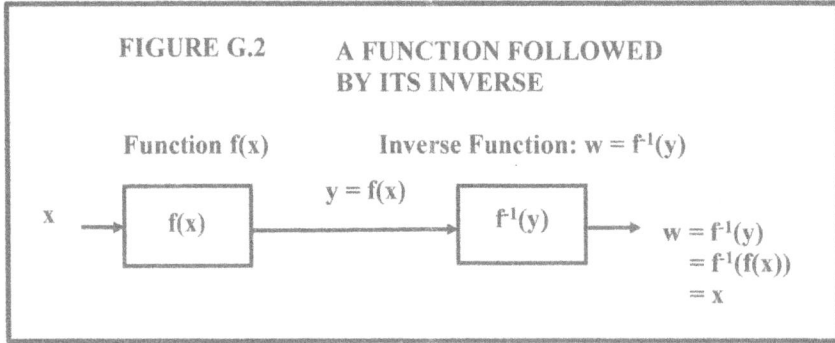

FIGURE G.2   A FUNCTION FOLLOWED BY ITS INVERSE

In the balloon example, above, if the balloon had originally half filled with helium when we blew in air, the sucking out of half the contents would *not* have resulted in the original variable (a balloon half filled with only *helium*), and would not have been a true inverse function. So other variables, or parameters often have to be specified. Let me redraw the flow of the function and the inverse function, taking into account that the operation of the function on x might require the application of an external variable or parameter, z.

The Witness and Spirit of Truth

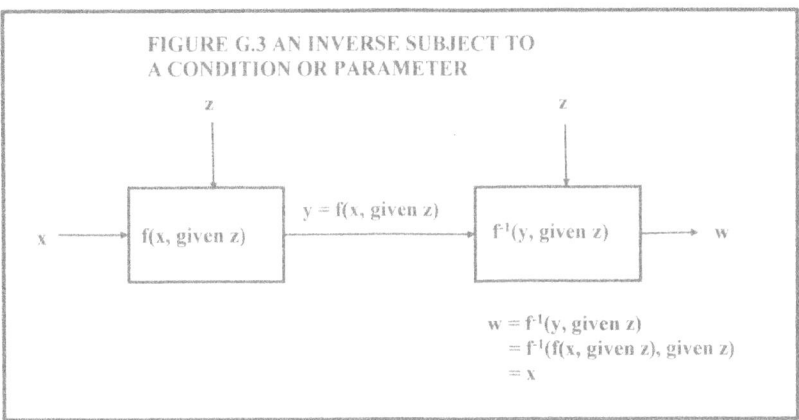

I ask the reader to follow with me as I explain how engineers have created inverse functions when they already had the original function available to them. An operational amplifier, also called a High Gain Stage, is inserted in a flow diagram with the original function, f, and a device that subtracts two things to provide a third:

G.2) The Synthesis of an Inverse

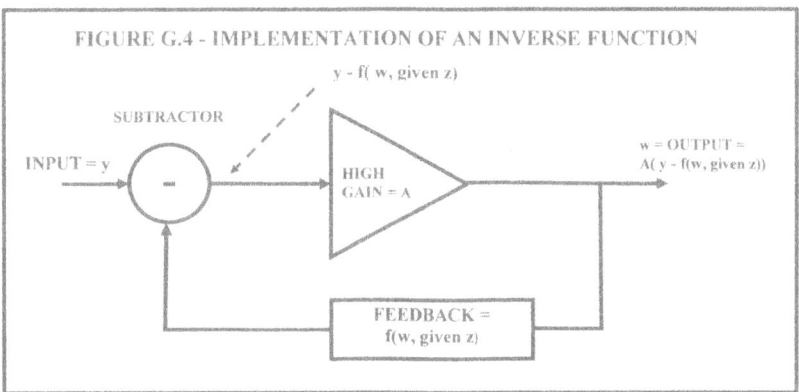

Note that $w = A(y - f(w, \text{given } z))$ or alternatively, by dividing both sides of this equation by A, we get the form:

$w/A = y - f(w, \text{given } z)$

In practice, A is greater than 10,000 and y has a magnitude much smaller than A (about 10) we get the practical equation assuming A is infinite:

$0 = y - f(w, \text{given } z)$
or $y = f(w, \text{given } z)$

But this is the definition for w being the inverse function of f, so

$w = f^{-1}(y, \text{given } z)$

Now, suppose the gain had really been infinite relative to w. The equation would have been exact and the output of our system would have been the exact inverse function. If such an inverse function were to follow the original function, the resulting output would be the original input x.

G.3) God's Plan of Sin Inversion Using A Sinless Substitute

Now I ask you to consider f(x) to be the sinless Person of Adam being stained with sin, z.. The question is how do we interpret our results? $f(x, \text{given } z)$ would have to be the function of z (sin) staining a sinless man Adam (x) Whereas, $f(w, \text{given } z)$ would have to be the function of staining a substitute sinless man (Jesus) with the same sin that Adam was stained by…no more and no less. The subtracter is the place where the sinner accepts the work of Jesus in redeeming him. The infinite gain amplifier, A, is the power of the Holy Spirit regenerating the resultant repentant sinner. Note that for each man, their sins are different sins in unique combinations. Each man must tell (confess to) the Holy One his sins or ask Him to read his heart to recover the knowledge of those sins. Jesus must use your sins to undo them (fire with fire, z against z). If the z used by Jesus in the inverse function does not equal the actual sins of the sinner, the inverse is not accomplished exactly. Additionally, if anything is brought to the cross except our sinfulness and our acceptance of Christ's work, the inverse will be corrupted, and the sinner will be left in an unpurified state.

The Mathematics of Salvation

Consider the symbols for an Operational Amplifier with an invertible function, f(x), in its negative feedback path in figure F4:

Then, let x be applied to the op amp noninverting side.
The output of the op amp will be
$$x_0 = A\{x - f(x_0)\}$$
or
$$x_0/A = x - f(x_0)$$
as $A \to \infty$ we have
$$x = f(x_0), \text{ or}$$
$$x_0 = f^{-1}(x).$$
That is, the output is the inverse function of the input.

Now consider f(sinless Man) to be the application of sin to a sinless man.

If that function is placed in the feedback loop of an infinite amplifier, read Holy Spirit, the sin of a man applied to the noninverting input of that amplifier will be removed completely, if and only if the amplification is infinite, and the substitutional Man is sinless.

Note that anything other than sin presented to Jesus will prevent the perfect inverse for sin. In fact, good works thought of as positive will become negative in this process. The gospel of Christ crucified must prevail over works, or the work of Christ is to no avail.

To see this effect, suppose the act of sinning was as simple as the addition of sin, x, to man ,x, then
$$y = x + z = f(x, \text{given } z)$$
since
$$f(f^{-1}(x, \text{given } z)) = x = f^{-1}(x, \text{given } z) + z$$
then
$$f^{-1}(x, \text{given } z) = x - z$$
but,
$$w = f^{-1}(y, \text{given } z)$$
$$= y - z$$
$$= (x + z) - z$$
$$= x \quad \text{as it should}$$

Now suppose however that the sin of Adam, z, is not exactly applied to Christ. Let the sin applied to Christ for Adam be z_2.

Then,
$$w = f^{-1}(y, \text{given } z_2)$$
$$= y - z_2$$
$$= (x + z) - z_2$$
$$= x + (z - z_2)$$
since

$(z - z_2)$ is not zero, Adam would still be stained.

Now suppose the sin applied to Christ also has some self-righteousness, r.
Then after the math,

$$w = x + (z - z_2 - r)$$

Now even if $z_2 = z$, there would still be a residual stain of "–r" on Adam.

Larry Sheets

Appendix H Parables of Jesus

Parable Kingdom Secrets Revealed

Builders and Foundations-Matt.7:24-27-Lk6:47-49

- If you are wise and build belief upon the solid rock of Jesus' Word, you will be safe in trouble.
- If you are unwise and build belief upon the sands of reason, you will suffer greatly.

Counting of the Cost-Lk.14:25-33

- Understand that the cost of loving Christ is everything.
- Be prepared to lose family, possessions and life following Christ.

Dishonest Steward-Lk.16:1-14

- The shrewd forgive or cover the sins or debts of others. If you do, your sins or debts will also be covered.
    - Such forgiveness is a currency of exchange.
    - You can choose to possess God's currency, or possess mammon.

Fig Tree-Matt.24: 32-51

- After the tribulation, including the Abomination of Desolation, the darkening of the sun and moon, heavens shaken, a sign of the Son of Man appearing in the sky, and the Rapture of His Elect, be prepared for His coming.
-
    - The evil generation that sees the first of these signs will see the Awful Day of the Lord.
    - The faithful servants will be blessed when Jesus comes or just before He comes.
    - The faithless servant is cut to pieces and going to Hell.

Friend at Midnight - Lk 11:5-8

- Persistence pays off when even friendship won't.

Fruitless Fig Tree-Lk.13: 6-9

- Jesus appeals to the Father not to destroy the sinner until after Jesus has done His work of making the soil better.
    - If the soil is better and there is still no fruit, then destruction awaits.
    - The soil is the condition of the heart toward God.

Good Samaritan - Luke 10:25-37

- The one who shows mercy is the true neighbor
- Go and show mercy.

Great Supper-Lk.14: 16-24

- The expected high officials and Priest classes of Israel rejected the invitation to Jesus' glory.
- The sinners of Israel and the Gentiles are invited to the glory.
- The expected are *Non gustabunt*, "they shall not taste of my supper."

Hidden Treasure-Matt.13: 44

- The kingdom of Heaven is a great treasure owned by God but available to man for a bargain if he is willing to forsake all he has for it.

Importunate Widow & Unjust Judge-Lk.18: 1-8

- Cry to God day and night, and He'll bring you quick justice.
- Jesus wonders if He'll find faith on earth when He comes again.

Laborers in the Vineyard-20: 1-16

- It does not matter when you become God's servant; we all receive the same reward.
- The Jews will be rewarded last, and the Gentiles rewarded first.

Leaven -Matt.13: 33-Lk.13: 20

- The understanding of the Truth of God happens slowly, like yeast rising.

Lost Coin-15: 8-10

- God is driven to restore the lost

Lost Sheep - Luke 15:1-7

- The act of repentance counts higher than righteous living.
- God seeks the lost.

Lost Prodigal Son - Luke 15:11-24

- The Father looks afar off for His lost ones
- The Father is quick to forgive.
- The gentiles are the young prodigal.
- The elder brother represents the Jews.
- The presence of the Lord compensates for the attention given the younger

Marriage Feast-Lk.22: 1-14

- God invited the Jews to accept Jesus, but they killed his prophets and rejected Jesus. He then invited the good and the bad to accept Jesus.
- Those few who are called and put on Jesus, the proper clothes, are chosen.
- Those many who are called but do not put on Jesus are damned to Hell.

Mustard Seed-Matt.13: 31-Mk.4: 30-Lk.13: 18

- The kingdom of heaven grows from almost nothing into a growth that helps the soaring ones.

Net-Matt.13: 47

- The good and the bad will be netted. The good will be gathered, and the bad thrown into Hell.
- At the end of the age the angels will take the wicked from the good and cast them into the furnace of fire.

Pearl of Great Price-Matt.13: 45

- The kingdom of Heaven is a great treasure owned by God but available to man for a bargain if he is willing to forsake all he has for it.

Pharisee & Tax Collector - Luke 18:9-14

- He who has a contrite heart will be justified.
- He who exalts himself will be humbled

Pounds (Money Usage)-Lk.19: 11-27

- God is toward saints as saints are toward Him.
- More to saint who has most, take from saint who has least.
- God's enemies die in His presence.

Rich Fool Farmer -Lk.12: 13-21

- Beware of every form of greed.
- Don't presume longevity.
- If you're rich toward yourself, be rich toward God-feed your brother.

Rich Man & Lazarus - Luke 16:19-31

- There is a great chasm between the good and the bad in afterlife.
- If Moses and Prophets not believed, then they won't believe Jesus.

Seed Growing Secretly-Mk.4: 26-29

- The Word of God grows in a way the preacher doesn't understand.
- When fully grown, the Word brings forth believers.

Sower on Four Soils-Matt.13: 3-23-Mk.4: 3-25-Lk.8: 5-15

- If you hear and don't understand, the devil takes it from the heart. This is the one on the side of the road
- If you hear, rejoice, but fall away with persecution. This is the one sown on rocky soil with no firm root.

- If you hear, but the worry and fast life chokes the Word. This is the one sown among the thorns.
- If you hear and understand you will bear good fruit X100, X60 and some X30. This is the seed sown on good soil. The principle of amplification.

Talents - Matt. 25:14-30
- If you are faithful with a few things, you'll be in charge of many, and He'll direct your path to heaven.
- If you consider God hard, He will be hard to you, and will cast you into Hell.
- God wants you to take a risk for Him because you trust His Love. That is faithfulness.

Ten Virgins-Matt.25: 1-13
- Believers must have the Holy Spirit with them when they receive the coming Lord.
- If you don't have the Holy Spirit, Jesus doesn't know you.

Two Sons-Matt.21: 28-32
- Sinners who repent do the will of God.
- The self-righteous don't do God's Will.

Two Debtors - Luke 7:36-50
- The more God forgives you, the more you love Him.
- Your faith in God's mercies saves you, and you'll have peace.

Unmerciful Debtor-Matt.18: 23-35
- If God forgives you, you must forgive your debtors from your heart.
- If you don't, you will be turned over to the torturers.

Unprofitable Servants - Lk.17:7-10
- First serve God properly clothed in Christ, and then you will be rewarded.

Wheat and the Tares - Matt. 13:24-30 &36-43
- God sows good seed
- The devil sows bad seed

- Don't hurt the good to get at the bad.
- Let both grow and reveal themselves
- Then burn the bad.
- Bring the good into God's barn.

Wicked Husbandmen-Matt.21: 33-46-Lk.20: 9-18
The Jews killed the prophets.

- The Jews killed His Son outside the city.
- The Kingdom of God was taken from the Jews because of this and given to the Gentiles.

L.L. Sheets Patents

PAT. NO.   Title

1) 8,320,584 — Method and system for performing audio signal processing
2) 6,477,250 — Adjustable hybrid having dial tone alignment configuration
3) 6,111,949 — Method of rapid automatic hybrid balancing
4) 5,974,137 — AGC amplifier for two-wire line conditioner
5) 5,963,638 — Adjustable hybrid having improved biasing configuration
6) 5,953,412 — Method and apparatus for controlling line conditioner equalizer
7) 5,862,200 — Ground fault detector for T1 span equipment
8) 5,691,998 — Data transmission protection circuit with error correction
9) 5,689,546 — Performance monitoring system for T1 telephone lines
10) 5,555,274 — Phantom data link for digital transmission lines
11) 5,444,776 — Bridge for a network interface unit
12) 5,437,023 — Noise-tolerant address transmission system for digital telecommunication network
13) 4,926,473 — Longitudinal balance system
14) 4,670,837 — Electrical system having variable-frequency clock
15) 4,467,149 — Compensation method and apparatus for use with nonideal test access lines
16) 4,176,248 — System for identifying and correcting the polarity of a data signal

Larry Sheets

Professional Activities
- Electrical engineer, Distinguished Member of Technical Staff at Bell Telephone Laboratories
- Director of Advanced Technology at Rockwell International
- Vice President of Engineering, and Chief Technical Officer at Teltrend *inc.*
- Awarded 16 U.S. patents.
- Hardwood tree farmer, having planted 120,000 hardwood Trees in Iowa
- Served three terms in the Iowa House of Representatives.

Education
- B.S. electrical engineering, Purdue University;
- M.S. electrical engineering, University of Michigan; and
- M.B.A., Illinois Institute of Technology.

Memberships and Activities
- Amateur Radio operator K9PAX since 1958
- Served as a member of the Moulton-Udell School Board,
- Moulton, IA Economic Development Association,
- Served 15 years on the Judson University President's Advisory Board,
- Served on the Hope Pregnancy Center Board, and
- Christian education church board (chairman).
- Conservation award recipient for planting 120,000 trees.
- Served as a Member of the Indian Hills Sustainable Agriculture Advisory Board.

Birth and Residence
- Born in 1943 in Hammond, Indiana.
- Resides in Centerville, Iowa

Family Members
- Seven sons and three daughters

Larry Sheets is available for book interviews and personal appearances. For more information contact:

Larry Sheets
C/O Advantage Books
info@advbooks.com

To purchase additional copies of these books, visit our bookstore at: www.advbookstore.com

Longwood, Florida, USA
"we bring dreams to life"™
www.advbookstore.com

www.ingramcontent.com/pod-product-compliance
Lightning Source LLC
Chambersburg PA
CBHW081209170426
43198CB00018B/2898